THE NEW CRAFT OF THE COCKTAIL

THE NEW CRAFT OF THE COCKTAIL

REVISED AND UPDATED EDITION

Everything You Need to Know to Think Like
a Master Mixologist, with 500 Recipes

DALE DEGROFF

PHOTOGRAPHS BY DANIEL KRIEGER

CLARKSON POTTER/PUBLISHERS
NEW YORK

I fell in love with the bars in New York City because of the uninhibited, disorderly, and surprising way life unfolds there: the regulars, the unexpected guests, the solitary drinker methodically working toward his end, the group of friends spontaneously celebrating another day on the planet. My life has been like a day behind the bar; the only logical progression has been the wealth of characters who have crossed my path, leaving their stories for me to ponder. And like the cocktails, some are sour, some are sweet, some are strong, and some are weak. I dedicate this book to all the friends and strangers who took a moment to tell me a great story to carry with me the rest of my life.

This new edition is especially dedicated to the late Gary "Gaz" Regan who taught the cocktailian community to change the world for the better, one customer at a time.

Also, to the pioneering post-Prohibition bartenders who helped restore the profession and set the stage for the craft cocktail revolution in the new millennium. A few of these notable men and women include:

Constante Ribalaigua Vert, owner of El Floridita in Havana, Cuba, from 1918 until his death in 1952, who hosted expat Americans in Havana all through the Prohibition. Ribalaigua raised the bartending profession to a new level of excellence during his long career.

Helen David, the pioneering post-Prohibition bartender and bar owner, who opened the Brass Rail in Port Huron, Michigan, in 1937 and presided over it for sixty-nine years until her death in 2006.

Harry MacElhone, owner of Harry's New York Bar in Paris from 1923 until his death in 1958, and author of *Harry's ABC of Mixing Cocktails* (1921) and *Barflies and Cocktails* (1927).

Ferdinand "Pete" Petiot, who trained under Harry MacElhone at Harry's New York Bar in Paris before presiding over the legendary King Cole Bar in the St. Regis Hotel in New York City for thirty years. Petiot is credited with popularizing both the Bloody Mary and the Red Snapper.

Harry Craddock, an American-trained English bartender who authored the legendary *The Savoy Cocktail* (1930) and cofounded the United Kingdom Bartenders Guild in 1934.

W. J. "Bill" Tarling, the first president of the IBA (International Bartenders Association) and author of the *Café Royal Cocktail Book* (1937).

Ernest Raymond Beaumont Gantt, aka Don the Beachcomber, who created a new kind of mixology after Prohibition that centered around mostly rum-based drinks served in a fantasy Polynesian setting.

Victor Bergeron, a bar owner in Oakland, California, who was inspired by Don the Beachcomber's unique rum mixology and went on to create the worldwide brand Trader Vic.

Fred Ireton, bartender of the Long Beach Yacht Club and pioneer of the first chapter of the United States Bartenders' Guild.

Valentine Goesaert, the bartender and owner who lost the Supreme Court case in 1948 to overturn the Michigan state law that prohibited women from owning and working behind the bar. Luckily, she lobbied the legislature and they repealed the law.

Joy Perrine, the Louisville bartender of forty years and coauthor of *The Kentucky Bourbon Cocktail Book* (2009).

Ray Foley, ex-bartender and founder of *Bartender* magazine and Bartender Hall of Fame, was the lone voice advocating for the bartending profession for many years.

Chris McMillian, cocktail historian and longtime New Orleans bartender and owner of Revel Cafe and Bar with his wife, Laura.

CONTENTS

THE NEW
MILLENNIUM

B. E. Rock and B. E. Windows were the two companies
I worked for from 1985 through 2001. They operated
two renowned restaurants that were also the two highest
restaurants in the world at the time: the Rainbow Room
at the top of 30 Rock and Windows on the World on
top of the World Trade Center. In 1999, we lost the
Rainbow Room in an unsuccessful negotiation with Jerry
Speyer of Tishman Speyer. Two years later, in 2001, we
lost Windows on the World in a catastrophe that changed
the United States more than any single event since the
Civil War.

Timing is everything. When the first edition of *The
Craft of the Cocktail* was released in 2002, the timing was
so right and so wrong. The 9/11 attacks in New York,
Washington, D.C., and in the sky over Pennsylvania
hit like a thunderbolt, turning our world upside down
overnight. Life as we knew it ceased: professions were
put on hold, entire sectors of the economy were frozen,
no one was sure what the future would bring. It was a
time of trauma and stark fear. The sudden downturn
had a huge impact on the hospitality and entertainment
industry. For me, it marked the end of a sixteen-year
episode. For America, it was the beginning of an era
with an uncertain future.

With the approach of the new millennium came the
promise of a cocktail resurgence. I assured young career
bartenders and anyone in the press who would listen,
that the recognition and notoriety of the star chefs of
the 1990s would be enjoyed by new bartenders of the
early aughts. Mixologists broke new ground and worked
the craft with creativity, achieving successes not seen
since the late nineteenth century. This would be the era
of the star bartender—complete with the rewards and
the pitfalls that the movers and shakers of the culinary
revolution had already experienced.

On the evening of September 10, 2001, I was at
Windows on the World hosting a session in a series we
called Spirits in the Skybox, presented in the Skybox,
a member's lounge that overlooked the main bar. My
session included a hands-on class in tequila cocktails
and a tasting of different expressions. At the end of the
session we all felt a bit buzzed and needed some food.
I had friends who had attended the class, and I asked
the evening manager whether he had a table in the
main bar large enough for the party to grow if needed.
I was supplying the fuel, Veuve Clicquot Champagne,
our Windows on the World special cuvée, to keep
things light and airy. We dined and then danced to the
music put on by a wonderful woman DJ and stayed
'til closing. The check I signed that night, along with
thousands of papers and documents, would be swept
away by the prevailing westerly winds and scattered from
New York Harbor to neighborhoods in Brooklyn. The
Baum Family was contacted by residents of Brooklyn

Spirits in the Skybox
at The Greatest Bar on Earth
September 10, 2001

Spirits Tasting:

Cuervo Gold

Tres Generaciones Plata

Herradura - Reposado

Suaza Tres Generaciones Anejo
(3-G's)

WINDOWS ON THE WORLD

COCKTAIL RECIPES

THE CLASSIC MARGARITA

1 ½ oz. Tequila
¾ oz. Cointreau
1 oz. Fresh Lime Juice
½ oz. Simple Syrup
Salt the rim of a martini glass. Shake and strain ingredients
into a glass. Garnish with a lime wedge.

LA RUMBA

1 oz. Tequila
1 oz. Cachaca
1 oz. Pineapple Juice
½ oz Fresh Lime Juice
½ oz Simple Syrup

Shake ingredients with ice and strain into a chilled cocktail glass.
Garnish with lime.

BANDITO LOCO

2 oz. Tequila
½ oz. Simple Syrup
½ Cointreau
Loco Soda
Fill with Loco Soda, build and serve in a highball glass.
Garnish with a Holland red pepper.

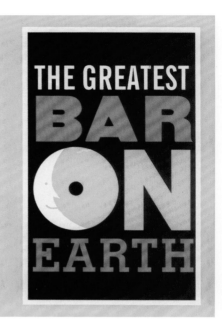

THE GREATEST BAR ON EARTH

who recovered papers from Joe Baum's archives in their backyards.

Our losses at Windows that day were heavy. We had booked a large breakfast event with two hundred guests. When the plane struck the North Tower, only a few of the client organizers were present, but a full complement of service staff—seventy-three Windows staff members—were setting up for the breakfast. Above the point of impact, they were unable to escape the building. The lives lost at Windows on the World that sunny Tuesday morning were among the 2,753 lives lost in the Twin Towers. It will take generations to recover from the loss.

After nineteen months of trauma, New Yorkers were still reeling but determined to find a path back to some sense of normalcy. As we began shifting into recovery mode, the fall season of 2003 exploded across the city: the bars and restaurants were back in business and then some. We were damned if terrorists were going to change our lifestyle, and we celebrated the holidays with a vengeance. With my book *The Craft of the Cocktail* as my passport, I went on the road, doing events around the country and in the United Kingdom, even taking a consulting job as the cocktail director for a small but influential London-based company called the Match Bar Group.

The cocktail bar business went into overdrive, its reawakening fueled by chat rooms that attracted aficionados from around the world, hungry for information about craft cocktails. London, New York, San Francisco, Portland, Seattle, and Sidney all had small communities of influential bartenders and bar owners involved daily in conversations. One chat room called DrinkBoy.com was the experiment of a project supervisor at Microsoft named Robert Hess, whose avocation was fine cocktails. He facilitated conversations with bartenders around the world, who shared recipes, techniques, products, and other resources. Debates over history and lore erupted in message-board threads that lasted for days at a time. Gurus of this online world emerged, including Ted "Dr. Cocktail" Haigh, whose influential 2004 book *Vintage Spirits and Forgotten Cocktails* inspired spirits producers to revisit the spirits and bitters products lost during Prohibition.

It was the beginning of a bull market for spirits, with companies large and small releasing premium and ultra-premium whiskey/y brands, tequila brands, and vodka brands. Grey Goose, an ultra-premium vodka brand on the market for a mere seven years, was purchased from Sidney Frank Importing Co. by Bacardi Limited for more than 2 billion dollars! Bitters, the defining ingredient of the cocktail category, were in the dead-letter box after Prohibition. But during the craft cocktail movement, they came roaring back, with more than a hundred brands producing several hundred flavors.

The cocktail community found an historical oracle in Dr. David Wondrich. A former college professor turned drinks writer for *Esquire* magazine, Wondrich wrote two books before publishing his seminal volume, *Imbibe!*, in 2007, a tour de force of drinks history, where real historical facts are typically as rare as dinosaur tracks. In 2010, Wondrich authored *Punch*, another volume of drinks history that changed the bar business. *Punch* was a deep dive into the birth of the spirit-based punch tradition that fueled high-society imbibing for 250 years, eventually becoming the blueprint for the cocktail itself. Craft bartenders around the world began serving classic shrub-based punches from the eighteenth century.

Meanwhile, *The Craft of the Cocktail*, my how-to book, was racking up printing after printing as bright young people leaving their business and professional studies to become bartenders began using it as their textbook. There must have been parents all over America gunning for this guy Dale DeGroff, whose book turned their son or daughter away from a *real* career for what—bartending!

Yes, indeed, it was starting to look as if there might be something to the notion that bartending could be a real profession again. Corporations that operated luxury hotel and restaurant brands realized that they needed beverage specialists with a broad knowledge of cocktails, spirits, wines, beers, teas, and coffees across cultures from the West to the East. The earnings ceiling for bartenders with these special skills was raised, and "the beverage specialist" became an emerging profession.

Large drinks companies that bet heavily on the rebirth of the cocktail and won big wanted to ensure that it was more than a flash in the pan. They put their dollars into the trade and invested in programs and events like Seagram's School of Spirits and Cocktails, Tales of the Cocktail, BarSmarts, World Class, and Bacardi Legacy. They dedicated themselves to the proposition that an educated consumer would reap huge returns in sales, and they invested in advertorials, researched and written by leading drinks writers like F. Paul Pacult, Dave Broom, and many others. They brought the consumer into the distilleries of Kentucky and the peat bogs and the barley malting floors of Scotland. I propose that the investment paid—and continues to pay—substantial dividends.

The drinks companies are not the only winners. Libbey glass and many smaller china and glass suppliers have prospered. The growth in just one glass category— the cocktail glass in all its iterations—from 1990 to 2018, is vast.

THE NICK & NORA GLASS

When we reopened the Rainbow Room in 1987, I needed a retro-style cocktail glass. Joe Baum sent me to Minners Designs, a venerable old house supplying china and glass to hotels and restaurants in New York for decades but sadly no longer in business. I described the glass I needed with a reference to *The Thin Man* movies: "Not the V shape, but a small bowl on a stem—the glass Nick and Nora Charles used when they made martinis." They referred me to their catalog of vintage items, with the disclaimer that they had discontinued many models, and because others were out of stock, new molds would have to be constructed.

Once I found the "Little Martini" glass in the catalog, that was it! We made the molds and used the glass for the lost cocktails with tradition at the Promenade Bar. Each time I ordered the glass, I called it the "Nick & Nora." In the new millennium, the china and glass company Steelite International bought some of the old Minners Designs catalog items, including the Little Martini; you will now find it described in their catalog as the Nick & Nora glass. Then, in 2005, Audrey Saunders used the Nick & Nora glass at New York's legendary Pegu Club, and within a few years the glass was adopted by craft bars around the world; today, even Libbey glass produces a version of the Nick & Nora.

Today, the cocktail seems to be everywhere, but most importantly, it is back in its rightful place in the thick of American cultural and culinary life. It is hard to thrill at the heights that the new millennium is taking the craft cocktail without looking back at how this unique American culinary art evolved for over two hundred years, a craft that we almost lost in the early days of the twentieth century with the "big mistake"—Prohibition.

PART ONE

THE CRAFT
OF THE
COCKTAIL

THE HISTORY OF THE COCKTAIL

The cocktail is, in a word, American. It's as big, diverse, and colorful as the country itself. Indeed, it could even be argued that the cocktail is a metaphor for the American people: it is a composite beverage, and we are a composite people. Let's begin by looking at what preceded its invention.

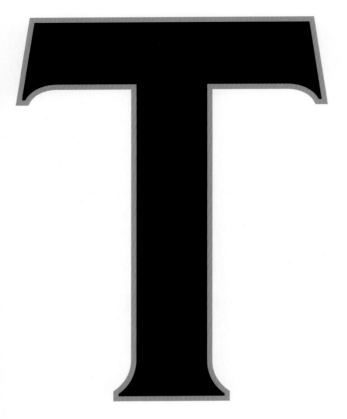

THE EARLY DAYS

Before Europeans settled in America, they had been cultivating beverage traditions for centuries. Around the Mediterranean, southern Europeans produced wine and eventually brandy, while beer and distilled-grain spirits were part of the tradition and culture of the peoples who inhabited the northern tier of Europe, where it was too cold for wine grapes to grow. (It is worth mentioning that in the time since this book was first published, climate change has expanded the grape-growing regions into areas previously too cool for successful vinification of grapes.)

The distillates produced from fermented fruits and grains were revered for their medicinal qualities, and came to be known as *aqua vitae* in Latin, *eau-de-vie* in French, *usquebaugh* in Gaelic, and "water of life" in English. These translations reveal how powerful their impact was. Consuming spirits was often perceived as a religious event, allowing imbibers to brush shoulders with the gods.

As technology advanced, distilled spirits were produced in greater quantities. Eventually spirits moved from the laboratory to the world of commerce, and alcohol as a beverage became firmly established.

DRINKING IN THE NEW WORLD

Once the Europeans established themselves in the New World, they put to good use the brewing, wine-making, and distilling skills they brought with them from the Old World. The early colonists were voracious experimenters, fermenting beverages from practically everything they could get their hands on: pumpkins, parsnips, turnips, rhubarbs, walnuts, elderberries, and more. They flavored their beer with birch, pine, spruce, and sassafras. They planted apple orchards to produce cider and, more importantly, applejack, which provided the base for many early colonial drinks. Applejack was popular because it could be made without the use of expensive distilling equipment, using an age-old technique. Fermented apple juice, or hard cider, was left out in the cold in late fall and early winter. As layers of ice formed on the surface of the cider, they were skimmed off, removing the water content and concentrating the alcohol in the remaining liquid.

New World spice and botanical ingredients fueled trade between the Old and New Worlds. In Italy and France, these plants found their way into fortified and flavored wines, aperitifs, amari, and digestivi, and eventually those products made their way full circle back across the Atlantic, where they would play a pivotal role in the development of iconic cocktails like the Manhattan and the martini.

Distilling in the new world for commercial use began as early as the sixteenth century. The Spanish colony that stretched from Central America to the tip of South America was called the Viceroyalty of Peru and was one of the sites of early distillation. By the close of the sixteenth century, colonial winemakers were distilling a small amount of brandy but exporting mainly wine to Spain. In 1641, King Philip IV prohibited imports of wine from the colony to protect producers in the Old World from losing their market to the cheaper imports. The growers retooled by increasing brandy production.

In the Dutch colony of New Amsterdam (now Manhattan), the director-general Willem Kieft set up the first still to make the Dutch grain spirit similar to genever, the first of the juniper-based spirits we know as gin today. In 1674, with the Treaty of Westminster, New Amsterdam became the English colony of New York. The genever stills were pressed into use making rum, the first commercially successful spirit of the New World. Rum distilling was already happening in the Dutch colony in northern Brazil. In their 1983 book *Rum: Yesterday and Today*, Anton Massel and Hugh Barty-King suggest that the sugarcane Pieter Blower planted on the island of Barbados in 1637 may have been sourced from Brazil.

THE DAWN OF THE MIXED DRINK

The English were also engaged in a lively trade in spices and tea in India and in Southeast Asia. David Wondrich, in his richly textured book *Punch*, tells how this trade between India and the growing British Empire led to the punch tradition. A drink made with arak, a local spirit of palm sap, sugarcane, and rice, combined with sugar, water or tea, citrus, and spice was a local specialty that found a home in the commercial outposts and on board ships bound back to the homeland. Its humble beginnings led to a high society tradition: the seventeenth- and eighteenth-century "cocktail party." Indeed, punch—a balanced combination of sweet, sour, strong, weak, and spice—would become the blueprint for the modern cocktail.

RUM & REVOLUTION

Rum production in the New World was sort of an accident. On his second voyage (1493–96), Christopher Columbus introduced sugarcane to the Western Hemisphere with the idea of creating lucrative sugar plantations. The Portuguese became the largest cane growers in the New World in the South American colony that is today known as Brazil. Rum was made by the ever-industrious colonists as a way to utilize molasses left over from sugar production. There was also a darker purpose: to subdue the slave population working in the cane fields. At the end of the seventeenth century, rum production in the British colonies dwarfed sugar production, leading the British to enact laws requiring a certain proportion of sugarcane crop to be used to make sugar. Rum had become the base for many colonial drinks and was produced throughout the Caribbean, South America, and to a great extent, even in New England.

The production of rum in the New England colonies started with clever ship captains making regular runs through the Caribbean, which fueled a growing underground economy. By 1733 it was a major export from New England. The New England rum distillers were purchasing the molasses from the cheapest sources in the Caribbean, the French, Spanish, and Portuguese. British rum distillers in the Caribbean were losing market share and losing the revenue from the molasses to the upstart colonial distillers. In retribution, the British Parliament passed the Molasses Act of 1733 to control and tax the flow of molasses into the colonies. The Sugar Act followed about thirty years later (1764), and then, in 1765, the Stamp Act required the use of a tax stamp on all transactions. These acts led to protests and revolt in the colonies, including the establishment of the Stamp Act Congress, a predecessor of the First Continental Congress, and more significantly to the beginnings of the American Revolution. So, you see, it was rum, not tea, that precipitated our break from Great Britain. (Well, maybe there were a few other minor concerns, but this is a book about cocktails, not lumber, oysters, cotton, tea, or tobacco.)

EXCISE TAXES & THE NEW REPUBLIC

The American victory over the British left the new republic deeply in debt. To the astonishment of most of his colleagues in the new government, Alexander Hamilton, our first secretary of the Treasury, decided to pay our war debts quickly by way of a federal excise tax on spirits. The tax was universally unpopular, but President Washington and the Congress, wishing to support a major initiative by Secretary Hamilton, passed the bill, and in 1791, it was signed into law. Thus began the tradition of paying for our wars by taxing spirits. A few years later the excise tax was repealed, but the precedent was set, and twenty years later—in 1812—the new nation found itself at war again with Great Britain. And for a second time in the nation's brief history, an excise tax was levied to pay for a war.

The British blockaded our coastline as they had done in the Revolutionary War, cutting off trade again with molasses producers in the Caribbean and all but finishing the dwindling rum production. This led to a tidal increase in the domestic production of grain spirits and eventually to the birth of the great American spirit, bourbon.

BITTERS & THE COCKTAIL

It was also during the period between the two wars with England that the word *cocktail* seems to have come into use. If you ambled into a colonial New England inn for a cold one, or just as likely a hot one, you'd probably order punch, ratafia, turnip wine, posset, bishop, flip, an ale, or a sling. Are any of these cocktails? No, but the sling, a poor man's punch, was the progenitor of the cocktail. The cocktail was first defined in print in response to a question posed by a reader. The year was 1806, the publication was called *The Balance and Columbian Repository*, and the editor wrote back:

> **Cock tail, then in a stimulating liquor, composed of spirits of any kind, sugar, water and bitters it is vulgarly called a bittered sling, and is supposed to be an excellent electioneering potion inasmuch as it renders the heart stout and bold, at the same time that it fuddles the head. It is said also, to be of great use to a democratic candidate: because, a person having swallowed a glass of it, is ready to swallow any thing else.**

The editor's reply gives us our first clear distinction of what constitutes a cocktail and separates it from all the concoctions that came before: the addition of bitters.

Bitters is a generic term that refers to both beverage and nonbeverage preparations, mostly alcohol-based and flavored with botanicals. Many of the botanicals used in these bitter concoctions were brought back to the Old World by explorers and botanists during the Age of Discovery and combined with botanicals whose origins date back to the ancient civilizations around the Mediterranean.

Nonbeverage bitters is a relatively modern term that separates the category from potable bitters that are taxed at a much higher rate. The bitters referred to in the 1806 definition of the cocktail began as medicinal preparations, which by no means meant they were undrinkable! They were popular as flavor additives in alcoholic beverages and by themselves. Doctor Richard Stoughton, a London physician, created the category in 1712 when he received a royal patent in the United Kingdom, only the second

medication to receive that distinction. Stoughton's may well have been the bitters formula that the editor referred to in the 1806 cocktail definition.

Stoughton's alcohol-based bitters, which contained nearly two dozen botanical flavors, became so popular as a beverage and as an additive to alcoholic beverages that word spread across the Atlantic—but, not the actual product itself. Colonial Americans were "entrepreneurial," to put the best face on their outright theft, and although a few wealthy colonists could afford to import the real thing, counterfeit versions emerged. It is no surprise that eventually Stoughton's was the victim of its own popularity, since it tasted different from city to city!

The most commercially successful bitters in the Americas, Angostura bitters, tasted the same no matter where it was purchased. It was developed in 1824 by J. G. B. Siegert. His product, like Stoughton's, tasted good and found an enthusiastic audience in the United States and eventually around the world. It was originally produced in the town of Angostura, now Cuidad Bolívar, in Venezuela, but things got too hot politically, and Siegert moved production offshore to Port of Spain, Trinidad, where the company prospers still today, making bitters as well as rum and other spirits.

The excise taxes on spirits were repealed in 1817, and during a long period of laissez-faire, the spirits industry took off with this open market. In 1861 that came to an end, when President Lincoln levied an excise tax on spirits to pay for the Civil War, a tax that stubbornly remains in place today and has been collected by the federal government as well as by individual states since the end of Prohibition. In the nineteenth century, clever producers beat the excise tax by marketing their alcohol-based bitter concoctions as medicines. Spirits were so expensive and difficult to find during the Civil War that the average foot soldier settled for one of these "medicinal" preparations—Hostetter's "stomach bitters"—which became the most consumed alcoholic beverage for Union soldiers during the war.

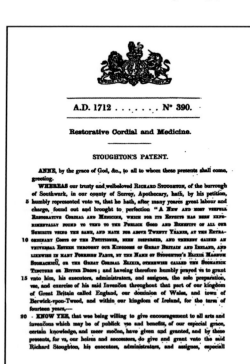

A.D. 1712 . . . . Nº 390.

Restorative Cordial and Medicine.

STOUGHTON'S PATENT.

ANNE, by the grace of God, &c., to all to whom these presents shall come, greeting.

WHEREAS our trusty and welbeloved RICHARD STOUGHTON, of the burrough of Southwark, in our county of Surrey, Apothecary, hath, by his petition, humbly represented unto us, that he hath, after many yeares great labour and charge, found out and brought to perfection "A NEW AND MOST USEFULL RESTORATIVE CORDIAL AND MEDICINE, WHICH FOR ITS EFFECTS HAS BEEN EXPERIMENTALLY FOUND TO TEND TO THE PUBLICK GOOD AND BENEFITT OF ALL OUR SUBJECTS USING THE SAME, AND HATH FOR ABOVE TWENTY YEARES, AT THE EXTRAORDINARY COSTS OF THE PETITIONER, BEEN DISPERSED, AND THEREBY GAINED AN UNIVERSALL ESTEEM THROUGOUT OUR KINGDOMS OF GREAT BRITAIN AND IRELAND, AND LIKEWISE IN MANY FORREIGN PARTS, BY THE NAME OF STOUGHTON'S ELIXIR MAGNUM STOMACHICI, OR THE GREAT CORDIAL ELIXIR, OTHERWISE CALLED THE STOMATICK TINCTURE OR BITTER DROPS; and haveing therefore humbly prayed us to grant unto him, his executors, administrators, and assignes, the sole preparation, use, and exercise of his said Invención throughout that part of our kingdom of Great Britain called England, our dominion of Wales, and town of Berwick-upon-Tweed, and within our kingdom of Ireland, for the term of fourteen yeares,—

KNOW YEES, that wee being willing to give encouragement to all arts and invencöns which may be of publick use and benefitt, of our especial grace, certain knowledge, and meer mocön, have given and granted, and by these presents, for us, our heires and successors, do give and grant unto the said Richard Stoughton, his executors, administrators, and assignes, especiall

The cocktail of 1806 was a novelty beverage, a "bittered" sling served without ice, which was a rare commodity at the time. Later in the century, Mark Twain would remark in his book *Life on the Mississippi*, "In Vicksburg and Natchez, in my time, ice was jewelry; none but the rich could wear it." The cocktail was a modern beverage, a post–Industrial Revolution phenomenon that needed technology. It would grow slowly through the early nineteenth century and pick up speed as alcohol beverage production became cheaper and more efficient with the invention of the continuous still. Ice became cheap and widely available with the commercialization of artificial ice production. The cocktail as an American iced drink on a wide scale became a reality.

THE STORY OF AMERICAN WHISKIES, BOURBON & RYE

After America's molasses supplies were cut off during two wars with the British, the transition from rum to whiskey as the most popular alcoholic beverage was well underway. The immigrants who fled the first potato famine in Ireland (1740–41) found the puritanical New England states less than welcoming, so many of them settled along the frontier of western Pennsylvania. These hardy souls cleared lands for small farms and did what they were schooled in: they distilled whiskey. Rye and barley, two grains not indigenous to the Americas, were widely cultivated. Some brought small stills with them; others simply built their own stills out of necessity. At first, whiskey was used in commerce in place of cash. Goods were purchased and debts were settled with "Monongahela," as the local rye whiskey came to be known in Pennsylvania along the shores of the Monongahela, the river that marked the western frontier at that time.

Hamilton's post–Revolutionary War excise tax on spirits drove many distillers out of the colonies altogether. They made their way through the Cumberland Gap and into the frontier territories that would become Kentucky, Tennessee, Ohio, and Indiana. These territories, then included in the state of Virginia, were ideal for whiskey production. The soil was rich, and the indigenous grain corn had higher per-acre yields than other grains. And there was a plentiful supply of pure iron-free water bubbling up through the limestone shelf.

The corn whiskey they made was used in a barter economy and was eventually floated down the Ohio and Mississippi Rivers and sold in towns downstream. Barrels of whiskey were sometimes in transit for many months; folks downstream as far away as New Orleans liked the way it tasted after all that time in a barrel and sent word back up north for more of that whiskey from Bourbon County, the name stamped on the barrels by many of the makers. (At that time, Bourbon County, Virginia, constituted most of what is now the state of Kentucky.)

Prior to the invention of the steam engine, all barge traffic on the river went very slowly in one direction only—south toward the Gulf of Mexico—on flatboats, barges, and wagons. But with the advent of steam-powered riverboats and the construction of canals in the northeastern United States, especially the Erie Canal, which was completed in 1825, the big cities in the Northeast could be reached by water. It was also at this time, around 1833, that the word *bourbon* was used to separate the whiskey of Bourbon County from the rye whiskey made on the Maryland side of the Cumberland Gap all the way up to Pennsylvania. The name bourbon comes from the House of Bourbon, the ruling house in France from 1589 to 1792, and was a tribute to France for supporting the United States through the Revolutionary War.

COCKTAIL'S GOLDEN AGE

The stage was set during the Civil War for what we look back on today as the golden age of the cocktail. In 1862, a seminal volume of recipes was released by Dick & Fitzgerald, a popular how-to publishing house. The book *How to Mix Drinks, or The Bon-Vivant's Companion*, authored by Jerry Thomas, was widely considered to be the father of the modern bartending profession. He certainly did not create the profession of bartending, but he sure made it popular! It would be egregious not to mention the 1882 tome Harry Johnson's *New and Improved Bartenders' Manual*. Thomas gave us the first collection of beverage recipes, but Harry Johnson gave us more than recipes; his volume was a detailed manual on how to open and run a modern cocktail bar, a manual just as useful today as it was in 1882.

Bars and saloons flourished during this period. In 1832, the Pioneer Inn and Tavern Law created a new type of license that allowed inns to serve alcoholic beverages without being required to lease rooms. This made official what had been happening ever so quietly when colonial-era regulations were relaxed after the Revolutionary War: the bar was officially open for business.

A BAR ON EVERY CORNER, THE RISE OF THE AMERICAN POLITICAL SALOON

The Industrial Revolution swept the Western world in the eighteenth and nineteenth centuries and had a powerful impact on every facet of American life. One result was that the alcoholic-beverage industry benefited greatly. Factories lured people to urban centers around the country and fostered a sea of change in the way people ate and drank and gathered. As cities grew larger, restaurants and hotels became an important part of the urban landscape. Between 1845 and 1855, the potato famine in the British Isles and a failing economy in Continental Europe fueled a mass immigration, bringing millions of people from the United Kingdom, Germany, and other central European countries to the bustling cities of our East Coast. Like the colonists before them, these new Americans brought with them their distilling and brewing skills, and they shared one important tradition: the love of communal drinking fostered in the pubs and taverns of Scotland, Ireland, and England and in the beer halls and beer gardens of Germany and eastern Europe, a tradition they indulged with great zeal.

Typically the new arrivals lived in the worst areas of these urban centers. But what they lacked in means, they made up for in ingenuity, creating their own social clubs that they stocked with whatever spirits or beer they could make or find cheaply, selling them to the neighborhood at large. These unlicensed establishments thrived in the immigrant neighborhoods of the big industrial cities, first in the Northeast, and then, as the frontier moved west, they populated those cities as well. But they caught the eye of powerful political bosses and were turned into political action centers.

Tammany Hall, the political organization that began as the party of Thomas Jefferson in 1789, when New York City was still the capital of the United States, morphed into a corrupt political machine. By the mid-nineteenth century Tammany politicians operated the city of New York like a bank using the city's treasury for their own enrichment. Tammany Hall had a long run, until the Great Depression in 1929, with Mayor Fiorello LaGuardia cleaning up the remains of the party when he was elected in 1934.

In the era that saw a massive increase in immigration, beginning in the mid-1850s, Tammany Hall mined the teeming ghettos for votes. They took notice of the illegal social clubs and unlicensed service of alcoholic beverages, and with the help of wealthy members in the alcohol beverage and the fixtures businesses, the American political saloon emerged. Popular neighborhood bars opened and Tammany was happy to license and fund them, but there was a quid pro quo. Soon enough, the saloon owners became the power brokers in their precincts, and the patronage system was perfected. Jobs in municipal government or in the police, fire, and sanitation departments were secured through the neighborhood saloons; all that was asked was to vote Tammany across the board.

THE AMERICAN POLITICAL SALOON

M. R. Werner, the author of *Tammany Hall*, published in 1928, a massive work on the rise and fall of Tammany Hall, shows the reach of the "pragmatic creed" that fueled that institution of corruption. In 1910, H. G. Wells wrote a book surveying the United States called *The Future in America*, asking the question, "Is the average citizen fundamentally dishonest? Is he a rascal and humbug in grain? If he is, the future can needs be no more than a monstrous social disorganization in the face of divine opportunities." In his book, Werner notes, "After he [H. G. Wells] had visited some American political saloons in Chicago with the boss of that city, Alderman [Michael] Kenna, better known as Hinky Dink, Mr. H. G. Wells wrote: 'It struck me that I would as soon go to live in a pen in the stockyards as into America politics'". The reach of the Tammany creed into New York State politics and by extension into the White House itself made Tammany Hall members kingmakers. And that pragmatic creed has been with human beings since they gathered in cities and tried to govern. Werner asks once again in his book: What brings real happiness? Money and power? Or justice, which brings happiness in the soul? It's a question also explored in Plato's *The Republic* 2,400 years ago.

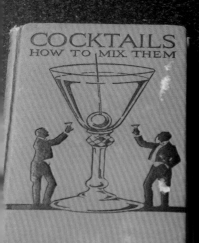

Cocktails: How to Mix Them by Robert Vermeire, a Herbert Jenkins Book, 1922

Drinks: How to Make and How to Serve Them by Bill Edwards, David McKay Company, 1936

Cups and Their Customs by John Van Voorst, Paternoster Row, 1869

The Artistry of Mixing Drinks by Frank Meier, Fryam Press Paris, 1936

Jerry Thomas' Bartenders Guide, Dick & Fitzgerald, 1887

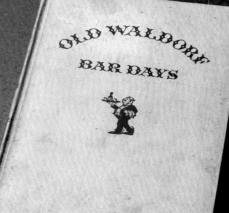

Old Waldorf Bar Days by Albert Stevens Crockett, Aventine, 1931

Jack's Manual by J. A. Grohusko, 1908, Alfred A. Knopf, completely revised and reset, 1933

Café Royal Cocktail Book compiled by W. J. Tarling, Pall Mall Ltd, coronation edition, 1937

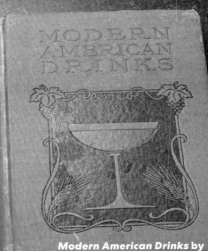

Modern American Drinks by George J. Kappeler, Saalfield Publishing Co., 1900

By the 1880s, the bar business was big and in full swing. More cocktail books and manuals were flooding the market, and cocktail bars of every description were flourishing in the big cities, from neighborhood haunts to the fancy cocktail palaces in big hotels. This was the era of the consummate professional—the barman. Service became as important as what was being served. In his 1882 *Bartenders' Manual*, Harry Johnson wrote a chapter titled "How to Attend Bar," in which he chides the novice to supply ice water immediately with every drink, to mix drinks above the counter where the guest can see, and to mix them in such a way as to be "neat, clean, and scientific." He also advises that professionalism affords a bit of showmanship when he instructs to "mix in such a way as to draw attention." Finally, Johnson instructs the bartender to be a caring friend: "If you think a customer is about spending for a beverage, when it is possible that he or his family needs the cash for some other more useful purpose, it would be best to give him advice rather than a drink, and send him home with an extra quarter instead of taking the dime for a drink from him."

One of the most stunning hotel bars in New York from the 1860s until it was shuttered in 1915, was the bar at the Hoffman House, with towering ceilings and an ornate fifty-foot mahogany bar, marble floors and walls, cigar counters, and an oyster bar. The barmen, pristine in their starched white jackets, were skilled practitioners trained in every aspect of beverage and service. Harry Johnson was the first to instruct ambitious acolytes in the opening and running of a solid bar business; Charles Mahoney took it several steps beyond Johnson in his 1905 publication *Hoffman House Bartender's Guide*. He dedicated the first 135 pages to setting up and running a first-class hotel bar. Each chapter focuses on a different aspect of bartender training: employer and employee relations, buying product, managing a cellar, wine and Champagne service, care and cleaning of fine silver—it is stunning in scope.

By the 1880s, all the elements were in place: the technology of refrigeration, charged water and tap beer systems, and mechanical ice machines. A growing variety of bottled spirits were available, both imported and domestic. Most importantly, a large, motivated, and well-trained workforce and a growing industrial economy fueled consumer spending. The 1880s right up to 1915 was the height of the cocktail's golden age, when many of the classics were either created or perfected: the Martini, the Manhattan, the sour, the fizz, the Old-Fashioned, the Pousse-Café, and the retooled Mint Julep made with American whiskey instead of brandy. Many of these remain classics today.

PROHIBITON & REPEAL

By the twentieth century, there were dark clouds on the horizon: a powerful women's temperance movement was gaining momentum across the country. They formed the Anti-Saloon League with the mission to end the production and·sale of all alcoholic beverages. They echoed the temperance sentiment that bars are "buckets of blood," where civility breaks down and is replaced by a predatory environment. They focused on the Christian heartland and, state by state, lobbied the governors and the state legislatures. By 1912, many states were already dry. Then in 1919, the Eighteenth Amendment to the Constitution was passed, and Prohibition became the law of the land. Speakeasies, the nickname for covert bars and private clubs where liquor could be found, flourished, often with the blessing of city officials and policemen who, behind the ruse of enforcement, were actually on the payroll of the powerful organized crime syndicates. These organizations not only controlled the supply and distribution of alcoholic beverages but in many cases operated the speakeasies and clubs where it was sold. But while booze continued to flow, the profession of bartending suffered immensely, and the arena for showmanship and excellence in the craft disappeared.

By the time Prohibition ended in 1932, the image of the bartending profession was badly tarnished by its association with organized crime. The gangsters did not suddenly disappear; they simply went "legit." Of course, after Prohibition there was great demand for bartenders, but the level of craftsmanship and respect for the profession as a serious pursuit was gone, and it would take decades for the profession to be rehabilitated.

Repeal was achieved by conceding control over the sale and distribution of spirits to the states. Under new laws, individual states—and even the individual counties within states—were granted enormous power over the alcohol beverage industry. A byzantine collection of regulations called the blue laws, which differed from state to state, made it very difficult for drink companies to conduct business nationwide. Control states like Pennsylvania and Washington purchased all beverage alcohol and sold it in state-owned liquor stores. Variety was not a priority and ingredients needed for many pre-Prohibition cocktails were not offered for sale or, in many cases, were no longer produced. Blue laws controlling on-premise sales were strange and inconsistent from state to state; some states only sold spirits in fifty-milliliter bottles, making cocktail production really difficult. Other states would not even allow liquor bottles to be on display at the bar! The tight controls and registering requirements that drinks companies had to deal with left the field open to the same sort of corruption that went on during Prohibition, with the ex-gangsters bribing public officials to carry their products exclusively, cutting out their competitors. This led to a dearth of smaller brands that did not sell in volume, or were not *represented* by the right distributors. The result dramatically impacted the range of cocktail possibilities.

Bartenders returning to the trade, or just getting started, found the shelves empty of many spirits and ingredients needed to make the classics of the nineteenth century. And when the Great Depression hit in 1929, the proverbial bottom of the barrel was reached.

After World War II, the fine-food and drink business entered the era of the bland. Cocktails suffered the ultimate insult: time-saving measures were introduced for an on-the-go society, some as a hedge against unskilled labor, but the result was technological advances that saved time and, of course, money, but diminished taste and quality.

COCKTAIL TRIVIA

Adrien Barbey, who owned and ran Hurley's bar and restaurant at Forty-Ninth Street and Sixth Avenue in New York City from 1979 to 1999, attributed much of his success to the men he put behind his bar. He would say about his bartenders, "I don't care what nationality they are, as long as they are Irish behind my bar." Hurley's Saloon is run today by Adrien's son Paul and, as of this writing, is located at 232 West Forty-Eighth Street.

A RETURN TO THE CLASSIC COCKTAIL

The 1950s was the era of the bland in both food and beverage. The technological advances that allowed large amounts of food to be shipped overseas to our fighting men in the two world wars were embraced by commercial food packagers. The supermarket was born. Pre-prepared and processed food products designed to make life easier flooded the market; TV dinners, baby formula, Kool-Aid, Jiffy Pop, and Tang were all the rage. Americans happily abandoned the fresh and natural, scooping up all that was processed and

canned. The cocktail bar was not spared. Presweetened, artificially flavored sweet-and-sour mixes, in the form of liquids or powders, made the scene. A product called 7-11 Tom Collins Powdered Mix, developed in the thirties, heralded the beginning of the end of the fresh-fruit cocktails of the pre-Prohibition era; by the 1960s, most bars in America had sour mixes in one form or another. Bartenders learned the "Kool-Aid" style of making drinks: ice, liquor, water, and a mix.

In 1959, when even "fine dining" restaurants featured vegetables from #10 cans, a ray of natural sunshine broke through the neon glare of fast-food joints and supermarkets. It began not at the bar but in the dining room on the culinary side of the business. Joe Baum, an executive of Restaurant Associates, in charge of the specialty restaurant division, and corporate chef Albert Stockli began working together in 1955 to develop unique restaurant concepts. Joe brought the chef and author James Beard on as a menu consultant. Beard shared Joe's vision of a new American cuisine that fused classic technique with regional glories and oddities and was prepared with fresh and seasonal ingredients. On the West Coast, author Helen Evans Brown published *Helen Brown's West Coast Cookbook* in 1952, which also pushed back against the growing trend of convenience foods from the grocery store shelves, emphasizing instead sourcing from local farms and fisheries. The idea resonated with both Baum and Beard, fitting neatly into their vision of a new American cuisine.

Under Joe's management in 1959, Restaurant Associates opened the Four Seasons restaurant in the stunning new Seagram Building on Park Avenue. The name of the restaurant tells the story. The kitchen was outfitted with fresh- and saltwater tanks for fish and shellfish, and Joe made deals with farmers in the nearby Hudson Valley for fresh produce. Joe was a locavore before the word even existed, and his daughter, Hilary, was a pioneer in setting up farmers' markets in Manhattan. The Four Seasons was an extraordinary success; as a single restaurant, it went on to have an extraordinary impact on fine dining in the United States.

In 1960, Baum opened La Fonda del Sol in the Time-Life Building. The restaurant celebrated Pan-American cuisines in a luxury setting for the first time. The recipes and ingredients were authentic; Joe's drink menu at La Fonda del Sol included cocktails made with pisco brandy, tequila, and mezcal, which had to be imported in 1960! Joe had a Mojito Criollo on that 1960 La Fonda del Sol menu. It would be twenty-eight years before Pisco Sours, Mojitos and mezcal drinks would appear on a menu again—my menu at the Rainbow Room. And it would be another ten years before they were widely available. Joe Baum was years ahead of his time. It would take the bar community another thirty years to catch up to the culinary side of the business.

Joe became president of Restaurant Associates in 1963 and created a flurry of theme restaurants, including two colonial tavern concepts, John Peel and Mermaid Tavern, and an Irish pub on Rockefeller Plaza called Charley O's, Joe's most successful bar until the Rainbow Room's Promenade Bar opened in December of 1987. Joe loved theatricality in restaurants but wanted menus with authentic recipes that would make sense to Americans. Michael Whiteman, Joe's business partner, captured that essence in a sentence, "Get rid of Beef Bourguignon on the menu—not the dish, just the description. How about beef braised in red wine sauce. Americans will order that!"

Between the 1950s and the 1980s, the American palate changed dramatically and Joe's impact was felt around the country. In the early 1960s a young U.C. Berkeley student named Alice Waters was studying abroad in France and fell in love with the French way of cooking. She made daily trips to the farmers' market to prepare her meals and it changed her life. Alice credits Joe's work at the Four Seasons as one of her inspirations for taking the big step to open Chez Panisse restaurant in Berkeley in 1971. At Chez Panisse, Waters would turn her love of market-to-table cooking into a business and eventually into a West Coast culinary movement.

In 1973, two French food critics, Henri Gault and Christian Millau, published their ten commandments of nouvelle cuisine. In their manifesto, they identified what young chefs like Paul Bocuse, Roger Vergé, Alain Chapel, and Michel Guérard were already doing; moving away from overworked dishes and heavy sauces to a simpler approach that let the ingredients speak rather than the sauces. The idea detonated like an atomic blast across the culinary world, even all the way to Berkeley, California, and the small restaurant operated by Alice Waters.

In 1973, the year that the manifesto hit the presses worldwide, Alice Waters brought in chef Jeremiah Tower to run the kitchen at Chez Panisse and help her explore the world of nouvelle cuisine. Tower had no formal culinary training, but his early exposure to the world of fine dining resonated with him. Being self-taught he

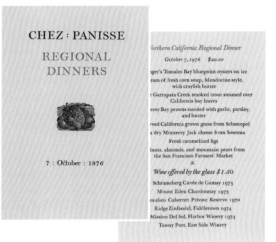

developed a unique and almost architectural approach to plating that was similar to the French nouvelle movement; he built sumptuous and appealing dishes. Early attempts at nouvelle cuisine by some were awkward, and I still chafe at the thought of my first encounter with nouvelle. My entrée arrived on a fifteen-inch plate with three sea scallops stranded in the middle and surrounded by eight colored dots that constituted the sauce.

Waters and Tower were together for five years and brought West Coast cuisine to the next stage. In October 1976, Tower's Northern California Regional Dinner, featuring all California wines and a menu that featured local oysters, Mendocino corn soup, Big Sur trout, preserved California geese from Sebastopol, Vella Monterey jack cheese from Sonoma. The dinner caused a sensation as word spread, even catching the attention of James Beard, who was in the midst of a monumental project with Joe Baum at the World Trade Towers in New York City. The work of Waters and Tower at Chez Panisse was christened at the time as "California cuisine." Chef Tower has largely been left out of the story of California cuisine; even Chef Anthony Bourdain felt strongly that the attention given Alice Waters eclipsed his role somewhat and he did something about that omission with a film called *Jeremiah Tower: The Last Magnificent*.

CALIFORNIA CUISINE

Chef, author, and television personality Anthony Bourdain believed that Jeremiah Tower didn't get the recognition he deserved for his part in developing California cuisine, so he decided to tell the story of America's first celebrity chef in the Zero Point Zero production *Jeremiah Tower: The Last Magnificent,* for which Bourdain was executive producer.

After six years of work on all the food service outlets in the two World Trade Towers, a daunting proposition to feed a small city of literally thousands of people a day,

Joe Baum opened Windows on the World in 1976, the crowning achievement of the whole project. Joe offered Tower the position of head chef, but Tower was still at Chez Panisse and had already begun talks with another group to open his own place in San Francisco. Tower opened Stars restaurant in San Francisco in 1984 and it was an overnight sensation. Tower took a keen interest in the bar at Stars. The drinks specials appeared on the mirror behind the bar, and over the years many regular customers were honored with their own specialties, including sixty-year veteran columnist Herb Caen of the *San Francisco Chronicle*, who enjoyed Herb's Picon Punch. Towers was one of the first chefs to move the bar in a culinary direction, using fresh ingredients and unusual garnishes, a direction that would become the signature of the craft bar movement in the new millennium. Stars had a fifteen-year run, and what a run it was!

During those fifteen years, the culinary world exploded. The death of James Beard in 1985 was a blow to that world, but it inspired Julia Child, chef Larry Forgione, and Chef Peter Kump to begin a fundraising campaign to buy James Beard's house left in his will to Reed College in Portland, Oregon, and create a home for chefs from around the United States to perform. The James Beard Foundation opened the house in 1986, and today it hosts more than two hundred events a year. In 1990, the James Beard awards for excellence in the culinary arts were instituted and they have become the equivalent of the Oscars for the culinary world. In 1993, the Food Network was launched on cable, garnering a devoted audience over a few short years. American chefs like Bobby Flay, Larry Forgione, Wolfgang Puck, Rozanne Gold, and Alfred Portale were opening restaurants and penning cookbooks throughout the decade, and a new language of the kitchen and the restaurant menu was emerging.

At Windows on the World, Joe hired a young man named Kevin Zraly to execute his vision of wine on every table. They got rid of the gold chain, the epaulets, and the snooty attitude and got down to the business of selling wine with passion and a smile. Joe Baum created concentric waves of change throughout the food and beverage world that touched many of the people who would go on to make dining in America the extraordinary experience it has become.

By now, dear reader, you may be wondering what all this culinary talk has to do with cocktails. In fact, the culinary revolution in the twentieth century played a critical role in the growth of the craft cocktail movement in the new millennium; it delivered a ready-made audience in love with big flavor and willing to take chances. An audience that embraced ethnic, regional, and fusion cuisines—and one that was demanding. When they sat down at the bar, they wanted that same quality that they were used to from the kitchen: drinks made from authentic recipes with only quality fresh ingredients.

A RAINBOW OVER MANHATTAN: DISHES & COCKTAILS WITH TRADITION

I started with Joe Baum in 1985 as the head bartender of a small fine-dining restaurant called Aurora with its Michelin-starred chef from Paris named Gérard Pangaud. We had a first-class Champagne and wine list, heavy on the wines of Burgundy, to accompany Chef Gérard's cuisine and I was a bit confused in my first interview with Joe, when he demanded a classic bar program of pre-Prohibition drinks, all fresh ingredients, no mixes. It would take a few months for me to understand why Joe made this odd request at a restaurant that was primarily focused on wine sales.

There was tremendous business at Aurora. We were in the Bankers Trust Annex Building, located at East Forty-Ninth Street between Madison and Park Avenues, with a built-in clientele of program traders. The stock market was through the roof, and the bar and restaurant were continually full for lunch and dinner. Joe was always busy with meetings at one of the half-round banquette tables across from the bar. He met with designers and artists like Milton Glaser, Phil George, and Dale Chihuly, and restaurant pals like George Lang. But when Benny Goodman pulled up a stool at my bar one day and announced he was here to meet with Joe Baum, I really wanted to know what I was missing. I asked the general manager and wine guru, Raymond Wellington, what was up. "It's Rainbow Room stuff. The Goodman orchestra is going to open the room." Sadly, Goodman passed six months before the Rainbow Room reopened.

The cocktail project Joe tasked me with had completely consumed me, and I almost missed the reason behind it. Aurora's cocktail program was a workshop, part of the preparations for the restoration of the legendary Rainbow Room on top of 30 Rockefeller Center. Dishes with tradition would be matched by cocktails with tradition. Joe always had a five-year plan. I instantly made it my business to discover everything I could about the restoration and expansion of the Rainbow Room.

I am deeply indebted to Joe's partner, Michael Whiteman, for his support in helping me craft a menu of classic cocktails. He sourced many of the historical books for me and, along with his wife Rozanne Gold, acted as a taster. Rozanne, a four-time Beard award winner, became Mayor Ed Koch's first chef when she was twenty-three years old, and she crafted the brilliant Little Meals menu at the Promenade Bar in the Rainbow Room. My challenge was translating nineteenth- and early twentieth-century cocktail recipes into menu items for Rainbow. I presented that menu to Joe and he liked it. I survived an interview with the GM, Alan Lewis, and in 1987, I got the gig as the head bartender at the Promenade Bar, and beverage manager to boot. Allen was unsure of my credentials when it came to the business side of the job, and much to my relief he hired a co-beverage manager to help me with the massive amount of work to build the inventory, hire thirty-six bartenders, and create the program. Bill worked with me for the first couple years, handling cost-of-sale issues and personnel problems, before moving on to another position.

Joe afforded me the opportunity to play an important role in reviving the great American cocktail. In December 1987, atop the Art Deco masterpiece at 30 Rockefeller Plaza, Joe's restoration of the legendary supper club opened to the public.

THE CRAFT COCKTAIL MOVEMENT

Keith McNally was one of the first restaurant owners in New York City to see this cocktail trend developing. He opened Cafe Luxembourg, Lucky Strike, Nell's, Pravda, Balthazar, Pastis, and more. Keith had the Midas touch. His secret weapon—like that of Joe Baum and Danny Meyer, the other great restaurateurs in New York City— was his attention to detail and his passion for excellence. Keith's legendary artist and gallery owners hangout, The Odeon restaurant, opened in 1980 and had a great bar, and his head bartender, Toby Cecchini, was the first to make a proper cosmopolitan in New York City.

In 1996, Keith opened Pravda, and he decided to make the bar the star of the place instead of the kitchen. Pravda was a vodka bar with gourmet snacks in an unattractive one-story building on Lafayette Street. He turned the basement space into a Moscow subway-station-themed bar, with a lounge that wandered through nooks and alcoves and even up the stairs to the main floor where he built a snug of a bar presided over by two extraordinary characters. The whole place was sexy, and it was an immediate and stunning success. Keith made a trip to the Rainbow Room with his management staff prior to opening at Pravda to show them the type of cocktail program he wanted. He engaged me shortly thereafter to train the staff and create the first drinks menu. I continued to consult with Keith at Balthazar and Pastis, doing staff training and some cocktail menu selections.

THE SURPRISE RETURN OF THE SPEAKEASY

A new millennium is a divide that few human beings in history have the opportunity to cross. Predictions of all sorts get made—like the Y2K computer meltdown. But wild theories aside, those of us who do live through the passing of one millennium to the next cannot help but feel a sense of awe. Big changes just seem inevitable. And the little corner of the cosmos that the cocktail industry occupies is one profession that has been experiencing big changes since the dawn of the aughts. New York City is not the only city to see this explosion of creativity, but it seemed to have the most concentrated collection of unusual new bars early on in the movement.

Craft bars opened in quick succession. From 1999 to 2000, I operated a downtown-style lounge uptown on Forty-Ninth Street called Blackbird. I call it a pop-up now after a premature closing but it had an impact, certainly on me. I finally had the opportunity to hire a talented friend, Audrey Saunders, who would go on to open the Pegu Club bar and lounge. Blackbird bar and restaurant lasted ten creative and lively months that seemed to pass in a moment. Fresh seasonal fruits were employed in the drinks inspired by my close relationship with the chef Michael Smith; he consulted me daily on orders for the bar as he placed them for the restaurant. The Blackbird experience was so rich that I decided with some coaxing from an agent friend, John Hodgeman, to write the first edition of *The Craft of the Cocktail*.

The year 1999 would see the start of one of the most influential bars in decades. Sasha Petraske opened a tiny bar on 134 Eldridge Street called Milk & Honey, in a basement site formerly occupied by a mahjong parlor. In a few short years, young bartenders around the world would imitate his unique approach to the craft of bartending. He brought back the jigger, all but discarded by upscale bars, where it was considered stingy, because he wanted precision in measuring. His exacting approach covered every detail of the drink—from chilling the ingredients and tools to predetermining shaking and stirring times in order to achieve the perfect balance of dilution and alcohol strength. These were details long since forgotten in most bars. Sasha rejected the metal-over-glass Boston shaker, replacing it with the metal-over-metal shaker to chill a drink faster.

Sasha was a problem solver, ignoring the long-standing norms. He never considered the garnish tray that every bar in the United States used because he knew they didn't keep the garnishes cold. Instead, he custom-built a stainless steel box with a drain and filled it with crushed ice to hold the garnishes. He even made his own ice in a used top-loading freezer that he picked up for fifty dollars, making slabs and block ice he could cut to the sizes and shapes he wanted.

The service at Milk & Honey was also unique. There was no menu: customers were queried about their likes and dislikes to arrive at the perfect drink, customized to their individual tastes. His standard of service was ladies and gentlemen being served by ladies and gentlemen. A speakeasy with locked doors and a password was not Sasha's intention; it was done out of necessity. He was serious about being a good neighbor in his building and in the neighborhood, which was mostly Chinese. He never put a sign above the door because he wanted to grow the business slowly. This unique approach garnered fans by word of mouth and he implored regulars to keep his name out of the press. Inevitably, the crowds started to gather outside his bar, and so he locked the door and only accepted reservations. He changed the bar's phone number every month and sent it to the regulars, always with the disclaimer "please don't bring anyone to my house that you would not be proud to invite in your own home." The details of Sasha's service, presentation, techniques, and tools, and the speakeasy style that Sasha resorted to out of necessity would become a popular new theme in bars around the country, and eventually around the world.

In 2003, Julie Reiner opened a large bar, Flatiron Lounge, on Nineteenth Street in Manhattan. She offered flights of cocktails prepared with all fresh ingredients in a classy deco-themed lounge. It was an instant success. In 2004, Keith McNally's employees of Pravda—most of whom I had trained—Dushan Zaric, Jason Kosmas, Henry LaFargue, Bill Gilroy, and Igor Hadzismajlovic—opened Employees Only at 510 Hudson Street in Greenwich Village behind a fortune teller's booth, which was a true speakeasy, featuring riffs on the classic cocktails. EO, as they have become known, began producing many of their own cocktail ingredients, like house-made grenadine and bitters. Sixteen years in they are busier than ever.

In 2005, Audrey Saunders opened an elegant bar lounge called Pegu Club on West Houston Street. Audrey is a wizard, a true apothecary, and she experimented constantly. She spent days on the simple Gin and Tonic, leaving nothing to chance and trying every combination that was available on the market to find perfection in the drink. Audrey's staff of bartenders schooled by her intense attention to detail went on to open iconic establishments of the craft bar movement, including Jim Meehan. He opened PDT in 2007 on St. Marks Place—a bar with a telephone booth entrance in the Crif Dogs hot dog joint. Jim and his partner weren't planning to open a speakeasy, but they had a dilemma: PDT was actually located in a separate street address from the hot dog place and if they cut a new door into the bar from the street, they would need another liquor license. It was not an option they could afford. That same year Death & Co. opened on East Sixth Street, headed by Phil Ward and Brian Miller, both of the Flatiron Lounge and Pegu Club family. Joaquín Simó, who now owns his own bar, Pouring Ribbons, and Jillian Vose, head bartender of the most celebrated bar in Manhattan, The Dead Rabbit, were both Death and Co. bartenders.

The family tree of bars and bartenders spread within New York and from city to city, and soon the craft bar movement was a global phenomenon. Robert Simonson penned a marvelous genealogy of the craft movement and its most important players called *A Proper Drink*; I highly recommend it. But now let's get to the spirits and the cocktails and learn more by tasting them!

THE LAST REQUEST

"High up there on the sixty-fifth floor they could look out over the sparkling city. . . . Manhattan gleaming like a beautiful queen wearing a billion dollars in diamonds. . . . They came to celebrate the greatest moments of their lives, and to dance on the revolving dance floor to the big band sounds of their youth. They came to rekindle romance, and be young again, if for only one night." These were the words of my friend and customer Jerry Yulsman, author, photographer for *Playboy* magazine, among other publications, and World War II tail gunner, who survived multiple bombing runs over Romania's Ploesti oil field and wrote a book about it, *The Last Liberator*. I fulfilled Jerry's last request after-hours in a day room at Interfaith hospital on Atlantic Avenue in Brooklyn, with our wives present. I made martinis for all, and we smoked Marlboro Reds in front of an open window, with a nurse guarding the door for us. Jerry was happy. It was the last time I saw him.

THE INGREDIENTS OF THE COCKTAIL

The craft bartenders of the new millennium have embraced the history, lore, and classic recipes, and they have taken the cocktail to a new place. The liquor purveyors have brought to market wonderful new products; let's take a look at these ingredients and, of course, the recipes new and old.

am a firm believer that spirits are gifts from the gods. How could man ever have figured out how to make them on his own? The hand of man is not needed to produce alcohol. Alcohol is the by-product of a natural process carried on by single-celled beasties from the fungus kingdom called yeast. There are over 1,500 species, and for our story we are especially interested in the ones that dine on sugar and produce ethanol alcohol, which is the drinkable type. They multiply by budding or splitting at an astonishing rate, and in the fermentation process, they eventually produce so much alcohol that they bring about their own demise. (We might take a lesson from these little beasties and put the brakes on the rate with which we are consuming the resources of this beautiful globe that shelters us from the uninhabitable vastness of space that surrounds us.)

DISTILLATION

Distillation is the process of removing the alcohol from the water, and it does require the hand of man and an apparatus that employs heat to separate the alcohol from the water. Basically, anything that contains sugar or starch can be turned into sugar, fermented, and distilled.

People have fermented and then eventually distilled every kind of fruit, grain, some vegetables, honey, and cane for thousands of years. Alcohol vaporizes at 178°F and water at 212°F, and that accident of nature accounts for a part of the human experience that has been with us since the first hunter-gatherers settled down and realized that they could make more than bread from the grains they were growing or the honey they were collecting. Throughout history there has been all sorts of equipment for the distillation of ethyl alcohol, from early methods in Asia, using ceramic vessels, and hollowed-out logs in colonial North America to the multicolumn fractional distillation machinery of today. The column or continuous still was invented in 1826 by Robert Stein but patented in 1831 by Aeneas Coffey. The continuous still was a huge leap forward for the alcohol beverage industry. The single batch or pot stills (also known as alembic stills) are charged with the liquid wash and distilled once after which the still must be emptied and cleaned before charging with a fresh batch of wash (low alcohol fermented beer or wine). The two-column patent still, as it is also known, is fed a continuous flow of liquid wash (fermented mash) at the top of the first column. As it is flowing down, it is heated to a vapor that rises again, and as it encounters the fresh wash coming down, it strips the alcohol and then passes to the second still, where that alcohol, a rich vapor, is condensed back into a liquid.

Distillers today have plenty of options, and the type of spirit a distiller wishes to produce will determine the equipment. Rich, oily spirits that retain characteristics (congeners) from the base ingredients might require a couple passes through a single pass "pot" or alembic-style still that allows many of the congeners or trace elements of flavor and aroma to remain in the mix. High-proof, very clean, almost neutral spirits can be efficiently produced in modern versions of the column still, some of which employ multiple columns with plates at intervals that can remove individual impurities with amazing efficiency.

FLAVOR AND AROMA

Alcohol is a hospitable organic compound that bonds naturally with other organic compounds, and this produces the flavors and aromas that we enjoy in spirits. High-proof, almost-pure alcohol can be diluted with water to produce vodka or flavored with botanicals to produce gin. It can take on a smoky flavor like Scotch whisky or artisanal mezcal. We can soften it and add flavors to enrich it with wood maturation, dividends returned as the spirit passes season after season in wood barrels. Unfortunately, alcohol molecules don't distinguish between good and bad flavors when they link with other organic compounds, so the distiller must be a brilliant matchmaker and introduce only the desired flavors and aromas. What flavors and aromas do you prefer? Choosing the spirits for a home bar, tasting them, and using them to make great cocktails can be a daunting task, but it can be a pleasant one as well.

There are a few fundamentals we should get out of the way before we start choosing brands and flipping cocktail shakers around: one of the most important is ice. The cocktail is by definition an American iced drink, and ice is a central ingredient.

ICE

Ice is the soul of the cocktail, it is an American iced drink. In the nineteenth century, cocktails were shaken and stirred with ice. We got hooked on ice-cold drinks because of our blazing hot summers; and we had the icy cold winters to harvest the ice bounty of the frozen lakes to store for summer use. Americans traveling in Europe are often vexed by the stingy amount of ice used in drinks. This wasn't always the case. As far back as the Greco-Roman civilizations, ice and snow were used to cool beverages, evidenced by the excavation of ancient ice pits used for storage. In Continental Europe there was easy access to ice and snow fields, but British winters were milder and ice was hard to source; there, it was used mostly for producing confections like ice cream and then later for the salmon fishing industry that thrived in the British Isles.

In the early nineteenth century, an American named Frederic Tudor pioneered an ice business by harvesting ice in the winter and then storing and selling it in the warm months and eventually in warmer climates. In the middle of the nineteenth century, artificial ice machines began to appear on the market. Inexpensive, readily available ice was a major factor in the growth of the cocktail.

Cocktail recipes called for different kinds of ice: block, lump or cubed, cracked, and snow ice. Block ice was the standard through the nineteenth and early twentieth centuries. The end user employed tools to break the block ice down into the types of ice needed, from nice large chunks for the punch bowl all the way down to snow ice shaved off the block for julep and frappé drinks.

Most of the twentieth-century commercial ice machines that made ice used in drinks (as well as by sportsmen and fishermen and in hospitals) were predominantly produced in the United States. The Kold-Draft company had a lock on the manufacturing of ice machines. Their machines produced a solid 1¼-inch ice cube that had a longer life in the glass and the pitcher, and even for the sportsman who required cooling for fish and game.

In the late twentieth century, the Japanese entered the market with efficiently designed machines modernized for speed of production. The machines produced shapes that were smaller, with increased surface area that filled the glass completely, giving the illusion of more liquid. Establishments replaced two older machines with one really efficient machine, providing real savings, but there was a cost. The downside was over-dilution. These new machines coincided with a change in drinking habits to lighter, juicier, and in many cases, sweeter drinks. The smaller cubes filled the glass and provided faster dilution that actually suited the lighter, sweeter-style drinks, making them less cloying and fresher, and for a while, the over-dilution problem went unnoticed.

The problem of dilution was experienced by those who consumed premium spirits over ice or strong spirits shaken and stirred into cocktails. Sipping premium spirits poured over two or three large cubes without over-dilution allowed the spirits to retain their richness and strength. The onset of the craft cocktail movement brought ice front and center again in cocktail production. Today's full-service craft cocktail bars use ice in many forms: snow ice for frappés and juleps, cracked ice for caipirinhas, 1¼-inch-square Kold-Draft ice cubes for shaking and stirring cocktails and large format 2 × 2-inch square cubes for straight spirits, and block ice for punch service. Craft bars have introduced a new type of ice called pebble ice, tiny ice balls, as a substitute for crushed or snow ice. I am not a fan and prefer the snow ice for juleps and frappés. Craft bars have returned to an earlier tradition, ordering—or in some cases producing—large blocks of ice to process into the formats they require, even an elongated cube used in highballs, a shape pioneered by Sasha Petraske at his bar, Milk & Honey, on Eldridge Street in Manhattan.

SASHA PETRASKE: THE ICEMAN COMETH

Shortly after Sashaa Petraske opened Milk & Honey, my friend Joe, who had a duplex apartment in the only loft building on the block, directly across the street, noticed a group of young people piling out of the ground-floor mahjong parlor across from his place. He approached and asked, "What were you guys doing in the mahjong parlor?" "That's a bar," they replied. Joe poked his head in and met

Sasha Petraske; he liked the place and popped in occasionally for a drink. He told Sasha that his favorite bar was the Rainbow Room's Promenade Bar and that he wanted to bring by his friend Dale. I met Sasha shortly after, and he had many questions for me, the first being about ice. At the time, I was like a missionary for the Kold-Draft machines and I mentioned that the cube was superior to anything else on the market. But the price and size of a machine was out of his reach. The next time I came in, Sasha had interesting oversize cubes, and I asked about his source. He had purchased one of those long chest-style freezers, the kind you could store a body in, for fifty bucks. He was making large blocks and cutting them down to the sizes he needed.

and even at home. Agave spirits like mezcal, bacanora, and sotol are showing up on back bars and in liquor stores, as are multiple amaro and beverage bitters brands; even the once-outlawed absinthe is legally available in the United States again. Pre-Prohibition-imported liqueurs gone for decades are being produced again. Domestic artisan spirits are coming into the market faster than we can keep up with them. Alcoholic beverages from Asia have followed in the path blazed by Asian fusion cuisine, with entries like sake, Korean soju and Japanese shochu, and the white spirit of China baijiu, which is currently the best-selling spirit worldwide, with 10.8 billion liters sold in 2018. It is about time we tried a taste! All these categories are finding a home in the craft cocktails of today. Where to begin? Start by assessing your needs—not for a single drink, but for your home bar.

WATER IS THE KEY

To illustrate how important water is to a cocktail, try the following experiment. Place a bottle of gin in the freezer and a bottle of vermouth in the fridge. Chill your glasses and your olives, get everything very cold. Prepare a martini without ice by simply mixing all the cold ingredients in the chilled glass and dropping in the olives; take a sip, and what you experience will not resemble a martini—it will be too strong and unpleasantly hot on the palate. The water created by dilution does many things to a cocktail: it mellows the alcohol burn and introduces the 80- or 90-proof spirit gently to the tongue, opening flavors and aromas that would be missed otherwise.

SPIRITS

In the original 2002 edition of **The Craft of the Cocktail,** I suggested brands at the end of the spirit descriptions of the "big seven" spirit categories. Today the growth in all spirit categories, as well as the arrival of new ones, has been so vast it is daunting. So, I have changed my recommendation process. I am branding many of the recipes. It is a better way to suggest the spirits that I recommend and the spirits that enhance the flavors in the drink.

A well-stocked bar should offer one or more selections from the big seven categories: gin, vodka, whiskey (bourbon, scotch, rye, blended, and Irish), rum, tequila, brandy, and liqueurs. But don't stop there. The big seven idea is a bit out of step with today's cocktail needs. New categories are fast becoming staples at bars

PRICE

Price doesn't guarantee quality, but in many cases you do get what you pay for. My feeling is choose the best ingredients you can afford. But there's no need to overspend on super-premium spirits—a VSOP Cognac makes a fine Sidecar. But don't grab the cooking brandy, either! There are three price levels that brand categories usually fall into: value brands, call brands, and premium brands. But the new millennium has continued the move toward luxury goods, adding ultra- or super-premium as a category, with prices ranging from above one hundred dollars into the thousands of dollars. Behind the bar at the legendary Hotel Bel-Air, I had orders for Christian Brothers brandy and soda and for Louis XIII and soda, and I was pleased to make them both.

LABELS & THE LAW

The information on bottle labels can range from minimalist-chic to the Gettysburg Address. The most important information is mandated by law: size, who makes it, where it's from, and alcohol by volume are the basics. Better labels tell you the process by which the spirit was made and, if it's been aged, how long, and under what conditions. Certain spirit categories like bourbon or rye whiskey, Cognac, Armagnac, and several others have strict production requirements that regulate what words can appear on the label. The alcohol strength on a label of spirits appears as a percentage of alcohol by volume, or ABV (for example, 40% ABV). The proof of spirits is double the percentage of alcohol: 40% equals

80 proof. The basic spirit categories—whiskey/y, vodka, gin, brandy, tequila, and rum—are required by the U.S. government to be bottled at a minimum of 40% ABV or 80 proof. The agency that sets the regulations in the United States is the Alcohol and Tobacco Tax and Trade Bureau, known more commonly as the TTB. In Europe the regulations are determined by the European Union, and the TTB regulations and definitions defining different spirits do not always agree with the EU regulations and definitions. But the fundamental TTB requirements must be adhered to if brands wish to export to the United States, for example base spirits like vodka, gin, whiskey, brandy, tequila, and rum must be a minimum of 40% alcohol by volume to be sold in the United States. It can be eye-opening to visit the TTB website and read through some of the requirements (www.ttb.gov).

Flavored spirits and liqueurs are permitted at lower proofs. Aperitifs, vermouths, and sherries are also lower, usually between 16% and 30% ABV, and liqueurs range widely from 16% to 55%. Today, knowledge about spirits and how they are made is much more widely available to the trade and consumers alike, thanks to a determined effort on the part of the drinks companies to educate consumers. The era of a colorful lore with no factual foundations is on the wane; more and more bartenders and consumers are choosing based on what is in the bottle and not what is in the public relations flyers.

AGE

The barrel-aging of spirits adds flavor and rounds out the harsh notes in young spirits. Most aging takes place in oak barrels. The size of the barrels, the climate where they are aging, their treatment, and the number of times they have been used are all factors that affect the resulting spirit. For example, bourbon aged in warehouses in Kentucky, with its hot summers and cool, damp winters, will age more rapidly than scotch aging in a warehouse on the island of Islay, with its damp, cool sea breezes and very little hot weather. The bourbon may reach maturity in four to six years, whereas the scotch will need six to twelve.

The aging of spirits is often used as a marketing tool and may actually have little to do with quality. A twelve-year-old designation on a bottle of spirits means nothing if it is poorly distilled. Don't rely exclusively on age declaration when choosing a spirit; look also for established, well-respected brands.

And in some cases, younger spirits may be preferred. The margarita is a clean, limey drink and is best with unaged silver or lightly aged reposado tequila. Save the expensive añejo or extra añejo tequilas for sipping or for richer cocktails. The same applies with rum for a daiquiri: use young or unaged silver rum with a bold cane flavor profile rather than aged rum with oak and vanilla notes that can get in the way of that clean, limey flavor profile. There are exceptions: the mai tai has lime juice as well, but it calls for an aged rum to stand up to the curaçao and the orgeat syrup that are also present in the cocktail.

All brandies, except eau-de-vie-style fruit brandies, which are rested in nonreactive containers, are much improved with barrel age. Many spirit categories—for example, American straight whiskey—have exacting regulations that designate the type, the size, and the preparation of the barrels that are used for maturing. A friend asked me about the requirement that American straight whiskeys be aged in new charred oak barrels, but other whiskeys from around the world didn't need to be. On the face of it, the first thought is that some well-connected barrel manufacturer used his lobbyist in Washington to effect the law. But in fact, American whiskey would not be the same without that requirement; directly behind the layer of char, there is a layer of caramelized sugars. Each time the whiskey passes that layer as it moves in and out of the barrel, it changes. Not to mention the myriad of compounds in the wood that the alcohol, which is a powerful solvent, carries back to the barrel. In 1964, the U.S. Congress did something good: they protected bourbon as an American heritage product after thoughtful study of the issues and arrived at smart regulations to carry that quality forward for future generations. Note: see Whiskey: American and Canadian (page 38) for the actual legal definition of bourbon and rye whiskies.

STYLE

Of all the considerations when buying spirits, the most important is style—it's also the most subjective. Gin is a good example. London dry style has multiple botanicals, but juniper is the most prominent. Genever, the original style of gin from the Netherlands and parts of France and Germany, is on the malty side and can resemble the flavor of a newly made whiskey.

Whiskey/y can be big, spicy, and bold; lighter bodied with grassy, floral, and fruit notes forward; or it can be smoky and oily. Whiskey/y can also have an almost sweet honey and vanilla character, like the American bourbon described above.

When you walk in the liquor store and are faced with rows and rows of bottles, the only way to make the final decision is to taste; you could buy small fifty-milliliter bottles of different brands and taste them first straight and then in your favorite cocktails. This is a slow and lonely approach. Why not round up a group of like-minded friends, each bringing their favorite bottle of whatever spirit you are exploring at the time for tasting and cocktail making. That's when the fun begins. I will be suggesting brands throughout the recipe section, sometimes because I think they suit the particular cocktail and sometimes because I really like the taste. I will never recommend a spirit that is not well distilled. But personal tastes are just that; no one can tell you that you're wrong to like something!

TASTING: THE NOSE KNOWS

The taste buds all over our mouths are counted in the thousands, but the olfactory receptors in our nasal passages are counted in the millions. Phillip (Pip) Hills, author of the wonderful book *Appreciating Whisky*, illustrates the importance of scent in our perception of taste with a fun little experiment: Close your eyes and pinch your nostrils shut. Have a friend place a small piece of apple and then a small piece of onion on your tongue. Don't chew; just taste. Until the aroma has had a chance to travel through the nasal passages at the back of your mouth, it will be difficult to tell the two apart. The nose *knows*, and it is critical in enjoying flavor.

Now don't go out and thrust your nose deep into a glass of spirits and inhale heartily; you will succeed only in numbing your olfactory receptors for the next half hour. Instead, begin by waving the glass of spirits under your nose, and as you move the glass closer, breathe through your nose and your mouth at the same time. Work your way around the rim of the glass and enjoy the subtle aromas that characterize the particular spirit. You might be tempted to swirl the glass as you would in a wine tasting—but don't. Distilled spirits are much higher in alcohol then wine, and swirling will just concentrate the alcohol vapors at the top of the glass. The glass that professional tasters use for spirit tasting is a glass with a round bowl and a chimney-shaped top, with or without a stem. The alcohol vapors are trapped in the glass, but the characteristic aroma of the spirit rises. However, a simple white-wine glass will be fine for a cocktail-party tasting. When you do finally taste, take a small amount of

the spirit, rinse your mouth, and spit; this will rinse away that bagel or your last cigarette and coat your mouth with the spirit you are tasting. Take a second sip and cup it in the center of your tongue. Let it slowly roll around your tongue from side to side and back to front, touching all the different taste receptors for sweet, bitter, salty, and sour located all over your tongue.

Spitting is wise if you are tasting several brands and evaluating them. Tasting for evaluation is a learned skill, so don't be discouraged if your more experienced mates start throwing around descriptors that you cannot find in the spirit; like any skill, it requires practice and is enhanced by building a library of aromas. If you want to get serious, start a tasting book and write down your perceptions. Build a library of spirits you have enjoyed, or not, as the case may be, listing their characteristic aromas and flavors.

If you're just partying with friends, then it's time to make cocktails with your favorite brands. Let's begin with the spirit that helped jump-start the craft cocktail movement that we are enjoying today: vodka. Surprised? Absolut Citron vodka was the base spirit of the Cosmopolitan, the cocktail that had a huge worldwide following and put cocktails back on the bar again.

VODKA

Vodka is the easiest spirit to discuss stylistically but the hardest when tasting for evaluation. As defined by law in the United States, vodka must be a pure spirit with no additives except water, non-aged, and basically tasteless and odorless. Well . . . almost no additives: two—glycerol and citric acid—are allowed by law in vodka production to "correct" the distillation, as described by the producers who lobbied in favor of the additions, but only in minute parts per million.

Generally, vodka is made from grain, with grain accounting for well over 90 percent of the production on the international market. But vodka can be made from any plant-based sugar. There are producers in the European Union countries that took exception to grape-based vodkas and called for a stricter definition of vodka production, but those voices are quiet lately and a live-and-let-live attitude has prevailed. Vodka is by definition distilled above 190 proof by rectification, usually in a column still or a multicolumn still fractionally (see page 30). The number of times distilled is a favorite marketing tool used by vodka producers, as are the means of filtration. In a multicolumn still, fractional distillation takes place at multiple copper plates assembled at intervals in each of the columns, and because of that fractional distillation within the columns, one could make a case for how many times the spirit is distilled by adding up the number of plates in each column. Many vodka brands use that as marketing to assure the drinker that their vodka is distilled multiple times, with quality results. The final and very important step in vodka production is filtering through activated charcoal or other more exotic and sexy-sounding mediums, like quartz crystals, glacial sand, or even diamond dust. Activated charcoal is widely used because the activation process multiplies the surface area of a gram of charcoal to 32,000 square feet. The charcoal is powdered and mixed with a solution of 25 percent calcium chloride, then dried, rinsed, and baked to create a super-fine porous carbon with enormous filtering capabilities. The process sounds simple but requires some sophisticated equipment to be successful.

The stylistic differences between vodka brands are subtle, since strong flavor is not usually a consideration, but as you taste your way through a range of vodkas, you will be surprised at the variations in flavor, aroma, and texture. The first and most obvious difference is the source

of the sugar used in production: grain, potato, or fruit. The most distinctive of all the vodkas I've tasted in any category of base material is a potato vodka from Sweden called Karlsson's; I always include it in vodka tastings because it is so distinctive. I would definitely recommend it to vodka drinkers, but not in a martini; it should be taken chilled and straight as a sipping vodka or possibly in savory- or spicy-style cocktails like a Bloody Mary or Bloody Bull.

The second stylistic difference in vodka is its texture on the tongue, or mouthfeel. I find that two of the very popular imported vodkas represent the two prominent styles: Absolut has an oily, almost viscous texture that is often found in pot-distilled spirits, and Stolichnaya has a clean texture and a slight medicinal finish. Alongside the texture, Absolut vodka has the aroma of pastry or bread dough and finishes with an almost milky texture on the tongue that is missing in the Stolichnaya. That hint of sweetness and the oily texture are due, in part, to glycerin, not added after but as a by-product of distillation that is present in trace amounts in all spirits.

Vodka, like any well-distilled spirit, should not be unpleasantly hot with a bitter or acrid aftertaste. All base spirits at 40% alcohol or more are going to be hot going in, especially when taken straight; that first sip will create some serious heat on the tongue. But a spirit that doesn't cool and become almost menthol-like with a couple quick intakes of air through the mouth, and instead remains hot and unpleasant on the tongue with an acrid bitter aftertaste in the back of the throat, indicates flaws in the distillation. This is a rule that can be applied to any spirit and is the first important step toward determining the difference between good and bad distillation. A skilled master distiller who is involved with every step, from storage of raw materials to the final bottling, will always make the difference. With the vodka category more than any other category, quality is not defined by price. Premium and super-premium-priced vodka brands are more often than not decisions made in the marketing department, not at the distillery.

THE SMIRNOV STORY

In the 1930s, Rudolph Kunett of Bethel, Connecticut, bought the name and formula for Smirnoff vodka, originally produced in czarist Russia, from Vladimir Smirnov, in Paris, the last surviving son of Pyotr Smirnov, the founder of Smirnoff vodka. Kunett's father had supplied grain in Russia for the original Smirnov vodka. In 1939, John Martin, then president of Heublein Inc. and grandson of its founder, bought the whole ball of wax from Kunett for $14,000, plus a small royalty to Kunett on every bottle sold for the first ten years. After World War II, Martin ceaselessly promoted his vodka with four main cocktails: the Bloody Mary, the Screwdriver, the Moscow Mule, and the Vodkatini. He employed gorilla marketing, serving Screwdrivers from a tank truck on Hollywood Boulevard. His most successful promotions established associations with Hollywood actors. He placed the Smirnoff bottle in movies, especially the hugely successful James Bond films. He hired the young actor and director Woody Allen for the Smirnoff print advertisements. His famous catch phrase to woo the lunchtime gin-martini drinker was "Smirnoff . . . It leaves you breathless." Martin's success was remarkable by any standard. Within thirty-five years, he took an unknown spirit with zero sales to the largest selling spirit in America.

FLAVORED VODKA

Flavored vodkas arrived thirty-five years ago with brands like Absolut Citron and Stolichnaya Pertsovka, (known as Stoli Hot today), but the Russians have been flavoring their vodkas for hundreds of years. So, do you need flavored vodka at your home bar? Sure you do. If you want to make a great cosmopolitan, then you need citrus vodka. How about whipping up a fabulous variation on Dick Bradsell's Espresso Vodka Cocktail (page 122) with a good vanilla vodka, Kahlúa, and cold espresso? Choose your favorite flavored vodka and have some fun with it.

GIN

The base spirit for gin is usually made from grain, but not exclusively, and then flavored with botanicals to give it that distinctive "gin" flavor profile. Though many botanicals can be (and are) used by individual producers, juniper is required and usually the most prominent fragrance and flavor note, the common factor that unifies all gins. Other botanicals include coriander, angelica, orris, lemon and orange zests, fennel, cassia, anise, almond, and many more too numerous to name here.

A Dutch chemist named Dr. Franciscus Sylvius purportedly created gin at the University of Leiden in the mid-sixteenth century. But Arnau de Vilanova, a

thirteenth/fourteenth-century physician and author from what is modern-day Spain developed an aqua vitae infused with juniper three centuries prior to Dr. Sylvius. In fact before Dr. Sylvius was born in 1614, a formula for *geneverbessenwater* ("juniper-berry water") was published in the first Dutch distilling manual, Philip Hermanni's 1562 *Constelyc Distilleerboek.* In1575, Bols distillery began operation in Amsterdam.

English soldiers fighting in the lowlands of the Netherlands adopted the taste for gin, which they called "Dutch courage." The production of gin in London was encouraged by the Dutch-born King William III (William of Orange), who ascended to the English throne in 1672, when he married his fifteen-year-old cousin Mary of the House of Stuart. William was the best friend of the English distillers banning French imports, including wine and spirits, and he freely offered distilling licenses to nearly anyone who wanted one. As a result, gin production soared from a half million gallons in 1690 to 18 million gallons in 1710. The bumpy road for gin in the eighteenth and nineteenth centuries makes good reading, and the best place to start is David Wondrich's *Daily Beast* article titled "Solving the Riddle of Old Tom Gin" (March 28, 2017). Like many other spirits, gin changed in character in the early nineteenth century with the invention of the continuous still. Today, gin is made around the world, but the London dry style is considered the benchmark for a dry martini.

TYPES OF GIN

Genever, or Hollands gin, as it was historically referred to, is 70 to 80 proof or 35% to 40% alcohol. Genever was originally pot distilled from malt wine (malted rye and barley) and flavored with botanicals, among them but not predominantly, juniper. The base grains were barley, rye, wheat, and spelt. This type is referred to as *oude* ("old") and must contain at least 15 percent malt wine. Oude genever can be aged in wood but is not required to be aged. Another older style of genever called *korenwijn*, made with a minimum of 51 to 100 percent malt wine, is the closest thing we have today to eighteenth-century genever.

A recent arrival to the market, Old Duff, makes a limited amount of single malt 100 percent malted rye and barley genever; it is imported to the United States, and you can source it if you are intrepid. In the mid-twentieth century, a new column-still style of genever called *jonge* ("young") emerged. Jonge is not describing age; it indicates a new style of genever. It is often, though not exclusively, made from grain (during grain shortages, alcohol derived from other sources like molasses has been substituted). Today's jonge style has 15 percent or less of malt wine and can be produced without it. Sugar content for jonge is less than the traditional styles at no more than ten grams per liter as opposed to no more than twenty grams per liter for the older styles. Genever is the only gin afforded its own official AOC, appellation d'origin or geographic place of origin by EU regulations for spirits. There are eleven AOC regions for genever in Belgium, and the Netherlands. Hollands gin was traditionally sipped neat, sometimes with beer or with snacks like cold smoked fish. In the mid-nineteenth-century United States, Hollands was the most common gin used in the gin cocktails like the Fancy Gin Cocktail, the recipe for which was first published in Jerry Thomas's *How to Mix Drinks*.

London dry gin is a highly rectified spirit (80 to 94 proof) enhanced using natural flavors only during distillation. The specific botanicals are chosen by the individual brands to give their own gin proprietary aromatic and flavor characteristics. Only tiny amounts of sugar are permitted in London dry gin by EU regulations.

London dry, however, is not protected by the EU for geographic origin.

Old Tom is similar to London dry, but it can be sweetened. The EU does not recognize Old Tom as a category, so the modern versions are all over the place, and many are not sweetened at all. As a style, Old Tom was very popular in the nineteenth century; in the United States, genever and Old Tom were the predominant gin used in cocktails during the mid-nineteenth century. Old Tom–style gin is experiencing a revival and finding a home again in the craft cocktail movement. The artisanal distilling has brought more than 1,600 gins to market worldwide. I'm sure that number will double, in time, and the market will then sort out the winners and losers.

WHISKEY

The first time someone walked up to my bar and said, "I'll have a whiskey and soda, bartender," I was stumped. Does he want Irish and soda, scotch and soda, bourbon and soda, or rye and soda? At first I would ask for clarification, but finally I realized only the English ask for whiskey and soda, and they usually mean scotch. (Now I just listen for the accent.) The bourbon drinker, on the other hand, never takes a chance; he or she always orders by brand, or at least specifies bourbon. Rye drinkers used to be cranky old men, but today they are just as likely to be young professional women as they are men. Rye is back and showing up in bars around the world.

IRISH AND SCOTCH

All whiskey drinkers have their loyalties, but we must pay tribute to our Irish and Scottish brothers who invented the stuff. Lore has it that whiskey of some sort has been made in Scotland and Ireland for more than seven hundred years. Before the "whiskey missionaries" migrated to the New World and discovered corn, whiskey in Ireland and Scotland was made from barley, wheat, rye, and even oats. Malt Scotch whisky was made from barley, which was encouraged to germinate, thus producing a chemical change that helps turn the starch in the seed to sugar; this is known as malting the barley. Germination has to be stopped in the malting process to prevent the plant from consuming all the sugar. This is done with heat in a kiln, which is where the Scots and the Irish diverge.

In the case of scotch, drying the malted grain is the stage in the process that adds the characteristic flavor that separates scotch from all the other whiskeys of the world.

Part of the drying process takes place over a peat-fueled fire, with the peat smoke coming in direct contact with the drying malt. Later, during fermentation and distillation, the smoky flavor of the peat-fired kiln is carried along as "baggage" by the alcohol molecules to the final product. Today malt whiskey with the smoke and peat character, although still predominantly made in Scotland, is produced in many countries. France, Japan, India, and the United States are now producing similar whiskies and, in some cases, buying the malt from Scotland.

Most modern Irish whiskey, on the other hand, has minimal peat flavor and usually no smoky flavor. The peat flavor can come from the water, and the malt used in the column-/pot-distilled blends have no smoke character because all the malt is dried in a closed kiln that is fired by coal or gas, and no smoke comes in contact with the malt. Irish whiskey is experiencing a tremendous revival, and older styles of production are returning. Pot-distilled whiskeys made from 100 percent malted and unmalted barley are finding a following again: among them are Redbreast, Yellow Spot, and Green Spot.

AMERICAN AND CANADIAN

On this side of the Atlantic, whiskey falls into two basic categories: straight or blended. Straight American whiskey like rye and bourbon must be made from at least 51 percent of the main grain, rye in the case of rye whiskey and corn in the case of bourbon. Rye however can be 100 percent rye, but bourbon cannot exceed 79 percent corn. Distillation must not exceed 160 proof, and the whiskey must be aged in new charred barrels for a minimum of two years. During the whole process, nothing can be added to the whiskey except water. The whiskey is bottled at no less than 80 proof.

Tennessee whiskey is similar to bourbon in almost every way, except something called the Lincoln County Process. Before the whiskey goes into the charred barrels to mature, it is slowly drip filtered through a vat of ten feet of sugar-maple charcoal. They cannot use the word *bourbon* on the label, as bourbon does not permit any additions or the removal of anything after distillation, and this filtration does both.

The mash, a mix of hot water and ground grain, for straight whiskey can be sweet or sour. Both begin with newly cooked sweet mash; but the sour mash process which makes up a large percentage of all straight whiskey production, mixes in a portion of fermented wash from the previous fermentation run to start the fermentation process. The same process is used in making sourdough bread, in which fermented dough from the previous run is saved and added to the new dough. This process carries forward the yeast strain, and that ensures flavor continuity. Sweet mash fermentation adds fresh yeast to the mash to begin the fermentation process.

CATHERINE SPEARS CARPENTER, A FRONTIER DISTILLER

Catherine Spears Carpenter was a mother of nine who survived the death of two husbands on the Kentucky frontier and supported her family with a textile business and a distillery. Her 1818 sour mash recipe included in a letter to a friend is the first recorded recipe for the sour mash method of making American whiskey. The time has come for Catherine Carpenter to be inducted into the Kentucky Bourbon Hall of Fame!

Blended whiskey is a diminishing share of the whiskey sales in the United States. (I speak more on the history of blended whiskey below. Blended American whiskey is a combination of a minimum of 20 percent 100-proof straight whiskeys that is blended with neutral grain spirit, and/or light whiskeys.

Today there are hundreds of artisanal whiskey distillers in the United States, and they make their own rules, producing malted barley whiskeys, wheat whiskeys, oat whiskeys, 100 percent corn whiskeys, whiskeys with nineteenth-century Irish mash bills or any mash bill they choose. A mash bill is simply a recipe for the types of grain and how much of each. More and more artisan distillers ignore the strict government aging requirements of a minimum of two years in new charred oak barrels. They are creating their own wood programs, using all sorts of combinations, toasted, charred and raw barrels, as well as used barrels that contained different types of wine and sherry. They aren't fazed by labeling restrictions on words like *bourbon* and *rye*, they simply don't use them on their labels.

In short, they are Americans doing what Americans do: whatever the hell they want! I know that there are European distillers, imprisoned by unyielding tradition, that look with envy on the American distiller.

COCKTAIL TRIVIA: STORING ALCOHOLIC BEVERAGES

Spirits that are 80 proof and above and some high-proof liqueurs like Cointreau can be stored, sealed, at room temperature, for an unlimited amount of time. Fortified wines like vermouth, port, Madeira, and sherry should be refrigerated after opening. The sweetest wines will last four to six weeks when refrigerated; the same for vermouth if it's refrigerated between uses. In all cases with wines of any type, refrigeration is crucial after opening. Still dry wines will oxidize after opening unless they are protected by a pump system or stored in a nitrogen or argon wine cabinet. All spirits and wines should be protected from long exposure to direct sunlight

BLENDED VERSUS STRAIGHT WHISKEY

Until the invention of the continuous still, whiskey was made in single-batch pot stills. At that time, whiskey consumption was confined mostly to Ireland, Scotland, and the United States; in England it was considered the poor relation to fine French brandy, and the English found the malt Scotch too strong in every way. All of that changed, however, with the invention of the Coffey still, which produces a light, higher-proof mixed-grain whiskey cheaply.

The nineteenth-century phylloxera epidemic wiped out Europe's vineyards, devastating wine and brandy production. That disaster was turned into an opportunity by many, including a small group of grocers and distillers in Scotland, among them Andrew Usher, a distiller from Edinburgh who figured out a solution to England's "too strong" complaint. Usher blended the light Coffey grain whisky with the heavy malt whisky to achieve a blended whisky that had the good qualities of both spirits and could be produced with consistency at a very good price. Usher was followed by Dewar brothers and many others. They made quality products and promoted them internationally.

Blending in American whiskey became big business post–Civil War. Lincoln's 1861 excise tax on spirits was the last nail in the coffin for many small whiskey distillers. Large industrial distillers used the opportunity to build up their business. These big rectifiers— rectifying is simply adding or removing something after the initial distillation—had the funds to take advantage of the new distilling technology. They were all about the money, but in a more cynical way than the Scots, who strived to create a quality blended whiskey. Quality was the last thing the large factory producers were looking for; rather, it was quite the opposite. They were buying up all the barrels of Kentucky straight whiskey they could get their hands on, then stepping on that whiskey ten times by adding cheap grain spirit and all sorts of nasty ingredients like pepper oil and creosote to trick the consumer into believing that they were experiencing a strong alcohol spirit. But in fact what they were tasting was these additives. The whiskey often contained less than 10 percent of the original Kentucky bourbon whiskey. They shipped it out west to the growing market of frontier saloons as *genuine* old Kentucky bourbon.

An entrepreneur named George Garvin Brown, a former pharmacist's assistant, pioneered a solution to protect the integrity of the Kentucky bourbon. Tamper-proof closures for dangerous medicines were a growing business, and Brown applied that same technology to bottle tops for Kentucky whiskey. At first, he was buying barrels of Kentucky bourbon and bottling them under the name Old Forrester (named after his former employer, Dr. Forrester), and the customer was guaranteed that what was in the bottle was 100 percent Kentucky straight bourbon. Brown sold only by the bottle to protect his brand quality, and it was a revolutionary change that led to branding on a wide scale. Brown's Old Forester (now with one *r*) is still popular today. It was my selection as our house bourbon at the Rainbow Room for all the years I ran the beverage program. It was quality whiskey at a good price and still is. Lincoln Henderson, Brown-Forman's master distiller for forty years, used Old Forester as the starting point to develop the super-premium Woodford Reserve brand in 1996.

Aged straight American bourbon and rye whiskey inventory was almost nonexistent in the United States after Prohibition, and the aged Canadian blends filled the vacuum and were popular until and even after the production of American aged straight whiskey could catch up to the market. Sadly, by mid-twentieth century all brown spirits, like whiskey, were losing market share rapidly to a clear spirit that mixed well with fruit juices and appealed to a lighter-drinking populace: vodka.

WHISKEY IN COCKTAILS

"Really smoky scotches, like the Islay malts, are the hardest of all the whiskies to find a home for in cocktails, though it's not impossible: Gary Regan's Debonair[e] Cocktail, matching ginger flavor with smoky scotch, is both successful and delicious." Those words from the 2002 edition of this book show the depth of change more than any others over the last eighteen years. Strong-flavored spirits like malt scotches and mezcals are now highly regarded in cocktails. A talented Australian bartender named Sam Ross, who worked with Sasha Petraske at Milk & Honey in New York and now operates Attaboy out of the same space, created a modern classic, the Penicillin cocktail, using the smokiest scotch on the planet, Laphroaig. Blended scotch can be easier to integrate into a cocktail, and there are many classics that employ it successfully, like the Rob Roy, the Blood and Sand, and the Bobby Burns, but today all things seem possible in the cocktail world. American whiskey is particularly cocktail friendly; it's that caramelized oak finish we spoke about that appeals in a cocktail. American whiskeys are found in Manhattans, old-fashioneds, sours, juleps, toddies, smashes, nogs, highballs, and punches.

COCKTAIL TRIVIA

When you see the designation "100 percent Single Malt Scotch Whisky," the whisky is made with only malted barley, and the word *single* means the whisky is the output of a single distillery in a single season.

TEQUILA

Conventional thought was always that tequila was the distilled version of a beer-like drink originally made by the Aztecs in Mexico called pulque, which was made with the fermented sugars of the maguey plant; *maguey* is the Taíno Indian name for agave. In fact, the maguey—and there are hundreds of varieties—was central in the lives of the indigenous peoples of Mexico, accounting for so many daily needs, from shelter to clothing. The pulque was just one of a myriad of uses for the agave plant. Spanish conquistadores didn't much like pulque, so they distilled the caramelized sugars of the agave plant into a spirit; the first to be produced from the maguey plant was called *vino de mezcal*, and today the general category to which tequila belongs is known simply as mezcal.

But did the art of distilling arrive in the New World with the Spanish? Some have raised another narrative: distilling may have been practiced by indigenous peoples in the Americas before the arrival of Europeans. Distilling technology originated in the Far East and spread to other parts of the world. Early stills in Asia were ceramic, similar to ceramic stills in use today in the mountains above Oaxaca, in southeastern Mexico. That opens the possibility that the first stills may have come from Asia to the Americas.

Early mezcal (the generic agave spirit) was produced in many parts of modern Mexico. By the late eighteenth century, mezcal production was centered around the town of Tequila, where experimentation with different maguey types eventually led to the selection of the variety classified as *Agave tequilana* 'Weber's Blue', commonly known as blue agave, the agave that all tequila is required to use. Pulque, by the way, is still made in Mexico, and I have enjoyed it in Oaxaca's large street market. Tequila, by law, is produced from blue agave plants grown only within regions of the Mexican states of Jalisco, Nayarit, Michoacán, Guanajuato, and Tamaulipas.

The agave plant can reproduce sexually by cross-pollination, primarily through bat populations looking for the honey. But it takes twelve to sixteen years for the plant to go to seed naturally, and the producer has to be willing to lose the piña (heart) for production; very few tequila producers are willing to take that path and grow plants from seed. The result is that the plant does not adapt and change because all the young plants are grown from clones of "pups" of the mother. There can be up to twelve or even more pups around the base of the mother agave plant that are easily removed and replanted.

Tequila falls into two main categories: *mixto* ("mixed") and 100 percent blue agave. Mixto is made from a mash of no less than 51 percent blue agave, with sugars from cane or other sources added during fermentation; it is often shipped in bulk and bottled elsewhere. Tequila designated 100 percent blue agave, or *puro*, is distilled from only the fermented sugars of the blue agave plants, and it must be aged and bottled in Mexico. According to Mexican law, there are four age categories of tequila: blanco (aged, if at all, less than sixty days), reposado (aged up to one year), añejo (aged more than one year), and extra añejo (aged more than two years). Aging takes place in oak, and the type is up to the producer: French and American oak are both used, but recycled barrels from whiskey production are the most common. All four age categories apply to mixto or tequila puro. Tequila labeled as *joven abocado*, also called "gold," is a sort of noncategory; it is almost always mixto tequila whose color comes not from aging, but from the addition of color, usually caramel.

The journey from mere plant to this unique spirit begins with the heart, or piña, of the blue agave plant, which resemble a giant pineapple; when separated from the outer leaves (*pencas*), the piña can weigh between fifty and one hundred pounds. Full of sweet juice called *aguamiel* ("honey water"), the piñas are taken to the distillery, where they are steamed or roasted in brick or concrete ovens for twenty-four to thirty-six hours (or alternatively in modern steel autoclaves that can cook the piñas in seven hours) to extract the caramelized sugars. The piñas rest and cool for another twenty-four hours, then they are crushed or milled and washed to remove the remaining aguamiel for fermentation. Distillation then takes place in either a pot still or a column still, depending on the producer, although handmade 100 percent blue agave tequilas are often distilled at lower temperatures in a pot still. Regardless, by law the tequila must pass through the still twice, the product of which results in a spirit with 55% alcohol that is ready for aging or bottling after rectifying it with pure water to bring it to commercial proof, usually 40% ABV, or 80 proof.

MODERNIZATION AT WHAT COST?

In traditional tequila production, agave piñas are slow roasted in ovens to turn the sugars into starch. The process caramelizes the sugars and creates flavor compounds that are present in the aguamiel, or honey water, that are extracted from the cooked agaves by crushing them and then washing the shredded agave with spring water to facilitate the process of collecting the aguamiel. The resulting slurry of water and aguamiel is transferred into fermentation vats. The fermented liquid is then distilled twice to about 55% alcohol. The flavor compounds called congeners, created in the cooking process and bonded to the alcohol molecules in fermentation, are also present after distillation, and they are the flavors of the agave that we look for in fine tequila.

Tequila production in the new millennium has seen major technological "advances," one of which—the giant diffuser—has encountered major pushback from aficionados and some general market sectors. The machine, a short city block long, extracts the starch, or inulin, from uncooked shredded agave fibers with blasts of high-pressure water. The resulting slurry may be cooked to turn the starch to sugar or, as with some producers, the starches are turned to sugar chemically by bathing the shredded agave with hydrochloric acid. The sugar yield from the agave piñas treated by diffusers is much higher than traditional tequila production and that results in a higher alcohol yield, but without the slow roasting of the agave piñas in ovens, there is no caramelization of those sugars, and none of the congeners that provides the classic agave character is created, and so the resulting alcohol loses much of the character that is present in tequila produced the traditional way. The reason for this advancement? The bottom line on the spread sheet looks much better.

MEZCAL: TEQUILA'S SIBLING

It's impossible to talk about tequila without mentioning mezcal. Mezcal is the Mexican spirit that was once bottled with the infamous worm, or *gusano*, in the bottom of the bottle. That was a marketing trick, but today these artisanal spirits and the *mezcaleros* who make them are getting the respect that they deserve. Mezcal is produced mainly around the city of Oaxaca. Traditional village mezcal from the mountain villages around Oaxaca was introduced to the wider market by *négociant* Ron Cooper and his partners in the Del Maguey company, who bought the total output of a village *palenque* (a mezcal distillery) and then bottled the output under the name of the village and the type of agave. Ron and his partners are now bottling from twelve different villages, each product bottled with the name of the village and the type of agave. Del Maguey broke the ice for many entrepreneurs, and the category of traditional mezcal is becoming competitive.

Mezcal is made from multiple types of agave, the primary source being the *espadín* variety. But several other varieties of maguey are also used, including some wild varieties like maguey *silvestre* and maguey *tobala*.

Production of mezcal is almost the same as for tequila, with the exception of the roasting of the piñas. In traditional or ancestral mezcal production, the heat for the cooking comes from wood charcoal. And although the piñas do not come in direct contact with the charcoal, they are impregnated with the smoke during the baking process, which takes place underground for two weeks or more, producing the smoky flavor that is apparent in the final product.

Steve Olsen and Fernando Caballero Cruz at Del Maquey's *palenque* or site of production.

TEQUILA AND MEZCAL IN COCKTAILS

Tequila is very mixable, combining easily with citrus and other fruit juices as well as with just tonic and ice. The vegetal character of tequila works well in savory drinks like the Bloody Mary and the traditional Tequila con Sangrita. Mezcal, on the other hand, is a banquet of rich flavors that change with the type of agave and the particular methods of the mezcalero. The applications for mezcal in cocktails have previously been limited to strong flavor matches like ginger or tropical fruits such as mango and passion fruit; however, the craft bartenders of the new millennium have tossed aside the traditional ideas about flavor combinations and are embracing big assertive flavors in spirits like mezcal, bitter aperitifs, and amaro in cocktail production. The venerable Old-Fashioned cocktail was transformed by craft bartender Phil Ward into the Oaxaca Old-Fashioned (page 175), employing two popular agave spirits—tequila and mezcal.

RUM

Rum is thought to be the first spirit of the New World, initially produced in Brazil, Barbados, and Jamaica in the wake of Columbus's introduction of sugarcane to the West Indies in 1493. That notion received some pushback since pisco production has been documented at the end of the sixteenth century. By the mid-eighteenth century, rum was being produced all over the Caribbean, in South America, and in New England, where it was the favorite spirit. The notion that rum originated in the New World has been called into question by several spirit historians, among them Hugh Barty-King and Anton Massel. The first line of their book *Rum: Yesterday and Today* reads, "The Hindu historian Udoy Chand Dutt tells of a drink which the inhabitants of ancient India made from pure cane juice called Sidhu, and another made from the brown sticky residue left after the juice had crystallized which they called Gaudi." It cannot be determined if it was distilled into spirit but sugarcane juice or molasses begins to ferment immediately so at the very least it was an alcoholic beverage. But there is a much earlier indication of distilling in Southeast Asia and India. In *The Archeology of Food: An Encyclopedia*, in the distillation section, it is noted that ceramic pots identified as alembic stills were found in a 2,500-year-old village in Northern India and Pakistan. Early molasses and rice-based spirit production in Southeast Asia was encountered by both the Dutch and the English explorers and merchants in the seventeenth and eighteenth centuries. In 2017, spirit historian David Wondrich wrote a two-part article in the *Daily Beast* that explores the history of distilling in Southeast Asia, called "Rediscovering the World's First Luxury Spirit: Batavia Arrack," and "The Rebirth of an Essential Cocktail Ingredient."

Rum is made from molasses, sugarcane juice, or a concentrated syrup called sugarcane honey, which is made by reducing the juice of pressed sugarcane. The rums made from these three sources have some things in common, but they can range dramatically in style depending on production methods and where they are made. David Wondrich, one of the partners at BAR (Beverage Alcohol Resource company), along with myself, F. Paul Pacult, Steve Olson, Doug Frost, and Andy Seymour, has come up with a common-sense way to classify rum: partly by country tradition and partly by technique.

THE ENGLISH TRADITION

The island of Barbados accounts for some of the first rums produced in the Caribbean. Early molasses-based rums from the English colonies, especially the Jamaican rums, were characterized as "pirate juice" by some, not unlike the strong flavored cane and rice distillates of Southeast Asia. It is not surprising that the funky, heavy-bodied rum would appeal to the English who colonized in India. The strong flavors were derived from the congeners or flavor compounds created during fermentation, and they remained through distillation to the finished product.

These funky rums with big estery flavors and aromas are enjoying new popularity. They are a favorite of my partners and I. Examples of this type of rum include Smith & Cross, Myers's, and Plantation, as well as more modern and less funky styles like Appleton Estate, Foursquare, and Mount Gay.

NATURE'S FLAVOR HOUSE

Esters are some of the "impurities" created during fermentation that are ganged up under the word *congeners*. Esters are natural chemical compounds formed when carboxylic acids react with ethanol—drinking alcohol—during distillation. They can be enhanced, creating multiple aromas of fruits of all sorts. Distilling to a very high proof, above 190°F, will break the chemical bonds that exist between the esters and the alcohol molecules.

OVERPROOF RUM

Overproof rum, usually Jamaican or in the English tradition, is a potent spirit of 75% ABV (that's 150 proof!) that is usually added as a float or a dash to finish a drink. Using overproof spirits of any kind

SONG OF A FALLEN ANGEL OVER A BOWL OF RUM PUNCH

by John Wilson

Illustration by Edward A. Wilson from *Full and By* (1925)

without diluting them can be very hard on the human body, but the overproof rums can have strong flavors that, when used with discretion, add flavor notes to many cocktails. Use caution: they are best kept well away from open flame.

THE FRENCH OR AGRICOLE TRADITION

The French and the Portuguese colonies both made rum from sugarcane juice rather than the by-product of sugar production, molasses. The style of rum really depends on the process. The French did what you would expect: they brought the technology of cognac to play in rum, using Charentais copper stills to produce a spirit with the attributes of fine brandy. Called *rhum agricole*, this style is popular in Martinque and Haiti. Agricole-style rums enjoy their own appellation d'origine contrôlée (AOC) for Martinique, including the rums of La Favorite, Clément, and Neisson to name a few that are available in the United States. Of course, today traditional "industrial" rums that employ continuous stills are produced alongside alembic-style rums. The agricole rums have a strong cane character.

In Brazil the scope of sugarcane distillation is vast; much of it is on an industrial scale. In 1972 the Brazilian government defined cachaça production, requiring that it be made from sugarcane juice rather than molasses, like most rum. The French rhum agricole has the same requirement. Cachaça is the third biggest selling sugarcane spirit worldwide but has yet to have a major impact outside of Brazil, with some exceptions like Germany and the United States, where it has a tenacious foothold in the craft bar movement. But a new breed of artisanal distillers experimenting with native-wood aging and alembic distillation could lead the way to a much bigger market for these unique rums. These producers are working to protect cachaça as a heritage product of Brazil. There is plenty of interest in cachaça in the craft cocktail community around the world, and that enthusiasm is spilling over to the larger market.

THE SPANISH TRADITION

The Spanish tradition rum started with Bacardí. Bacardí was founded in Santiago de Cuba in 1862 by Don Facundo Bacardí Massó, who developed a lighter style, molasses-based rum called Carta Blanca to compete with the heavy "pirate-style" products from the rest of the Caribbean. Today Bacardi Limited is second only to Tanduay in the Phillipines in worldwide rum sales. Don Facundo's lighter rum was the first rum to use charcoal filtering after aging. That process and the proprietary yeast defined a modern, clean distillate that was enthusiastically received. Originally pot distilled and filtered, Bacardí is made today in modern column stills and filtered after aging in barrels. Bacardí became the biggest selling rum in the world for some years, with distilleries in Mexico and Puerto Rico. They brought their remaining Cuban production to Puerto Rico in 1960, when Fidel Castro confiscated their Cuban holdings. Today Bacardí has diversified, with production facilities around the world that also produce vermouth, gin, whiskey, and vodka, and they recently acquired Patrón tequila, elevating their total U.S. sales to number two, behind Diageo alcohol beverage company.

INTERNATIONAL TRADITION: RUM AROUND THE WORLD

The three traditions—English, French, and Spanish—don't cover the whole explosion of rum production around the world. The remainder, ganged up under the heading "international tradition," are mostly molasses based and column distilled to a higher alcohol content, leaving fewer congeners. Of course, that produces a much lighter style of rum that has more in common with vodka than the cane-driven rums of the other traditions. Many of the rums in this category rely heavily on wood aging—typically, used American whiskey barrels—for the majority of their flavor.

- **AUSTRALIA:** *Australia has been producing rum since the nineteenth century, making white, gold, and black varieties. Bundaberg is available online in the United States, but twelve states and five American territories do not allow Internet sales.*

- **BARBADOS:** *Barbados rums are medium to heavy. Mount Gay rum is the oldest rum brand in continuous production. The estate Mount Gilboa was purchased in 1663 by William Sandiford. It is unclear when rum production began but in 1703, when the estate was purchased or inherited by John Sober, there was a working still. Some years later, a family friend, Sir John Gay Alleyne, became the distillery manager. The estate was renamed Mount Gay in honor of Sir John Gay Alleyne's success in growing the business. Maison Ferrand, a French company, produces their Plantation Barbados and XO rums in Barbados. After aging first in the Caribbean* in bourbon barrels, the XO continues aging in France in French oak. Foursquare's Richard Seale is a talented third-generation Barbadian distiller making Foursquare, Doorly's, and the Real McCoy rums, among others. R. L. Seale & Company also produces one of my favorite cocktail ingredients, John D. Taylor's Velvet Falernum.

- **BRITISH VIRGIN ISLANDS:** Pusser's rum—the most famous of the British Navy rums—is made with a blend of rums from Barbados, Trinidad, and Guyana. Its strong flavor blends well in punch-style drinks.

- **CUBA:** Havana Club is the best example of Cuban rums, made from a blend of molasses and sugarcane juice in continuous stills. Sand-filtered Havana Club rums are sadly still out of reach of U.S. citizens.

- **DOMINICAN REPUBLIC:** These rums are just beginning to attract attention in the United States, mostly because they have been available for only a few years. The leaders are Brugal and Ron Bermúdez.

- **GUATEMALA:** Zacapa rums are aged in the highlands of Guatemala at 7,000 feet above sea level, in a much cooler environment than any other rum on earth. Master blender Lorena Vásquez bucked the strong tradition of all-male master distillers when she took over as master blender for Zacapa.

- **GUYANA:** The Demerara rums of Guyana are medium to heavy in the English tradition. Produced along the Demerara River in Guyana, they were exported to London to be blended into British Navy rum, once rationed to every sailor in the British Royal Navy. Navy rums were also sourced in Guiana and Trinidad. El Dorado is a well-known rum from Guyana and made from a blend of pot- and column-distilled rums. Cadenhead's Classic is a full-bodied, mostly Demerara rum blend from Guyana weighing in at a bold 50% ABV.

- **HAITI:** Haiti is known primarily for Rhum Barbancourt, a wonderful sipping rum made with sugarcane juice instead of molasses. Aged eight to twelve years, it has a beautiful Cognac-like finish. Scottish bottler Cadenhead's produces in Haiti, as well, with a Cadenhead Green Label 9- and 11-year, with some specialty bottlings even older.

- **INDONESIA:** Batavia arrack is the funkiest of the cane spirits, due partly to its fermentation with red rice cakes. Thanks to our historical oracle David Wondrich, we can enjoy batavia arrack punch again.

- **JAMAICA:** Jamaica is known for its heavier-bodied rums in the best examples of the English tradition. The Wray & Nephew distillery, the largest in Jamaica, makes a range of medium rums and a flavorful overproof rum under both their own and the Appleton labels. Myers's dark rum is a favorite in the United States and a key ingredient in Planter's Punch.

- **MARTINIQUE:** Rhum Clément is one of the best from Martinique, and thanks to importer Ed Hamilton, we have the two most authentic and flavorful rhum agricoles from Martinique: La Favorite and Neisson Rhum. Ed has made bartenders all over the United States very happy by bringing Hamilton Ministry of Rum Collection 151 Demerara Overproof rum from the banks of the Demerara River. Now they can finish their Mai Tai cocktails with a float of a proper overproof rum.

- **PUERTO RICO:** Produced primarily in Puerto Rico, Bacardí rum is the best example of the international style, much lighter, with fewer congeners. Rums of Puerto Rico markets all the rums from the island, including Bacardí, Don Q, Ron del Barrilito, Ron Llave, and Palo Viejo.

- **TRINIDAD:** Local producer Angostura has finally decided to increase export of their rums to the United States. Angostura aromatic bitters is one of the oldest trademarked brands sold in the United States, a very good reason to increase their rum exports.

- **U.S. VIRGIN ISLANDS:** Cruzan rum and Captain Morgan rum are two fine examples of the cocktail-friendly rums produced in the U.S. Virgin Islands.

- **VENEZUELA:** Pampero makes the premier rums here, and their aged Aniversario rum is ranked among the best by bartenders.

INDEPENDENT BOTTLERS

Cadenhead's is Scotland's oldest independent bottling company. They bottle rums, gins, Cognacs, and whiskies. Their rums are purchased from distillers all over the Caribbean, then shipped to Campbeltown, where they are aged and bottled. They pride themselves on bottling their rums at 46% ABV versus many who bottle at 40% ABV, and on aging them longer. Their Green Label rums from Guyana and Haiti range in age from nine to eleven years, with special bottlings even older.

RUM: WHAT'S IN A NAME?

Where did rum get its name? One theory employs the Latin name for the species of grass we call sugarcane, *Saccharum officinarum*, both of which words end in "rum." The Spanish called it *ron*, the Swedes and Russians called it *rom*, the French called it *rhum*. The English, however, didn't mince words when they called rum "kill-devil." In his book *Rum, Romance and Rebellion*, Charles William Taussig writes that the word *rum* was derived from the West Indian word *rumbullion*. But Hugh Barty-King and Anton Massel, authors of *Rum: Yesterday and Today*, find the origin of the word in Chaucer, who writes in "The Clerk's Tale"—*Canterbury Tales* (Fragment IV)—"a people delitynge ever in rumbul that is new." Taussig cites a 1676 periodical describing the substance as "made of sugar canes distilled; a hot, hellish and terrible liquor made on the island of Barbados."

RUM IN COCKTAILS

Though colonial America loved rum, the Revolutionary War and subsequent War of 1812 destroyed the rum industry here in the United States. It wasn't until Prohibition that we discovered rum again, but it wasn't in this country; it was in Cuba. Havana became *the* destination for bohemians, the well-heeled, and especially the Hollywood elite. The talented bartenders of Cuba were prolific in their rum creations.

BRANDY

Brandy is a liquor distilled from grape wine or other fermented fruit juices. The name derives from the Dutch *brandewijn* ("burned wine"), referring to the technique of heating the wine during distillation. A number of subcategories fall under the broad definition of brandy, including grappa, marc, pomace, pisco, and eau-de-vie. The finest grape brandies traditionally come from two regions in southwestern France: Cognac and Armagnac.

Armagnac is the brandy that the French drink; 65 percent of the Armagnac produced is consumed in France. Exports are minimal, and that probably makes the French very happy. There are only 15,000 hectares of vines in the three areas of Armagnac versus 89,000 hectares of grapes in the Cognac region.

The French region of Normandy has produced apple and pear ciders for four hundred years. The apple brandy of Normandy was the neglected sibling of Cognac and Armagnac. During the reign of the Sun King, Louis

XIV, from 1643 to 1715, the sale of apple brandy was prohibited outside of Normandy.

Philippe Gironi's roving Armagnac still

And here in the United States, a surprising number of excellent examples come from several producers. Gallo has taken the lead in the last few years, buying the prestigious Germain-Robin brand and growing their own Argonaut label brandies.

SPANISH BRANDY

Spain also produces some top-quality brandies, the brandy de Jerez solera gran reserva. Spanish brandy and Spanish sherry both come from the Andalusia region in southern Spain. Many of the towns in this area are described by the phrase *de la frontera* because, historically, this was the frontier between Christian Europe and the Moors to the south. In the center of this area is the town of Jerez de la Frontera, settled by the Phoenicians, then the Greeks, Romans, Vandals, Goths, Moors, and finally Christians. The vineyards of this area prospered in ancient times, and though the Moors didn't drink alcohol, they developed an alembic still to distill alcohol for medicinal and cosmetic purposes. It is believed that the Moors, in fact, are responsible for the first distilling of any kind in Europe, in the town they called Sherisch, which later became the town of

Jerez. (Note the similarity between *Sherisch* and *sherry*.) When the Spanish Christians recaptured the "frontier" from the Moors in 1262, they made wine to supply the large contingent of soldiers stationed there. Those wines would eventually accompany the Spanish on their exploration of the New World; the practice of fortifying the wines with alcohol preserved them for the long voyages in warm weather. The end of the fifteenth century ushered in the dawn of the Age of Discovery. Spanish expeditions sailed west, bringing with them the sweet grapes that they planted in their colonies along the west coast of South America. Those grapes adapted well to the terroir and eventually were used in the production of the brandy pisco in the area on either side of the Peruvian-Chilean border.

COGNAC

As early as the tenth century, English and Norse seamen came to the western region of France for salt. After repeated journeys, they also began to buy wine. The Dutch were prodigious traders along the Charente River 350 years ago and were instrumental in supporting the early distillation of the local wines. Commercial distilling was in place in Amsterdam in 1575. The Dutch built the first stills in Cognac, France, for the express purpose of distilling the wine at its source. The wine didn't travel well and was boiled down to save it from oxidation, to economize on space, and to avoid taxation, which was levied by bulk. Until the early nineteenth century, Cognac was shipped in barrels and aged and bottled at its destination. In the nineteenth century, the Cognac producers began to age and bottle the Cognac themselves.

Today, Cognac is exported to 160 countries and enjoys a much wider audience than Armagnac. The region of Cognac has just under 89,000 hectares, about 220,000 acres producing, only a third of the area that was under vines before phylloxera ravaged them in the 1870s. Most of the production is concentrated in the first four of the six designated growing areas listed: Grande Champagne, Petite Champagne, Borderies, and Fins Bois. Bons Bois and Bois Ordinaires are large areas, but the eaux-de-vies from these areas are used only occasionally and never in the finest Cognacs.

The most common grape in Cognac is Trebbiano, known in France as Ugni Blanc or Saint Emilion, and it accounts for 90 percent of the base wine for Cognac. The wine produced is high in acid and low in alcohol, which gives Cognac its attractive flavor profile and the ability to improve with oak aging for years. The

wine goes through a double-distillation process in an alembic or pot still, emerging as raw Cognac to be aged. Because the oak used for aging is so porous, an amount equivalent to what the French people consume on a yearly basis, or to put a number on it, 3 percent, is lost. That's the equivalent of 25 million bottles. The loss, due to the evaporation, is romantically known as the "angels' share." There are about 175 Cognac producers that range in size from the small farmer to the multinational shipper.

The *paradis* ("paradise") is the inner sanctum of the aging cellars where the very oldest blending reserves are kept in demijohns—large glass containers—some from the mid 1800s. Cognac is a blended spirit but vintage Cognacs are occasionally permitted by the French government under strict guidelines. The aging and the vintage have to be well documented, but they don't just take the word of the producer: carbon dating tests are also required to establish the actual age. Cognacs are labeled VS (very superior), aged for two years minimum; VSOP (very superior old pale), four years minimum; and XO (extra old), six years minimum.

ARMAGNAC

The region of Armagnac is located in Gascony, in southwestern France; the brandy known as Armagnac was first produced in the fifteenth century. The three designated districts for Armagnac are Bas-Armagnac, Armagnac-Ténarèze, and Haut-Armagnac; Bas-Armagnac and Armagnac-Ténarèze produce the world-class selections. Ten grapes are grown in the region for Armagnac production, but four dominate: Ugni Blanc, Baco Blanc, Folle Blanche, and Colombard. The grapes are picked before they are fully ripe and mature to ensure high acidity, a key component in the finished product. The low-alcohol wine (9% to 10%) is immediately distilled in a unique hybrid still with elements of both continuous and batch distillation. All the wine must be distilled by April 30, the spring following the harvest.

Limousin oak and Tronçais oak are used for aging Armagnac, an element as important as the grapes or the soil in producing the distinctive flavor that makes Armagnac unique. Armagnac will continue to improve in oak for up to about fifty years, at which point the flavor of the fruit dries out. Armagnac may or may not be vintage dated. It may also be blended. If it is both vintage dated and blended, the vintage indicated will denote the youngest year in the blend. Traditionally Armagnac had a stronger flavor than Cognac, but today's Armagnac and Cognac styles overlap.

CALVADOS

This apple (and pear) brandy is a specialty of northern France. The Calvados appellation is located in western Normandy and a small area east of Rouen. While apple brandy (called applejack in this country) is distilled in other parts of the world, Calvados is considered the best. It is made by double-distilling fermented apple cider, then aging it in Limousin oak barrels for no less than one year, some as long as forty years. In Normandy, Calvados is often taken between courses of a fine meal to prepare the palate. The best Calvados is aged between ten and fifteen years.

Calvados does well in cocktails, especially the American applejack cocktails, like the Jack Rose. Frank Meier, the head bartender at the Ritz bar in Paris in the 1930s, has an impressive Calvados recipe in *The Artistry of Mixing Drinks* (1936) that he calls the Applejack Cocktail. Today's craft bartenders have really embraced Calvados.

THE SOLERA SYSTEM

Spanish brandies are aged in a particular way that distinguishes them from their French counterparts: the solera system. Unlike Cognac and Armagnac, which age slowly in individual oak casks, Spanish brandy is moved through a series of oak casks arranged in rows called criaderas. The last layer of this system is called the solera, and it contains the oldest brandies. The solera level is the last stop before bottling. The layer above the solera is called the first criadera, then the second criadera, and so on. New brandy, after five years in oak, begins its trip through the casks at the top level. To move it through the criaderas, an equal amount is taken from each cask and transferred to the cask below. In this way, the new brandy is disciplined by the older brandy. The blending takes place horizontally as well, moving wine from the old barrels to even older barrels across the bottom row to ensure a good supply of very old wines for blending with the younger ones. In three years, this system achieves an aging equivalent to that of brandy or Cognac held in individual casks for fifteen years.

BRANDY IN COCKTAILS

Brandy, whiskey, and gin were the three base spirits for all the early cocktails, fancy cocktails, and crustas. These three original cocktails contained essentially the same ingredients: spirits, bitters, and a sweetener, usually curaçao. The difference was in the garnish and preparation. The first juleps were made with Cognac and/or peach-flavored brandy. All the pousse-café and shamparelle recipes were topped with brandy. In the nineteenth century, many woke up to the brandy-based Morning Glory cocktail and went to bed with the brandy-based Stinger cocktail. Before Prohibition, the Coffee Cocktail, made with brandy, port, egg, and sugar, was the after-dinner alcohol confection of choice.

FORTIFIED & AROMATIC WINES

Aromatic or flavored wines are one of the oldest alcoholic preparations known to man—Hippocrates, for example, steeped herbs and flowers in wine to make medicine in the fourth century B.C. In most cases, aromatic wines are fortified with grapes or other spirits. Aromatized wines like vermouth are highly processed, and the character of the base wine is not apparent in the finished product; the base wine is simply the palette upon which the flavors are assembled. These wines are between 16% and 18% alcohol by volume. Fortified wines are also preserved by adding eau-de-vie of grape but the grape varieties in fortified wines are everything. Vintage Port wines usually blend up to six grapes for one vintage and they can also make a single varietal.

VERMOUTH AN AROMATIZED WINE

When it comes to cocktails, the most important of the aromatic wines is vermouth. The word *vermouth* comes from the German word for the bitter digestive herb wormwood, *Wermut*. Wormwood-flavored wines are mentioned in the seventeenth-century diary of Samuel Pepys. But Antonio Carpano of Turin, Italy, is credited with producing the first commercial vermouth in 1786, and becoming the inspiration for others who followed The House of Cinzano, today a famous producer in the category, was established in 1757, but as a confectionary company. It didn't produce the Cinzano aromatized wine until the nineteenth century. The Martini & Rossi Company was founded in 1863, when Alessandro Martini, Teofila Sola, and Luigi Rossi took over a vermouth distillery in Turin. They made a vermouth that was sweeter, more herbal, and less spiced than the Carpano vermouth. The Italian and the French vermouths are all made from white grapes, and color is added to the sweeter reds.

In 1813, Joseph Noilly of Marseillan, France, introduced a new, white, drier-style vermouth. Although

Italian and French vermouths differ slightly, the basic formula consists of base wine and mistelle (sweetened grape juice and brandy) flavored with herbs, roots, bark, and flowers. The manufacturing process is fairly complex. Herbs and flavors are steeped in the base wine and the eau-de-vie of grape. The eau-de-vie, like any high-proof spirit, is a much better choice for maceration of the herbal and spice ingredients than wine, but all the houses have their own proprietary methods. After steeping, mistelle and brandy are blended mechanically in large vats. The mixture is blended, pasteurized, and refrigerated for two weeks to allow any impurities to crystallize, then it is filtered and bottled.

An eighteenth-century taste du vin or tasting cup

In 1815, vermouth was made in Chambéry, newly returned to the Duchy of Savoy after the defeat of Napoleon at Waterloo. Modern Chambéry, located in the alpine eastern region of the department of Savoie, France, produces a premium dry vermouth from the French Alps, and it was the only vermouth with its own appellation d'origine contrôlée (AOC). Sadly, it seems that that AOC has not been renewed. Chambéry also pioneered the demi-sec-blanc style of white vermouth. Dolin Vermouth de Chambéry was a standard in the late nineteenth century in the United States, but never returned after Prohibition. But in 2009, Eric Seed, the founder of Haus Alpenz, an importing company that specializes in long-tail market brands sought after by the craft cocktail bartenders, imported Dolin dry and sweet (rouge) vermouth back into the American market. Haus Alpenz is also the importer of Cocchi vermouths: the "it" brand of vermouth in the craft bar world.

Other aromatized and fortified wine producers include Lillet, Dubonnet, Amer Picon, and St Raphaël from France; and Rosso Antico, Cocchi, Punt e Mes, Cynar, and Barolo Chinato from Italy.

Aromatized wines are found in the superstars of the cocktail world, the Martini and the Manhattan, and in countless other cocktails, modern and classic.

SHERRY, PORT & MADEIRA: THE FORTIFIED WINE

Rupert Croft-Cooke, in his 1956 book **Sherry** *writes,* "There is sherry, and there are all other wines." Sherry is a versatile wine that fits the bill as an aperitif, a table wine, and a cocktail ingredient. Sherry is fermented like all wines, but after fermentation is complete, there is an additional step in the production of sherry that separates it from other wines: it is fortified with unaged grape brandy. Like Spanish brandy, sherry is aged by the solera system (see page 48). Though this fortified wine ranges widely in color, flavor, and sweetness, there are really only two distinct sherry categories: fino and oloroso. Fino is the drier style, on the surface of which a thin layer of flor, or yeast cells and perhaps some bacteria, is encouraged to grow (see page 246). Finos are lighter-bodied wines than olorosos because flor can't grow on a wine with alcohol content higher than 15.5%. And oloroso wines are fortified to 18% alcohol. When a fino loses the flor, it begins oxidative aging and becomes part of the amontillado category. Usually aged for six years after losing its flor, the darker, softer amontillado has a rich, nutty character. The driest fino is Manzanilla, uniquely pungent because it ages near the sea, in the town of Sanlúcar de Barrameda. Pale cream sherry is fino that has been sweetened.

Oloroso, fortified with up to 18% alcohol, is not protected by flor and, therefore, is much darker in color, from gold to brown. There is a very thick, sweet style of oloroso that some consider a separate class unto itself called Pedro Ximénez (the grape name) that is sometimes used as a flavoring additive in brandy and whiskey. Cream sherries are highly sweetened olorosos of less distinction and less age. Some olorosos are also known as amorosos, Old Brown, and East India. Palo cortado is sort of a non-category of sherry that varies from producer to producer. In palo cortado, producers often blend the two contrasting styles of dry amontillado and oloroso.

Sherry predated the cocktail as a colonial favorite in drinks like the Sherry Flip and in the mid-nineteenth century as a housewives' summer cooler recipe called the Sherry Cobbler. Two of my favorite cocktails, the Flame of Love and the Valencia-Style Martini, are both made with fino sherry, which is the driest, in place of vermouth.

The alcohol content for different sherries varies with great subtlety:

- **FINO:** *15% to 16% alcohol*
- **AMONTILLADO:** *16% to 20% alcohol*
- **OLOROSO:** *18% to 20% alcohol*
- **PEDRO XIMÉNEZ:** *20% to 24% alcohol*

PORT

Port is produced in the Douro Valley in Portugal from thirty varieties of red and white grapes. Some of the red grapes are Touriga Nacional, Touriga Francisca, Mourisco Tinto, Malvasia, Bastardo, Tinta Cão, Tinta Barroca, Tinta Francisca, and several more. Some of the sanctioned white grapes are Arinto, Boal, Cercial, Esgana Cão, Malvasia Corada, Malvasia Fino, among others. The two basic categories of port are vintage port and wood port. Vintage ports are aged two years in oak barrels and then bottled and aged usually for a minimum of ten years, often much longer—fifty or sixty years in a good vintage. The decision to produce a vintage port is made by the winemaker late in the season, between mid-September and mid-October, based on many factors, the weather and the quality and sugar content of the grapes among them.

The wood ports, which include the ruby, tawny, and white ports, are aged in the barrel until they are ready to drink, then blended and bottled. Ruby port is aged usually for two years and is ready to drink as soon as it is bottled. Tawny ports can be aged for many years in oak barrels and blended from many vintages. The long barrel aging and filtering and fining (clarifying) gives the older tawny a light golden color. Usual fining

agents are gelatin, egg whites, and isinglass. They absorb or create a bond with suspended particles and colloids like tannins (phenolics in the wine that can have a bitter aftertaste).

Fermentation is short—usually thirty-six to forty-eight hours—for port and is halted by the addition of brandy, which kills the yeast and stops the fermentation, leaving residual sugar in the wine. These are dessert wines that are aged for long periods and the sugar acts as a preservative. Port-style wines are produced in many countries, including the United States and Australia, but all true port is from Portugal.

MADEIRA

Madeira from the Portuguese island of the same name is similar to port and sherry in that it is also fortified with brandy. Madeira is the longest lived of the fortified wines, sometimes topping a hundred years. It is aged in a solera, similarly to sherry, but there is a critical difference. By the time the wine is bottled from the solera, 50 percent of the wine in the bottle is from the vintage year listed on the bottle. After discovering how Madeira changed and seemed to improve in the steamy holds of sailing ships bound for America, Madeira producers re-created the temperature in their aging cellars. Madeira was popular in colonial America, because it was the least expensive of the imported wines. A lighter, younger Madeira was exported to colonial America; today we refer to it as Rainwater Madeira, and it is terrific in cocktails and punches. There are four types of fine Madeira, determined by the degree of sweetness and named after the grapes from which they are produced. Beginning with the driest, they are Sercial, with a pale golden color and a rich aroma; Verdelho, sweeter than the Sercial but still on the dry side; Bual, medium brown in color and sweeter than the other two; and Malmsey or Malvasia, the sweetest and biggest bodied. Port and Madeira make a wonderful float in some punch and cobbler drinks.

CORDIALS & LIQUEURS

The historical distinction between cordials, which are fruit based, and liqueurs, which are herb based, doesn't really exist anymore, and the terms are now interchangeable in some cultures. Today in Europe, cordials often refer to nonalcoholic flavors, like elderflower cordial—confusing, but when every country has a finger in the pie, things get messy. What we do know is that the liqueurs originated in the thirteenth century; pioneers like Catalan chemist Arnau de Vilanova experimented with distillation and with the extraction of plant essences by steeping them in alcohol at France's University of Montpellier. Like many intellectual pursuits during the Middle Ages, experiments with herb-infused spirits were conducted in monasteries and universities.

The Combier Distillery, designed by Gustave Eiffel

Many of the liqueurs created by the monks have survived to the present day, such as Bénédictine and Chartreuse. The Italians, in particular, excelled in the creation of fruit, nut, and herbal liqueurs; many of today's most popular brands of liqueurs are Italian, such as amaretto, Strega, Tuaca, and sambuca, to name only a few.

Liqueurs, by definition, are spirits flavored with between 2.5 and 40 percent sweetener. Their flavorings vary widely and may include herbs, roots, fruits, nuts, and spices. The alcohol base can be derived from grain, grape, or other fruits or vegetables, and it may be flavored in four different ways: distillation, infusion, maceration, or percolation (see Four Ways to Make Liqueur, opposite). Liqueurs should not be confused with fruit brandies, which are distilled from a mash of the fruit itself and are usually dry and high in proof. Some producers mistakenly label their liqueur products as brandies, such as blackberry brandy or apricot brandy, when they are not. Food colors are permitted in liqueurs, and some lesser brands of liqueurs use artificial flavors. The alcoholic strength of liqueurs is generally between 40 and 80 proof.

The United States makes great whiskey and reasonably good spirits in most categories, but liqueurs are not our strong suit. Price is a real consideration in the liqueur category, more than many other spirits; you have to pay for quality. Those eight- to twelve-dollar bottles of liqueurs are good for the bottom line but bad for your cocktails; they are too sweet and too low in alcohol. Macerating fresh fruits, herbs, and other botanicals is expensive, and no amount of compounding of oils and artificial flavors can replace the real thing. The French, the Swiss, and the Italians have been at it a long time, and they get it.

FOUR WAYS TO MAKE LIQUEUR

- **COMPOUNDING** is the process of blending together base alcohol, flavoring agents, and sugar.

- **INFUSION** is the steeping of mashed fruits or herbs in alcohol, often with the application of heat, then filtering the liquid, adding sugar and then adding water to bring the liqueur to bottle proof, then bottling.

- **MACERATION** is the steeping of herbs or fruits in alcohol, then rectifying—redistilling—it with or without the material in the still, filtering, adding sugar, and finally bottling.

- **PERCOLATION** is like the process inside a coffeepot: circulate the alcohol through a container holding the materials from which the flavor is extracted over and over.

ABSINTHE, PERNOD, RICARD & PASTIS

Absinthe filled the gap left by the phylloxera epidemic that destroyed the grapevines in Europe in the 1870s. It was made from beet- or grain-sourced distillate and infused with botanicals—anise, licorice, hyssop, melissa (a type of mint), coriander, veronica, chamomile, and other herbs, the most important of which was *Artemisia absinthium*, or wormwood. The formula was sold by a French national living in Switzerland to Henri-Louis Pernod in 1797, and by the late nineteenth century it was one of the most popular liqueurs in the world. By the year 1919, however, absinthe had been outlawed by every nation except Spain and Portugal. There are trace amounts in wormwood of the psychoactive compound thujone, which is classified as a convulsant poison that attacks the nervous system if taken in large doses. The trace amounts in absinthe never posed any danger, but the spirit was a whopping 130 to 140 proof, which could do plenty of damage if taken straight on a regular basis.

Enter the absinthe substitutes: Pernod (which tends toward anise in flavor and aroma) and Ricard (which tends toward licorice in flavor and aroma). Both are proprietary brands made in France—without any trace of wormwood oil. They are readily available here in the United States, as are several brands of pastis, a liqueur from Marseille flavored with both licorice and anise. The return of true absinthe in 2007 has slowed sales of these substitutes. Here in the United States, we have our own absinthe wannabe, produced in New Orleans, called Herbsaint.

After the phylloxera epidemic, the recovering wine and brandy producers launched an all-out PR attack on absinthe to gain back lost market share. They succeeded beyond their expectations. Today absinthe is available again in most countries, including the United States. Jade Liqueurs makes a line of true absinthe in Saumur, France, that I highly recommend.

AMARETTO

Though there's no doubt it was created in Saronno, Italy; a legend surrounds its creator. It is said that the artist Bernardino Luini, a student of the da Vinci school, was painting frescoes at the Sanctuario della Beata Vergine dei Miracoli in Saronno and needed a model, so he used a poor young woman who worked at the inn where he stayed. She showed her gratitude by making a sweet liqueur from almonds and apricots that is said to be the original recipe for what is surely one of Italy's most famous liqueurs. Many producers are making amaretto today.

AMARO & AMER

A category of Italian digestivo liqueurs and bitters, this is a growing category in the United States, especially among craft bartenders. They are wonderful and complex and can bring new dimension when used as additives in cocktails. Traditionally, amaro was an aid to digestion after a rich meal. I am glad to see a little movement in the category—no pun intended. The French version, amer, is well represented by Amer Picon, a once popular French

cocktail ingredient that disappeared from the American market but is available again online from the UK, but not (yet) on the shelves of your local liquor store.

ANISETTE

The oldest of the anise-based liqueurs, anisette was one of the first commercially available liqueurs. The pioneering French spirit company Marie Brizard began the production of anisette in 1755.

BÉNÉDICTINE AND B & B

Bénédictine is the oldest of the liqueurs made on the Continent, beginning in 1510 in the Benedictine Abbey of Fécamp, when a monk named Dom Bernardo Vincelli first infused spirits with a secret formula of herbs. The area of Normandy around the abbey was swampy, and malaria was prevalent. Later, Dom Vincelli's elixir was used to prevent malaria, suggesting that one of the ingredients was bark of cinchona, the source of quinine from the New World. In the nineteenth and twentieth centuries, Bénédictine was popular mixed with brandy or Cognac, prompting the company to create B & B—a bottled brandy-and-Bénédictine mixture.

BERENTZEN APPLE LIQUEUR

This premium apple liqueur made in Germany is getting a lot of notice because of the boom in popularity of apple drinks, such as the Sour Apple Martini. It mixes well with many other spirits, but it is a match made in heaven when mixed with bourbon.

CRÈME LIQUEURS

Despite their names, this category of liqueurs doesn't actually contain any dairy products; flavored with fruits, flowers, herbs, and nuts, crème liqueurs are perceived to be creamy because of their heaviness on the palate. Today the most popular are cacao (white and dark), menthe (green and white), and banana.

DRAMBUIE

The actual formula for this scotch-based proprietary liqueur made with heather honey remains a secret of the MacKinnon family, who has produced it since Prince Charles Edward Stuart presented the recipe to them in 1746, in gratitude for their support in his failed bid to defeat the Duke of Cumberland at the Battle of Culloden and become the king of England. Bonnie Prince Charlie, or the Young Pretender as he came to be nicknamed, spent the rest of his life of exile in Italy.

GALLIANO

This proprietary Italian herb liqueur is based on grape eau-de-vie infused with a vanilla top note. The Harvey Wallbanger cocktail put Galliano on every American bar in the late 1960s; it consists of vodka and orange juice in a highball glass with a float of Galliano. The companion to Harvey quickly became the Freddie Fudpucker, a tequila version of the same drink.

MARASCHINO

The Italians make several brands of maraschino, a sweet, clear liqueur made from Marasca cherries and pits, and two of them are widely available in the United States: Luxardo and Stock. Maraschino was a popular ingredient in early punches and cocktails, especially when paired with Champagne; it is almost never taken straight. The Cuban bartenders added it to daiquiris, and it is a primary ingredient in the famous Aviation Cocktail. The floral nose of maraschino makes it a successful ingredient in cocktails that have a lighter, subtler flavor profile; it works especially well with gin, Champagne, and light rums.

PETER HEERING CHERRY LIQUEUR

This is almost entirely the opposite in every way from its sister cherry liqueur, maraschino. Made in Denmark from local cherries, it is dark red with a bold taste that can stand up to the biggest flavors in cocktails, such as in the Blood and Sand, where it is mixed with scotch, sweet vermouth, and orange juice.

ORANGE LIQUEURS

These are for the most part listed under proprietary names. An exception is curaçao, the original orange liqueur made by the Bols company from the curaçao oranges that grow on the Lesser Antilles, islands off the coast of Venezuela. In the middle of the nineteenth century, when the cocktail was an emerging phenomenon, many of the first cocktails consisted of a base spirit, such as gin, whiskey, or brandy, dashed with bitters and sweetened with curaçao. In the 1880s, vermouth began to become more widely distributed,

and it gradually took the place of curaçao as a sweetener and flavoring in cocktails. By the turn of the century, curaçao was offered in many different colors to jazz up the look of cocktails, such as the Pousse-Café. Although the Dutch originally pioneered the orange liqueur, the French have several very successful versions: Cointreau is a proprietary version and a drier style of triple sec. Besides Cointreau, there are Combier, Grand Marnier (considered the aristocrat of the curaçao-based orange liqueurs), and—newly arrived in the United States— Joseph Cartron Curaçao Triple Sec. I have left out the value American brands. They are not the same quality as the European selections.

SAMBUCA

An anise-and-elderberry-flavored herbal liqueur made in Italy, sambuca is popular after dinner, often taken with coffee. Sambuca con Mosca, literally translated as "sambuca with flies," is the popular way of serving sambuca: "up" with three coffee beans floating like flies in the glass. Although Romana sambuca is by far the most popular version consumed in the United States, in Italy Molinari sambuca reigns supreme.

COCKTAIL TRIVIA

When serving Romana sambuca with coffee beans, never use an even number of beans: it's considered bad luck by superstitious Italians. An even number of beans supposedly proves disastrous for lovers, presumably sipping from the same glass.

SCHNAPPS

A German and Dutch word that translates literally to "a snatch," *schnapps* came to mean a quick shot of spirits. There's a whole category of less expensive flavored liqueurs called schnapps in the United States. De Kuyper pioneered this category with its wildly successful Peachtree schnapps, which was embraced by the disco generation, in cocktails like Sex on the Beach (vodka, Peachtree schnapps, cranberry juice, and orange juice) and the Fuzzy Navel (Peachtree and orange juice). The Old World definition of schnapps can refer to fruit brandies or eaux-de-vie that are distilled from the base fruit and are usually above 40% alcohol.

Here's to beefsteak when you're d[...]
Whiskey when you ever wa[...]
All the girls you ever wa[...]
And heaven when you di[...]

[...] LADY COCKTAIL
½ Lime — Ice
[...]am — 1 Jigger Gin
[...]enadine
[...]Cocktail Glass

"Happy are we met, happy have we been,
Happy may we part, and happy meet again.

TOM COLLINS
Gin, 1 Glass
[...]wdered Sugar, 2 Teaspoon
[...] of 1 Lemon, 15 shake
[...]n 8 oz. glass.

THE TOOLS, TECHNIQUES, AND GARNISHES OF THE COCKTAIL

Any craftsperson, whether a carpenter, a chef, or a bartender, needs tools. Having the correct tool to do a particular job and the skill to use it are equally important. In the last twenty years, the craft of the cocktail as an integral part of the larger culinary arts world has reemerged, along with a generation of talented young bartenders. A support community of designers has supplied the tools to do the job. Let's take a look at the extraordinary array of tools, some harkening back to the first golden age of the craft, and some cutting-edge technology.

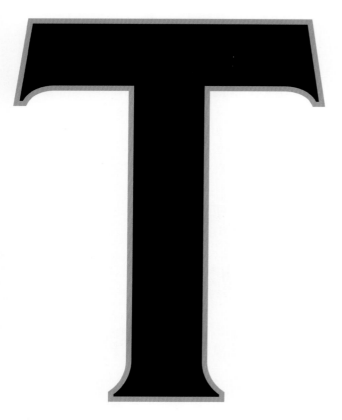

a smaller cap, which unscrews to reveal a strainer. The shaker is simplicity itself to use: add ingredients, secure the top and cap, shake, unscrew cap, and strain. The cobbler has been executed in hundreds of shapes and designs.

THE BOSTON SHAKER SET

The more mundane Boston shaker set takes a little more practice but offers more versatility than the cobbler style. It's also more fun to use, and it is the choice of most professional bartenders these days. The Boston shaker consists of two parts: the larger is twenty-six to thirty ounces and usually made from stainless steel; the smaller is usually about sixteen ounces and can be glass or stainless steel. The craft bartending community has embraced the metal-on-metal Boston shaker, often with one in each hand while they execute a series of very skilled moves to seal, shake, and unseal; then strain both simultaneously into two prepared glasses. Assemble the cocktail in the smaller part of the set. Combine the two parts and create a seal. Always shake with the smaller side on top.

Look for glass with a *T* on the bottom if you're choosing the metal over glass shaker; this means it's tempered to avoid cracking when first chilled to freezing and then plunged into hot water. Buy a fitted set rather than separate pieces to insure a good fit. The two parts should create a tight seal. If they don't, it is not a good tool. See page 228 for more on purchasing a proper tool.

Making drinks is a bit of a show, so always prepare the drinks in front of your guests, whether at home or working behind a bar. Free-pouring ingredients without using calibrated measuring jiggers is a risk, especially for the home bartender. That type of drink-making is executed by professionals after years of experience and requires significant hand-eye coordination. My rule in adding ingredients follows a strict order: sour first followed by sweet, then flavor modifiers and dashes, and finally the base ingredient. Ice is added last, just before shaking. The exceptions to this rule are strong stirred drinks like Manhattans and martinis, and in those cases add the ice first, then follow the rule of base ingredient last, just before stirring.

THE SHAKER &
OTHER TOOLS

The cocktail shaker and accompanying tools evolved slowly with the addition of ice, fruits, and citrus juices to simple cocktail and punch recipes over a hundred years. The earliest patent for a cocktail shaking apparatus I have been able to find was in 1872, documented in *Vintage Bar Ware*, by Stephen Visakay (1997).

Since that first patent, the cocktail shaker has inspired hundreds of inventors to patent their unusual and unique versions, from penguin-shaped shakers to bell shapes that utilize the handle of the bell for shaking. In the 1870s, the U.S. Patent and Trademark Office was flooded with shaker designs from hopeful inventors. The designs broke down into two basic styles: the cobbler shaker and the Boston shaker.

THE COBBLER SHAKER

The glamorous three-piece cobbler-style shaker is the one we associate with all those madcap cocktail drinkers in 1930s movies. They are usually all metal (often stainless steel, sometimes silver, rarely glass), with a top that has

SHAKING A DRINK

Place the larger half of the Boston shaker over the smaller half while it is resting on the bar. Strike the upturned end of the large half twice with the heel of your free hand to create the seal. The shaker should seal so tightly that the whole assembly can be picked up as a single unit. If the metal and glass halves fail to seal properly, try again, and if they don't seal, then there is a problem with one of the parts, and it should be replaced.

After creating the seal, turn the whole assemblage over so the smaller half is now on top and the metal half rests on the bar. Strike the upturned smaller side one more time with the heel of your palm to ensure a seal. Now grasp the unit with the large half resting securely in the palm of one hand and the fingers of the other hand wrapped securely over the top of the smaller half, giving you complete control of the unit. Shake hard; even if the seal were to break, the liquid would be mostly contained within the larger metal half, and there's less danger of splashing cocktail ingredients all over your guests. The shaking should sound like a machine gun; I shake most cocktails vigorously but with style to a slow count of ten. Shake drinks that contain eggs longer and harder to emulsify the egg. A limp shake is a bad show, so have fun. Shaking with style takes some practice.

After shaking, grasp the unit firmly in one hand with two fingers wrapped around each portion of the shaker to control both halves. Using the heel of your other hand, hit the top rim of the larger half sharply. This will break the seal. Keep in mind that pressure has built up inside the cold shaker, so breaking the seal can be difficult. If it doesn't work the first time, turn the whole unit slightly and try again until it works.

ROLLING A DRINK

When making Bloody Marys and other drinks containing tomato juice, always shake them lightly or roll them. Rolling means pouring the drink back and forth between the two parts of a cocktail shaker. Vigorously shaking drinks containing tomato juice creates an unpleasant foamy consistency.

STRAINERS

The final step in the preparation of a stirred or shaken cocktail is pouring and straining the drink into a proper glass with style and flourish. There are two popular types of strainers used for cocktail service: the Hawthorne strainer (the one with the spring) and the julep strainer (the one with the holes), both of which are perfect companions for the Boston shaker set. The smaller julep strainer works efficiently with the smaller half of the shaker; and the Hawthorne, with its metal tabs around the edge designed to rest on the rim, works well with the metal larger half of the shaker. Hawthorne strainers come in many styles and designs today. Oxo has a neat,

ergonomically designed version. Don Lee of Cocktail Kingdom (see Tools & Books, page 228) designed my favorite, the Koriko Hawthorne strainer, which works well with martini beakers and the Boston shaker glass.

Straining the liquid from the shaker into the glass is a one-handed affair. After breaking the seal of the Boston shaker, place the Hawthorne strainer on top of the larger half of the shaker. The index finger and sometimes the middle finger keep the strainer in place. The thumb, little finger, and ring finger hold the body of the shaker (see photo on the title page). Hold the metal shaker tightly and strain slowly at first to avoid splashing. When straining into a martini or cocktail glass, pour the liquid in a circular motion, delicately swirling around the insides of the glass (this will also help avoid spillage). The graceful circular motion slows down as you empty the glass shaker. For the last ounce, draw your hand up high over the middle of the cocktail glass, emptying the last of the liquid. When the liquid is drained from the shaker, the final motion should be a sharp snap of the wrist to punctuate the ceremony and draw attention to the drink.

JIGGERS

Get a set of two jiggers, both of which should be stainless steel and feature two different cup sizes—one calibrated by quarter ounces up to one ounce and the second calibrated by half ounces up to two ounces. Today you can source a single jigger with all the calibrations up to three ounces, the standard pour for fortified wines.

LONG-HANDLED COCKTAIL SPOON

The standard cocktail spoon is a long spoon with a twisted stem; a simple tool that, when properly used, is at the heart of the most elegant of the bartender customer interactions, stirring a proper Martini or Manhattan. Making a martini without the ceremony is a lost opportunity for one of those special ceremonies in life. When I was stirring martinis behind the busy bar at the Rainbow Room, I had Zen moments when I could see the whole room almost in slow motion while I took my time stirring. It simply can't be rushed. I stir to a slow thirty count unless otherwise indicated in the recipe.

When making stirred drinks, add dashes and small amounts first. The in-and-out martini is an example of this in action. The bartender dashes the vermouth over the ice, swirls the mixing glass to season the ice, then tosses out the extra vermouth before adding the gin or vodka.

1. Microplane grater
2. TAG barspoon
3. Hand-turned muddler
4. Swiss peeler
5. Koriko Hawthorne strainer
6. Spanish twisted bar spoon
7. Mini bar strainer
8. Teardrop barspoon
9. OXO Hawthorne strainer
10. TAG julep strainer
11. Custom chef's knife
12. Japanese bar knife
13. Paring knife
14. Cocktail Kingdom julep strainer
15. Caviar strainer

SWIZZLES

The original nineteenth-century swizzle from Jamaica and other islands in the Greater and Lesser Antilles was a much more important tool than the ones we use here in America today. In fact, the swizzle was so distinguished that its name was given to an entire category of drinks. The Swizzle is attributed to the Georgetown Club in British Guiana, where the plantation owners gathered at the end of their day to "tell the government what to do next."

KNIVES & CUTTING BOARD

I have a selection of knives in my kit, but I travel with a four-inch paring knife, a chef's knife, a channel knife. Wooden cutting boards are prohibited in commercial establishments by health department guidelines but are fine in the home. Kitchen-safety studies show the rubber-composition boards made by companies are easier to clean and less likely to harbor bacteria. Separate the boards used for raw meat or chicken, and do not use them for any other purpose.

STIRRING VERSUS SHAKING

There are long-standing guidelines regarding stirring versus shaking: Drinks that contain spirits only—such as martinis, Manhattans, and Rob Roys—should be stirred. Drinks that also contain fruit or citrus juice and sweet ingredients should be shaken. The difference between stirring and shaking is most noticeable in the look of the drink and the texture on your tongue. Shaking adds millions of tiny air bubbles to a cocktail, which is fine for a cocktail like a daiquiri or a margarita; those concoctions should be effervescent and alive in the glass when you drink them. As Harry Craddock said in *The Savoy Cocktail Book* (1930), a cocktail should be consumed "quickly while it's laughing at you." Conversely, martinis and Manhattans should have a cold, heavy, silky texture, not light and frothy. I always stir them. Mind you, shaking doesn't permanently change the flavor of gin or vodka; it temporarily fills the solution with air bubbles that change the texture on the tongue. After a minute, the bubbles will disperse and the drink will taste the same as if you had stirred it. But don't let me dissuade you. Enjoy your martinis well shaken, if that's your pleasure.

CORKSCREW

A corkscrew, cork extractor, or wine key should be chosen on the basis of ease of handling. Two other types are widely available: the winged corkscrew that you crank from the top, and the waiter's corkscrew that looks sort of like a switchblade knife. Screwpull is one of the leading manufacturers of cork extractors for the home, and they are simple and easy to use and priced for all budgets. I highly recommend them.

PIANO WHIP & FRENCH WHIP OR WHISK

The piano whip is a must if you are a fan of coffee drinks; it has the thinnest-gauge wire of all the whips, and it can whip up a pint of heavy cream to the right consistency for Irish coffee in two minutes. I like to use a thick-wire French-style whisk to extract juice from watermelons. The heavy-gauge wire is stiff enough to break down the melon and release its juice. Dice the melon to smaller pieces and place them in a large china cap strainer over a big bowl, then break the melon down with the whisk to release the juice.

FUNNEL

Talk about follow-up: you will need a funnel when it comes time to fill that decorative bottle with simple syrup or lemon and lime juices. Bonus points: try to find a funnel with a built-in strainer to help remove seeds and pulp from citrus.

CHANNEL KNIFE

The channel knife cuts a thin strip of peel from a lemon, lime, or orange to make a wonderfully decorative garnish. This is really an optional tool for the bartender who wants to get creative with spirals of citrus, but it is a must to re-create the Horse's Neck cocktail. Buy one that has a fat, ergonomically designed handle at a good kitchenware store; I recommend OXO brand.

JUICERS & JUICING

CITRUS JUICER EXTRACTOR

All of my recipes require lots of fresh juices, so if you don't yet have one, get a serviceable citrus juice extractor. There are many shapes and sizes on the market, but I recommend one that is large enough to juice a grapefruit. Inexpensive electric citrus juice extractors are not powerful enough for commercial use but fine for household use. Power juicer extractors like those made by Hamilton Beach and KitchenAid are pricey and really not necessary unless you make lots of juice. A vegetable and fruit juicer is an extra indulgence if you enjoy exotic tropical or vegetable-based smoothies.

HINTS FOR JUICING

The first rule of thumb is always choosing fruit that is intended for juicing. They are fruits with the thinnest skin; if you have doubts, ask a good grocer for help. There are other points to remember as well:

* *Be sure to remove all agricultural stamps and stickers with the knife, either pulling them off or scraping them away.*

* *Always wash fruits.*

* *Never refrigerate lemons, limes, or oranges that are meant for juicing, because cold fruit is stingy with juice. If the fruit is cold warm the fruit in the sink in warm water. Roll fruit under the palm of your hand across a cutting board to break down the cells and release more of the juice. Follow these simple steps and you can almost double the amount of juice you extract.*

* *Strain fruit juice through a fine strainer to remove seeds as well as pulp. Some people like fruit juice with lots of pulp, but it can present some problems with glassware, especially those washed in a dishwasher. The pulp becomes baked on the inside of the glass and, even though the glass is sterile, it looks dirty and is unusable. Always store juices in the refrigerator to safeguard against bacteria growth. Remember that fresh-squeezed juices are not pasteurized like some commercial juices, and they will spoil a lot faster. Fresh-squeeze juices as needed. Orange, lemon, and grapefruit will store in the fridge but lime should be squeezed fresh.*

FRUIT FOR DAIQUIRIS

Fresh-fruit daiquiris are usually prepared as frozen drinks, but they can also be prepared as "up" drinks—served without ice. Strawberries, bananas, papayas, and mangos make wonderful frozen drinks. They can be prepared ahead of time for a party and stored in simple syrup. Most fresh fruit will hold in the syrup for a couple days, but ideally they should be used the same day. Note: Frozen fresh fruit purées, once available only for commercial use, are now offered online for household use. One source is the Perfect Purée of Napa Valley, which has a marvelous range of flavors.

GARNISHES

I've always been amused by the definition of garnish *in* the dictionary as "something on or around food to add color or flavor." Beverage garnishes, I guess, don't make the cut. That's fine with me, because my definition of a cocktail garnish is something that adds both color *and* flavor. That thin sliver of dried lemon peel or the half wedge of oxidized lime that bobs to the surface of your drink is not a proper garnish.

For me, there are three words that are paramount to garniture presentation: *decorative, bountiful,* and *fresh.* A garnish should be chosen for size, beauty, and freshness. And when I say size, I am not implying bigger is better. A juice orange is not acceptable for garnish because its skin is too thin. Then again, the large, thick-skinned navels that make wonderful garnishes are very stingy in the juice department—not to mention expensive. The orange must be just right. Preparation is important, too. That big, beautiful navel is often butchered down to little chunks that retain nothing of the original shape and beauty of the whole fruit.

The first cocktail books in the mid-nineteenth century took a simple approach to the question of garnish. In his 1862 book *How to Mix Drinks, or The Bon-Vivant's Companion,* Jerry Thomas instructs us to "dress" or "ornament the top with fresh fruits in season."

LEMON AND LIME WEDGES

Wedges should be cut in the following way:

* *Begin by cutting the ends, or poles, off of the fruit; cut about ⅛-inch nub off each end, being careful not to cut into the fruit.*

* *Cut the fruit in half lengthwise (through the poles) and lay the halves facedown on the cutting board.*

* *Holding 1 half at a time, make 2 cuts lengthwise at a 45-degree angle, creating 3 wedges; then do the same with the other half. With larger fruit it's possible to get 4 wedges (instead of 3) out of each half.*

* *Cut lemons will remain fresh for 2 days if covered with a damp cloth and refrigerated. Cut limes, however, oxidize quickly, turning the edges brown and unusable for garnishing after 1 day. (Use the day-old lime wedges for muddling in drinks such as the Caipirinha.)*

* *Depending on the time of year and the source, some lemons may have more seeds than at other times, and if so, one more step is necessary: After the final cut, you'll notice that the seeds are generally gathered along the center line of the wedge. With a quick cut, remove that quarter-inch of seed-filled gutter.*

PINEAPPLE WEDGES

For garnishing, cut off both ends of the pineapple, then cut 1-inch-thick slices crosswise (through the equator, not pole to pole). Cut each slice into 8 wedges, leaving the skin on.

FLAMED ORANGE & LEMON ZEST COINS

The aroma and flavor in citrus fruits is concentrated in the oil cells of the peel. Chefs and bartenders often extract this oil along with the juice to add the essence of the fruit to various dishes and drinks. In cocktails, the oil in the citrus peel provides an additional advantage because it can be flamed.

- *Always use firm, fresh fruit: the skin will have a higher oil content.*

- *Use thick-skinned navel oranges and large lemons; ask your grocer for 95-count (a grocer term to indicate approximate number of pieces in the case) lemons as opposed to juice lemons (which are 165 count).*

- *Cut thin, uniformly sized oval or round peels, about an inch across. These are called* coins *by bartenders. If you are just developing confidence and skill with kitchen knives, begin with this easier technique: First cut a ½-inch nub off each end as described on page 61 for the wedges. Place the fruit on the cutting board with one of the cut poles resting on the board. Hold it down firmly on the cutting board and, using the paring knife, cut thin oval-shaped twists about 1 inch by 1½ inches long, slicing down toward the cutting board and away from your hand. The peel should be thin enough that the yellow shows all around the circumference, with just a small amount of white pith visible in the center. This type of peel will maximize the amount of oil expressed into the drink and minimize the amount of bitter white pith on the twist. Cut twists in a downward motion from the middle of the fruit to the bottom, following the curve of the fruit and turning the fruit after each cut until you have circled the fruit completely. Then turn the fruit over and perform the same operation on the other half. Navel oranges should yield 12 twists. If the large, fancy lemons are not available, choose the largest lemons available and be sure the skin is fresh, firm, and full of oil (as the fruit dries out, the skin will feel softer and have much less oil).*

Now that you have the peels, you can create festive pyrotechnical displays for your guests with the oil present in the skins. Here's how to flame the oil:

- *Hold a lit match in one hand and very carefully pick up a twist in the other hand, as if holding an eggshell; if you squeeze the twist prematurely, the oil will be expelled.*

- *Hold the twist gingerly by the side, not the ends, between thumb and forefinger, skin-side facing down, about 4 inches above the drink.*

- *Hold the match between the drink and the twist, closer to the twist. Snap the twist sharply, propelling the oil through the lit match and onto the surface of the drink. (Be sure to hold the twist far enough from the drink to avoid getting a smoky film on the surface of the drink.)*

LEMON/ORANGE PEEL SPIRAL GARNISH

Here's a fun and extravagant garnish used for drinks that are served in a tall chimney-style glass, like the Horse's Neck and Gin Sling. You will need a channel knife to cut a small groove in the skin of the fruit, creating a long spiral of lemon peel. Begin the same way as you would make peels above:

- *Remove the small nubs at each end.*

- *Grasping the lemon in one hand and the channel knife in the other, begin cutting at the pole farthest from you, cutting in a spiral around the fruit until you reach the other pole. Maintain steady downward pressure so the blade will cut into the skin.*

- *The half-inch-wide spiral peel left on the lemon is the garnish for the Horse's Neck cocktail, and it has to be carefully cut from the lemon using a paring knife. Take the paring knife and cut the thicker spiral peel from the lemon, keeping the knife tilted slightly inward toward the fruit to avoid cutting through the peel.*

- *Store the peels in ice water and the spirals will tighten up and become springy. The thicker spiral peel for the Horse's Neck garnish has to be placed in the serving glass before the ice and ingredients. Hook the curved end of the peel over the rim of the glass and drape the remaining length of peel in a spiral down inside the glass until it reaches the bottom. Hold the portion of the peel curled over the rim of the glass so it doesn't fall into the glass. Put the ice cubes in the center with the peel around the outside. The ice will hold the spiral garnish in place.*

The thinner spiral peel can be cut into shorter lengths and used on the rim of a glass, like a champagne flute, as a garnish for Champagne cocktails.

ORANGE/LEMON SLICE GARNISH

- *Choose fresh thick-skinned navel oranges or thick-skinned fancy lemons.*

- *Cut both ends off the fruit; note that some navel oranges have skin up to an inch thick at the poles that has to be cut away before you reach the flesh of the fruit.*

- *Next, cut the fruit in half lengthwise, through the poles, then place both halves facedown on a cutting board and cut ½-inch slices crosswise, following the line of the equator, not from pole to pole. (If your glassware is small, halve the slices of orange into quarter-round pieces.) When you combine an orange slice with a maraschino cherry, you have the famous "flag," a popular garnish for collins and sour drinks.*

MINT AND OTHER HERBS

A mint garnish has been a part of the American beverage since colonial times, when it appeared in the first brandy and peach-brandy juleps that were signature early American drinks. When choosing mint for beverage applications, look for springy young spearmint. Some varieties are more suited to garnish and beverage application. Avoid what I call the elephant-ear mint, with large floppy leaves; the leaves look wilted on top of a drink. A mint garnish should look generous and bushy. Drinks garnished with mint should be served with straws.

After muddling gently or shaking mint in a drink, strain the drink through the julep strainer to remove the bits of mint that are floating in the drink. It is not necessary to shred the mint when muddling, only to bruise the leaves to extract flavor. The action of shaking with ice will do the rest of the job. With mint leaves, I don't want to tear them into tiny pieces because the tannins are bitter.

FROSTING THE RIM OF THE GLASS

I sometimes shudder while sitting at a bar and watching the bartender take the glass from which I will be drinking, turn it upside down, dunk the rim into a container with some wet spongy material in it, and then dip the rim into salt. The rim of the glass is coated inside and outside with salt, not to mention the mysterious wet spongy stuff. Yuck.

Here's the right way to do it: Take a small widemouthed bowl and fill it with kosher or margarita salt, granulated sugar, or whatever you are frosting the glass with; never use iodized salt for frosting glasses. Using a fresh lemon, lime, or orange slice, carefully moisten only the outside rim of the glass in the desired width. Then, holding the glass sideways with the stem or bottom tipped slightly upward, dab the rim into the salt while turning the glass slowly, until the whole moistened rim is covered with the coating. Hold the glass over the sink or the trash container and tap the bowl of the glass gently to knock off the excess salt or sugar. The effect is a delicately salted rim that looks almost frosted. Tommy's Mexican Restaurant, a San Francisco restaurant that is famous for its margaritas, has a clever tradition: they salt only half the rim of the glass so the drinker can go back and forth between the salted and the unsalted parts of the rim.

MUDDLE THIS OVER

Muddling is a constant theme running through the recipes in this book. The standard muddler available at cocktail websites or in retail stores is not the same as the natural, hardwood muddler that I'm accustomed to using behind the bar; mine is made of hard fruitwood. Muddle herbs more gently than fruits.

Other useful muddling herbs include pineapple sage, which has a wonderful aroma that would enhance lots of drinks, like my Pineapple Julep, or even tropical drinks with pineapple as an ingredient. Black peppermint, besides adding a dramatic visual to a drink with its dark maroon stem veins, packs the most concentrated peppermint aroma of any in the category. Shiso leaf is the green or red-tinged leaf you find on the plate under sashimi. It has a strong, distinctive flavor and aroma. Bartenders are including more Asian spirits in cocktails, and shiso brings authentic flavor notes as both an ingredient and a garnish in these drinks. Verbena and lemon verbena have dark green leaves that add a refreshing lemony note as a garnish or muddled into citrus-based vodka, gin, and rum drinks. Simple syrup (page 225) can also be flavored by macerating or heating it with different spices like cinnamon. Try your own flavored syrup with spices of your choice.

FRUITS CUT FOR MUDDLING

- **LEMONS AND LIMES:** *Quarters work better for muddling than the wedges used for garnish. Wash the fruit and cut the nubs from both poles, then cut the fruit in half through the equator. Place both halves facedown on the cutting board and cut each into 4 equal quarters. The quarters are more compact than wedges and are easier to muddle and mash in the bottom of a mixing glass. One lemon make 2 sets of 4 quarters for muddling.*

Spiral orange peel and lemon garnish for Horse's Neck

**Jalap
skin gar**

Scored lime and lemon wedges

**Nutmeg gr
and be**

Bordeaux cherries

Wide orange peel spiral
for Café Brûlot (page 100)

Lemon/lime half wedges
for muddling or garnish

Pineapple leaf garnishes
and pineapple wedges

- **ORANGES:** *Because of their size, I muddle oranges cut into slices.*

- **PINEAPPLE:** *Cut off both ends and the rind. Remove the hard core. Cut 1-inch-thick slices crosswise (through the equator, not the pole). Cut the slices into 8 wedges, and use the pieces for muddling.*

There are two types of actions I perform with the muddler: bruising and muddling. I will bruise herbs by muddling them gently for a short time just to release some flavor without pulverizing them. I will aggressively muddle fruit like lemon, orange, and lime, or topical fruit like pineapple, kiwi, and mango, among others.

GLASSWARE

Glassware needs today are far simpler than they were in the nineteenth century. In his 1888 book, *Harry Johnson's New and Improved Illustrated Bartender's Manual or How to Mix Drinks of the Present Style*, Harry Johnson recommends six different wineglasses, five different beer glasses, and thirteen different drink glasses.

A good rule when choosing glassware is the old-fashioned idea of closely matching the glass size to portion size. Sure, there are times when an oversize glass is appropriate: An oversize Burgundy or Bordeaux glass adds elegance to wine service, and a scotch on the rocks looks and feels better in a double old-fashioned glass with some heft. However, there is little to no advantage to a ten- or eleven-ounce cocktail glass. Although they may appear to be crowd-pleasers, they are a losing proposition; filling them is bad for the bottom line and will end the party quickly, and not filling them looks stingy. The cocktail is intended to be a door opener at a cocktail party, a before-dinner appetite stimulant, not an evening ender.

Purchase a cocktail glass with size, balance, and style as your guide. Keep in mind that many classic cocktail recipes are 3 to 3½ ounces total before dilution and are designed for 5- to 7-ounce cocktail glasses that are never filled to the brim. Many glasses on the market are simply too big. At the Rainbow Room, I eventually switched to a 6-ounce cocktail glass, which at first garnered negative customer reactions. Eventually, though, check averages increased, as people felt free to enjoy more than one drink; this was not my intention, but it was an unexpected benefit on the bottom line. I think a smaller glass is perceived as not only manageable but also elegant and classic, like the drinks served in them. There's no reason why you shouldn't do the same at home.

PONY, LONDON DOCK & POUSSE-CAFÉ GLASSES

- *The pony looks like a miniature port glass, usually only one ounce.*

- *The London dock is used for Spanish sherry, and dessert wines, about five ounces.*

- *The pousse-café glass stands slightly taller than a copita, has straighter sides, and flares out at the top instead of inward to accommodate the layered pour.*

IRISH COFFEE & HOT DRINK GLASSES

If you're a big fan of hot coffee drinks, a classic Irish coffee glass with a tulip shape and medallion in the stem would be a good investment for aesthetic as well as practical reasons. The classic Irish coffee glass is only eight ounces, so after the whiskey and the brown-sugar syrup are poured in, there is room left in the glass for the exact amount of coffee (four ounces), then a nice, generous one-inch thick float of cream.

PITCHERS, BOWLS & CUPS

Group drinks served in pitchers, fancy punch bowls, or any large container are a big part of home entertaining. I serve a rum punch at my Super Bowl party in a big plastic cooler, just like the one the winning team dumps over the head of the coach at the end of the game. And a premade cocktail by the pitcher can solve the problem of getting a drink into the hand of each guest upon arrival. I like to keep a couple of nice glass pitchers, between thirty-two and forty-six ounces, on hand for parties.

PREPPING GLASSWARE

Always assume that your glassware is at least in need of polishing and probably in need of washing before use. That doesn't mean your day-to-day dinner glassware; we're talking about those special cocktail glasses and wineglasses that have probably been shelved for some time. Holding a glass up to the light can reveal streaks and cloudiness that will not enhance the look of a martini or a glass of Champagne. Polish glassware with a lint-free cloth (in a pinch, use paper towels—Viva is the choice of food stylists). Chill martini and cocktail glasses by placing them in the freezer before a party. If your freezer can't accommodate several glasses, fill the glasses with ice cubes and water before use, and they will chill up nicely.

WHICH GLASS FOR WHICH DRINK?

Below are must-haves for cocktail bars, but in the home, a wide range of glassware is really unnecessary.

- **NICK & NORA:** *Retro "up" cocktails*
- **V-SHAPED COCKTAIL:** *All "up" cocktails*
- **COUPE:** *All "up" cocktails*
- **FIZZ OR DELMONICO:** *Fizz drinks with egg and sometimes cream were served without ice in a highball-style glass (six to eight ounces)*
- **HIGHBALL:** *Soda and beer (colloquially called a tumbler)*
- **ROCKS OR OLD-FASHIONED:** *Spirits over ice, cocktails over ice (six to ten ounces)*
- **DOUBLE OLD-FASHIONED:** *Mai Tai, Negroni (twelve to sixteen ounces)*

- **ALL-PURPOSE WINEGLASS:** *Red and white wine, frozen drinks (eight to twelve ounces, but do not fill more than halfway)*
- **CHAMPAGNE FLUTE:** *Champagne and Champagne cocktails*

OPTIONAL GLASSWARE

- **SPECIALTY, COPA GRANDE, HURRICANE:** *Frozen drinks and tropical rum drinks*
- **PILSNER, PINT, OR STEIN:** *A must-have for the beer-drinking household, Pilsner twelve to fourteen ounces, pint or stein sixteen ounces*
- **BRANDY SNIFTER:** *London dock glass is a fine substitute, though not as good aesthetically*
- **SHOT:** *For the crowd that enjoys shooters. Shot glasses are an extra, unless, of course, you are a fan of shooters or of los tres cuates ("the three chums"): salt, tequila shot, and lime*
- **COLLINS OR CHIMNEY:** *Zombie, collins (twelve to fourteen ounces). Note: Zombie can also be served in an oversize specialty glass.*
- **PUNCH BOWL AND CUPS:** *Traditional shrub-based or holiday punches*

A NOTE FROM LEGENDARY BARTENDER "COCKTAIL BILL" BOOTHBY

"Just because a particular recipe calls for a particular ingredient not possessed by the home mixer, he [or she] should not become discouraged. He [or she] must remember that many of the finest beverages have been discovered by substitution . . . or, in some instances by omission of an ingredient."

PART TWO

COCKTAILS
AND
BAR TALES

THE RECIPES

The years that followed the release of *The Craft of the Cocktail* in 2002 were important to the growth of the craft cocktail movement. A new generation of bartenders added their voices and their creativity to the art of making drinks, tinkering and retooling the classics, and borrowing both ingredients and techniques from the culinary world. That opened the door to a new era: the cocktail as a companion to the explosion of creativity in the culinary world and a love affair with big flavor. **In this chapter, you will find many of these talented men and women and their recipes represented with this + symbol.** Some of these recipes are destined to be the modern classics that will endure.

Today the offerings from drinks companies have grown exponentially. Rather than a separate list of recommended brands as I did in the original edition, **I have branded many of the recipes with my recommended favorites, and labeled my original recipes or variations on classics with this * symbol**. This is an opportunity to introduce you to quality and sometimes unique brands from the vastly expanded repertoire of spirits. The result is a much tighter focus on flavor and a better drink. Time to roll up our sleeves and shake, muddle, stir, and roll some great cocktails.

DRINK NAMES, RECIPE SEQUENCE & INDEX

Some drinks go by many different names. What one person calls a Buck's Fizz, another calls a Mimosa. It's usually a matter of opinion as to who's right or wrong, and often they are both right. Sometimes it's impossible to even guess. So I have used the name that has the widest use, and that's where you'll find the recipe. I created a number of special features—such as Manhattan, Martini, Fizz, and Bloody Mary variations—to group together all the members of these tightly knit families, so if you don't find it alphabetically, check those sections.

All drinks are listed alphabetically in the index.

STRAIGHT UP

The straight-up recipes are between 3 and 4 ounces before shaking or stirring. Proper shaking or stirring should add about 1 ounce water. Water is as important as any other ingredient to the flavor of a proper cocktail. With the water content, the "up" recipes are all designed to be served in a 5½- to 7-ounce cocktail glass.

HIGHBALLS

Highball recipes generally contain between 1½ and 2 ounces total alcohol.

ON THE ROCKS

Drinks on the rocks should contain between 2 and 3 ounces alcohol, with Martinis and Manhattans in the upper range, and spirits on the rocks in the lower range.

FLAMING

Throughout the recipe library, I call for flamed orange and lemon coins. This is a neat trick that was a regular part of the drink service at the bar of the Rainbow Room. It brought a little theater *and* added a wonderful burnt orange or lemon flavor to the drinks. The technique is easy to master: just follow the instructions on page 62.

ABBEY COCKTAIL

Aviation gin, created by bartender Ryan Magarian, is a nice example of the "new Western" style; it's more floral, with juniper in the middle of the aroma instead of on top.

1½ ounces Aviation American gin
¾ ounce Lillet Blanc
1 ounce fresh orange juice
Dash of Regan's Orange Bitters No. 6
Flamed orange zest coin (see page 62),
**   for garnish**

Shake all the ingredients (except the garnish) with ice and strain into a chilled cocktail glass. Garnish with the flamed orange zest coin.

ABSINTHE DRIP

The drip technique is critical to the success of this absinthe classic. The *louche*, or clouding, happens when the alcohol content is lowered and the bonds between the essential oils and the alcohol molecules are broken. Shocking the absinthe by pouring in water all at once will cause the essential oils to clump together. This manifests as "scales" that float on top of the surface of the drink, which is definitely not the way we want to present the drink. Finally, the sugar that is used traditionally is not necessary with fine absinthe, and I recommend using the reservoir apparatus to deliver the water that does not employ sugar.

4 ounces spring water
2 ounces Jade 1901 Absinthe Supérieure

Fill the reservoir container with the water and place it on top of the glass, then watch as the magic happens. Note, the resevoir apparatus is a glass or metal container that sits on top of an absinthe glass and delivers water to the absinthe drop by drop through a fine hole in the bottom of the container.

ABSINTHE SUISSE

In his book the *Roving Bartender*, 1946, Bill Kelly suggests orgeat as a replacement for anisette, which was more popular; others recommend French vermouth.

1½ ounces Jade 1901 Absinthe Supérieure
¾ ounce Dolin Blanc vermouth
¼ ounce orgeat
¾ ounce emulsified egg white (see page 204)
Grated Marcona almond, for garnish

Shake all the ingredients (except the garnish) very well with ice, making sure to completely emulsify the egg white. Strain into a coupe glass and top with the grated almond.

ABSOLUTELY BANANAS+

David Thompson of the Capital Hotel in London won first prize with this drink in the first annual London Absolut Vodka Cocktail contest in 1996. If this cocktail is shaken very hard to a slow ten count, a handsome layer of foam from the pineapple juice will float on top of the drink and make a great presentation.

1½ ounces Blue Shark vodka
½ ounce Tempus Fugit Crème de Banane liqueur
1½ ounces pineapple juice

Shake all the ingredients very well with ice and strain into a chilled cocktail glass.

ADAM & EVE*

This recipe is my original, created for the now-closed Gin Lane bar in New York City.

1 ounce Pama pomegranate liqueur
1 ounce Żubrówka Bison Grass flavored vodka
4 ounces fresh apple cider
Dash of Dale DeGroff's Pimento Aromatic Bitters
Slice of green apple, for garnish

Build all the ingredients (except the garnish) in a highball glass over ice and stir. Garnish with the green apple slice.

ABSINTHE SUISSE

ADONIS COCKTAIL RETOOLED

The original Adonis Cocktail was created in 1884 and named after a Broadway musical. The ingredients as listed in most books are simply sherry, vermouth, and bitters. I substituted a couple of my favorites.

2 ounces Lustau fino sherry, or your favorite fino
1 ounce Martini Riserva Speciale Ambrato vermouth
3 dashes of Dale DeGroff's Pimento Aromatic Bitters
Orange zest coin (see page 62), for garnish

Stir all the ingredients (except for the garnish) with ice and strain into a chilled Nick & Nora glass. Garnish with the orange zest coin.

AIR BALLOON⁺

Recipe by Ms. Franky Marshall. Franky Marshall is an accomplished craft bartender, educator, and unrepentant hedonist.

1½ ounces Clément Premiére Canne rum
¾ ounce Nardini Acqua di Cedro liqueur
¼ ounce green Chartreuse
½ ounce fresh lime juice
¼ ounce Simple Syrup (page 225)
Sage leaf, for garnish
Dehydrated lime wheel, for garnish

Shake all the ingredients (except the garnishes) gently with ice. Strain into a fine stemware over pebble ice (see page 31). Garnish with the sage leaf and lime wheel.

AIR MAIL COCKTAIL

1 ounce Clément Premiére Canne rum
½ ounce fresh lime juice
¼ ounce Simple Syrup (page 225)
¼ ounce Honey Syrup (page 224)
4 ounces Champagne

Shake the first four ingredients with ice. Strain into a large cocktail glass and top with the Champagne.

ALABAMA SLAMMERITOS*

MAKES 4 SHOOTERS

This is a trip back to your *salad days*, so you want to take it easy—keep to small doses, served as shooters. This recipe makes four shooters, so find three fellow travelers to accompany you on this bit of time travel.

¾ ounce Southern Comfort 100 Proof
1½ ounces Tito's Handmade vodka
¾ ounce Plymouth sloe gin
3 ounces fresh orange juice

Shake all the ingredients hard with ice, then strain into four 1½-ounce shot glasses. Bottoms up!

ALAMBIC FIZZ⁺

This original cocktail is from Jeff Bell at PDT (Please Don't Tell) in New York City. Jeff and sommelier Thomas Pastuszak were the consulting blend masters for Bertoux brandy, a pot-distilled California brandy that is a blend of brandies from three- to seven-year-old that are aged in French and American oak.

2 ounces Bertoux brandy
¾ ounce Blandy's 5-year-old Bual Madeira
Dash of Dale DeGroff's Pimento Aromatic Bitters
1½ ounces Lindemans Pêche Lambic Belgian beer

Shake all the ingredients except the beer hard with ice, strain into a chilled coupe glass, and top with the beer.

ALEXANDER

This may be served "up" or as a frappé over snow ice.

1 ounce gin or Cognac
1 ounce Tempus Fugit crème de cacao
2 ounces heavy cream
Freshly grated nutmeg, for garnish

Shake the ingredients (except the garnish) with ice and strain into a small cocktail glass. Garnish with the nutmeg.

ALGONQUIN

Ted Saucier collected drinks from around the world in his 1951 book *Bottoms Up*. The Blue Bar at New York City's famous Algonquin Hotel offered the following recipe.

2 ounces Banks Island Blend rum
½ ounce Marie Brizard No 21 blackberry liqueur
¼ ounce Bénédictine
½ ounce fresh lime juice
Bordeaux cherry, for garnish

Shake the ingredients (except the garnish) with ice and strain into a small cocktail glass. Garnish with the cherry.

ALLEGHENY

I found this in *The Ultimate A-to-Z Bar Guide*, and I include it here with a thank-you to the authors. For extra flavor, muddle in a piece of lemon.

1 ounce bourbon
1 ounce Noilly Prat Original dry vermouth
½ ounce Marie Brizard No 21 blackberry liqueur
½ ounce fresh lemon juice
Lemon zest coin (see page 62), for garnish

Shake the ingredients (except the garnish) well with ice and strain into a chilled cocktail glass. Garnish with the lemon zest coin.

ALLIANCE*

Tony Abou-Ganim, aka the Modern Mixologist, and I collaborated on this cocktail for the Trade Board of Peru to feature the iconic Peruvian brandy, pisco.

1 strawberry, for garnish
¼ ounce strawberry purée (see Note)
½ ounce lychee purée (see Note)
1½ ounces BarSol Primero Quebranta pisco
¼ ounce Ginger Syrup (page 224)
¼ ounce Simple Syrup (page 225)
1 ounce fresh lemon juice
2 ounces Champagne
½ lemon wheel, for garnish

Hull the strawberry and slice it lengthwise (through the stem end) to get heart-shaped slices. Set aside.

Add all the ingredients (except the Champagne and garnishes) to a large wineglass and stir. Fill the glass with ice about one-third full and slowly top with the Champagne; stir very gently. Add the strawberry slices and half lemon wheel to the glass as you would for sangria.

NOTE You can premix the two purées in bulk to expedite service of the drink. Source the purées from the Perfect Purée of Napa Valley (www.perfectpuree.com).

TRYING IS FOR STUDENTS!

In early 1989, just months after we had opened the Rainbow Room, I was called to the executive floor at 30 Rock for a one-on-one with Joe Baum—that was not good news. As I entered, Joe threw a magazine across the desk and said, "Read this." The magazine was *Gastronome*. The article by Karen MacNeil was "Cocktails? Of Course." Though I didn't know I'd be quoted, it was my first real ink, and I was smiling, but that did not make Joe happy.

He underlined the spot he wanted me to read: "Here [at Rainbow] we're trying to re-invent the feeling, style, and professionalism . . ." Joe slapped the desk so hard that I jumped out of my seat. He shouted, "**TRYING** IS FOR STUDENTS. WE DON'T **TRY**, WE DO! GET THE HELL OUT OF MY OFFICE."

It was actually a good meeting. I never heard the words "you're fired." And I got my first and most important lesson on how to handle the press. It was also sloppy fact checking. The Rainbow Room Bronx Cocktail, in our beautiful retro Nick and Nora glass, was attributed to Gordon's in Chicago, and the Blond Bombshell from Gordon's was attributed to the Rainbow Room.

ALPHONSO COCKTAIL

ALPHONSO COCKTAIL

This retooling of the classic Champagne Cocktail (page 107) was served at the French resort of Deauville in Normandy around 1920.

1 sugar cube soaked with Angostura bitters
1 ounce Dubonnet Rouge
Champagne or sparkling wine
Lemon zest coin or spiral (see page 62), for garnish

Place the bitters-soaked sugar cube in a white-wine glass with a couple of ice cubes. Add the Dubonnet and fill with Champagne. Garnish with the lemon zest coin or spiral.

AMBER DREAM

The Amber Dream is a Bijou cocktail with dry vermouth and sweet and yellow Chartreuse instead of green Chartreuse.

2 ounces Beefeater gin
1 ounce Dolin dry vermouth
¼ ounce yellow Chartreuse
Dash of orange bitters
Flamed orange zest coin (see page 62), for garnish

Place the ingredients (except the garnish) in a bar glass with ice and stir. Garnish with the flamed orange zest coin.

AMERICAN BEAUTY

¾ ounce Argonaut brandy
¾ ounce Dolin dry vermouth
¾ ounce fresh orange juice
¼ ounce grenadine, homemade (page 224) or store-bought
¼ ounce Marie Brizard No 33 white crème de menthe
½ ounce Sandeman Founder's Reserve ruby port
Food-grade rose petal, for garnish

Shake all the ingredients (except the port and garnish) with ice and strain into a chilled cocktail glass. Float the port on top. Garnish with the rose petal.

AMERICANO HIGHBALL

This cocktail was bottled and sold around the world by Martini & Rossi in the 1890s. Note that most aperitif, sherry, and vermouth drinks should be served in stemware, but the Americano Highball should obviously be in a highball glass.

1½ ounces Italian sweet vermouth
1½ ounces Campari
Soda water
Flamed orange zest coin (see page 62), for garnish

Pour the vermouth and Campari into an ice-filled highball glass and top with soda water. Garnish with the flamed orange zest coin.

ANOTHER SHADE OF GREYHOUND*

I created this variation on the theme for Holland America Line's ships.

1½ ounces Blue Shark vodka
½ ounce St-Germain elderflower liqueur
4 ounces fresh grapefruit juice
Dash of Bitter Truth grapefruit bitters
Grapefruit zest coin (see page 62), for garnish

Build all the ingredients (ecept the garnish) in a highball glass over ice and stir. Garnish with the grapefruit zest coin.

AÑEJO HIGHBALL*

I created the Añejo Highball as a tribute to the great bartenders of Cuba, in particular Constantino Ribalaigua Vert, from Havana's El Floridita bar, one of the leading bartenders of the twentieth century.

1½ ounces Bacardí añejo rum
½ ounce Pierre Ferrand dry curaçao
¼ ounce fresh lime juice
2 dashes of Dale DeGroff's Pimento Aromatic Bitters
2 ounces ginger beer, homemade (see page 222) or store-bought
Lime wheel, for garnish
Orange slice, for garnish

Build the first four ingredients over ice in a highball glass and fill with the ginger beer. Stir and garnish with the lime wheel and orange slice.

APERATIVO CALIFORNIA*

This was a menu item I created for Keith McNally's Morandi Italian restaurant.

1½ ounces China Martini liqueur
¾ ounce fresh orange juice
¾ ounce fresh grapefruit juice
2 dashes of Regan's Orange Bitters No. 6
Lime wedge
Thin English cucumber wheel, unpeeled, for garnish

Build all the ingredients (except the lime and the cucumber garnish) with ice in a double old-fashioned glass. Stir. Squeeze the lime wedge into the drink and discard it; garnish with the fresh-cut cucumber wheel.

APPLEJACK COCKTAIL

This is adapted from a drink served at the Ritz Bar in Paris and published in *The Artistry of Mixing Drinks* by Frank Meier (1936).

2 ounces Laird's Straight Applejack 86
¾ ounce Pierre Ferrand dry curaçao
¼ ounce fresh lime juice
2 dashes of Bitter Truth orange bitters
Apple slice, for garnish
Orange zest coin (see page 62), for garnish

Shake all the ingredients (except the garnishes) with ice and strain into a chilled cocktail glass. Garnish with the apple slice and the orange zest coin.

APRICOT COCKTAIL*

I started playing with the recipe for a Bermuda Rose (gin, apricot, lime, and grenadine) and came up with the Apricot Cocktail. It's a good match for either spicy tuna tartare or spicy tapas.

1½ ounces Hendrick's Orbium gin
¾ ounce Marie Brizard Apry liqueur
¾ ounce fresh orange juice
½ ounce fresh lemon juice
Flamed orange zest coin (see page 62), for garnish

Shake the ingredients (except the garnish) well with ice and strain into a chilled cocktail glass. Garnish with the flamed orange zest coin.

AQUEDUCT

I can't resist a drink named after a racetrack.

1½ ounces vodka
½ ounce Marie Brizard No 1 triple sec
½ ounce Marie Brizard Apry liqueur
¾ ounce fresh lime juice
Thin lime wheel, for garnish

Shake all ingredients (except the garnish) with ice and strain into a chilled cocktail glass. Float the thin lime wheel on top of the drink.

ARANCIO AMERICANO*

This was a menu item I created for Keith McNally's
Morandi Italian restaurant.

¾ ounce Aperol
¾ ounce Martini & Rossi sweet vermouth
1 ounce fresh orange juice
2 ounces Mionetto Prosecco Brut Valdobbiadene
Half orange wheel, for garnish

Build the Aperol, vermouth, and orange juice in
a highball glass filled three-quarters full with ice
cubes. Stir and top with the prosecco. Garnish with
the half orange wheel.

ANGEL'S SHOOTERS

"Angel" drinks are the original shooters created during the Jazz Age. The following recipes are designed, as they were originally, to be layered in a one-ounce pony-style glass. If you wish to serve this drink in a larger glass, the recipe amounts need to be adjusted accordingly.

ANGEL'S KISS

The layers are achieved by pouring the alcohol slowly over the back of a spoon held against the inside of the glass (see Pousse-Café, page 187).

1 part Tempus Fugit crème de cacao
1 part Cognac
1 part heavy cream

Layer the crème de cacao and Cognac in a pony glass. Pour the cream over the back of a bar spoon to float on top of the other two ingredients.

ANGEL'S TIP

1 part Tempus Fugit crème de cacao
1 part heavy cream

Pour the crème de cacao in a pony or cordial glass and pour the cream over the back of a bar spoon to float on top.

AVIATION COCKTAIL

The Internet cocktail crowd has breathed new life into this chestnut.

2 ounces Fords gin
½ ounce Luxardo maraschino liqueur
½ ounce fresh lemon juice
Splash of Simple Syrup (page 225; optional)
½ ounce Giffard crème de violette
Bordeaux cherry, for garnish

Shake the gin, maraschino liqueur, lemon juice, and simple syrup with ice and strain into a chilled cocktail glass; pour the crème de violette through the drink. Garnish with the cherry.

B-52

This was one of the first disco-era layered shooters, and it is still one of the best. See Pousse-Café (page 187) for help with layering.

¾ ounce Kahlúa
¾ ounce Baileys Irish cream
¾ ounce Grand Marnier

Layer the ingredients in a cordial glass in the listed order, starting with the Kahlúa.

BACARDÍ COCKTAIL

The Bacardí Cocktail was the cosmopolitan of the 1930s. Add orange juice and you have the Robson; add dry vermouth for Frank Meier's version from the Ritz Bar in Paris. Stork Club bartender, Johnny Brooks, created the Cubanola by adding fresh orange juice, pineapple juice, and egg white to the regular Bacardí Cocktail. I added my own touch with less grenadine and some simple syrup, which is not without historical precedent.

In the mid 1930s Bacardí waged a lawsuit against a New York hotel that was making the drink with another rum; the New York Supreme Court ruled that the Bacardí Cocktail must be made with Bacardí rum. The ruling was unenforceable but worth a fortune in publicity.

2 ounces Bacardí light rum
½ ounce fresh lemon juice
½ ounce Simple Syrup (page 225)
4 dashes of grenadine, homemade (page 224) or store-bought
Bordeaux cherry, for garnish

Shake all the ingredients (except the garnish) with ice and strain into a small cocktail glass. Garnish with the cherry.

BAHAMA MAMA

¾ ounce light rum
¾ ounce añejo rum
¾ ounce dark rum
¾ ounce Clément Mahina Coco liqueur
¾ ounce Tempus Fugit Crème de Banane liqueur
2 ounces fresh orange juice
2 ounces pineapple juice
¼ teaspoon grenadine, homemade (page 224) or store-bought
Dash of Dale DeGroff's Pimento Aromatic Bitters
Bordeaux cherry, for garnish
Pineapple slice and pineapple leaf, for garnish
Orange slice, for garnish

Shake all the ingredients (except garnishes) with ice and strain into a boca grande or other specialty glass. Garnish with the cherry, pineapple slice and leaf, and orange slice.

BAKUNIN

This drink was created at Pravda bar in New York, which, next to the bar at The Odeon, was Keith McNally's most successful bar.

1½ ounces Stolichnaya Ohranj vodka
¾ ounce Grand Marnier
1 ounce fresh orange juice
½ ounce fresh lemon juice
Dash of Bitter Truth orange bitters

Shake all the ingredients well with ice and strain into a large coupe glass over crushed ice.

BALM COCKTAIL

If you can find fresh lemon balm, shake a leaf with this cocktail and use a sprig as an additional garnish.

2 ounces Dry Sack Medium sherry
¾ ounce fresh orange juice
½ ounce Cointreau
2 dashes of Angostura bitters
2 orange slices
2 sprigs of lemon balm, for garnish
Flamed orange zest coin (see page 62),
    for garnish

Shake the sherry, orange juice, Cointreau, bitters, and orange slices with ice. Fine strain into a chilled cocktail glass. Garnish with the lemon balm and the flamed orange zest coin.

BANANA DAIQUIRI (FROZEN)

I use only a small amount of banana liqueur so I get the flavor from the fruit itself.

1 ounce light rum
1 ounce amber rum
1 ounce Tempus Fugit Crème de Banane liqueur
¾ ounce fresh lime juice
2 ounces Simple Syrup (page 225)
½ small banana, sliced

Pulse the ingredients in a blender with cracked ice and serve in a Boca grande glass.

BANSHEE

A Grasshopper made with crème de banane liqueur instead of crème de menthe.

1 ounce Tempest Fugit Crème de Banane liqueur
1 ounce Tempest Fugit crème de cacao
2 ounces heavy cream

Shake well with ice and strain into a large coupe glass.

BARCELONA (FROZEN)*

I created this for the James Beard House in New York City during the 1992 Barcelona Olympics. The frozen Barcelona was served with dessert.

¾ ounce Gran Duque d'Alba Spanish brandy
¾ ounce Dry Sack sherry or your favorite
    medium sherry
¾ ounce Cointreau
¾ ounce fresh orange juice
¾ ounce heavy cream
1 ounce Simple Syrup (page 225)
¾ cup ice
Ground cinnamon, for garnish

Blend all the ingredients (except the garnish) in a blender. Serve in a large coupe glass. Garnish with a light dusting of cinnamon.

BATIDAS (FROZEN)

These Brazilian milkshakes are made in many flavors; choose your favorite fruit purée or nectar.

2 ounces cachaça
2 ounces tropical fruit purée or nectar
1 ounce sweetened condensed milk
1 ounce Simple Syrup (page 225)
Grated nutmeg, for garnish

Blend all the ingredients (except the garnish) with ice and serve in a stem glass. Garnish with grated nutmeg.

BEE'S KISS

This is modified from a recipe from the Ritz Bar in Paris as printed in Frank Meier's *The Artistry of Mixing Drinks* (1936).

1½ ounces Bacardí rum
1 ounce heavy cream
¾ ounce Honey Syrup (page 224; see Note)

Shake all the ingredients with ice and strain into a chilled coupe glass.

BEE'S KNEES

2 ounces gin
¾ ounce Honey Syrup (page 224)
¾ ounce fresh lemon juice
Lemon zest coin (see page 62), for garnish

Shake the gin, honey syrup, and lemon juice with ice and strain into a chilled cocktail glass. Garnish with the lemon zest coin.

BELFAST COCKTAIL⁺

This was created by Francis Schott, partner in the landmark New Brunswick, New Jersey, restaurant Stage Left Steak—purveyors of fine food and drink for thirty-seven years as I write this.

1½ ounces Sandeman Founder's Reserve
   ruby port
1½ ounces Pierre Ferrand Ambre Cognac
½ ounce Trimbach Poire William brandy
½ ounce Cinnamon Syrup (page 223)
Dash of Bitter Truth orange bitters
Dash of Dale DeGroff's Pimento Aromatic Bitters
Orange zest coin (see page 62)
Freshly grated Ceylon cinnamon stick,
   for garnish

Combine all the ingredients (except the orange zest and cinnamon) in a cocktail mixing glass with ice and stir to chill. Strain into a chilled cocktail glass and express the oil of the orange zest coin over the top of the drink and discard. Garnish with the cinnamon.

THE BELLINI

The Bellini was invented by Giuseppe Cipriani in 1948, at Harry's Bar in Venice. Originally the drink was made only during four months of the year, when the sweet white peaches used for the purée were in season. But when the Cipriani empire spread to New York City, Giuseppe's son, Arrigo, found a flash-frozen peach purée that he could use year-round. He colored the purée slightly with raspberry juice or grenadine to create the perfect Bellini color.

2 ounces of colored and chilled white peach purée
   (see Notes)
3 ounces dry prosecco, such as Mionetto Prestige
   Collection DOC Treviso Brut
½ ounce Marie Brizard No 11 peach liqueur float
   (optional)

Put the peach purée in the bottom of a mixing glass without ice. Slowly pour in the prosecco while gently pulling the colored peach purée up the side of the glass to mix with the prosecco; stir gently to avoid losing the effervescence. Strain into a champagne flute and float the peach liqueur, if desired.

NOTES I recommend flash-frozen purée from the Perfect Purée of Napa Valley (www. perfectpuree.com). I bought frozen peach purée by the liter, thawed it for use, and then colored the whole liter with 1½ tablespoons of raspberry juice or grenadine syrup for use in Bellinis.

Bellinis are often made by the pitcherful. To do so, choose a pitcher that is wider at the top than at the bottom and fill it one-third full with colored peach purée. Slowly pour prosecco down the side of the pitcher, and using a long bar spoon, pull the purée up the side of the pitcher. Stir gently to avoid losing the effervescence of the prosecco.

BETWEEN THE SHEETS

This drink is a relative of the Sidecar (page 202). There are other versions that omit Bénédictine and use rum instead. I'm a fan of this recipe that I sourced from *Bottoms Up* (1951) by Ted Saucier. If desired, frost the outside rim of the glass with sugar (see page 63).

1½ ounces Cognac
½ ounce Bénédictine
½ ounce Cointreau
¾ ounce fresh lemon juice
Flamed orange zest coin (see page 62), for garnish

Shake all the ingredients (except the garnish) with ice and strain into a chilled cocktail glass. Garnish with the flamed orange zest coin.

BIG SPENDER*

I created the Big Spender for the 2005 Broadway revival of *Sweet Charity* largely because the Beckmann family of Jose Cuervo tequila were the "angels" behind the show. The original drink was made with Cristal Rosé Champagne.

1 ounce Gran Centenario añejo tequila
1 ounce Clément Créole Shrubb orange liqueur
1½ ounces blood orange juice
2½ ounces rosé Champagne
Orange zest coin (see page 62)

Combine the tequila, liqueur, and blood orange juice in a large bar glass with ice and stir. Strain into a champagne flute and top with the Champagne. Stir gently, flame the orange zest coin over the drink, and discard.

BIJOU

This is *The Savoy Cocktail Book*'s version, with the green Chartreuse upgraded to V.E.P., which stands for *vieillissement exceptionnellement prolongé*, meaning "exceptionally prolonged aging." I had the Bijou on my second menu at Rainbow's Promenade Bar. It was a delicate cocktail to balance, maybe ahead of its time for my audience in 1988, but today it would be a hit.

2 ounces Plymouth gin
½ ounce green Chartreuse V.E.P.
½ ounce Martini & Rossi sweet vermouth
Dash of orange bitters (see Note)
Lemon zest coin (see page 62)
Bordeaux cherry, for garnish

Stir the gin, Chartreuse, vermouth, and bitters with ice, and strain into a chilled Nick & Nora glass. Express the lemon oil over the drink and discard. Garnish with the cherry.

NOTE For this recipe, I like to use Pegu Club's blend of two parts Regan's Orange Bitters No. 6 to one part Fee Brothers orange bitters.

BLACK RUSSIAN

This is a classic.

1½ ounces Kahlúa
1½ ounces Russian Standard vodka

Build over ice cubes in an old-fashioned glass.

NOTE For a White Russian, add 1 ounce cream, shake, and serve over crushed ice.

BLACK VELVET

This unusual drink dates to the death of Queen Victoria's Prince Albert, in 1861, which set off deep mourning throughout the country. In this recipe, even the Champagne is draped in black. James Squire Four Wives Pilsener is the perfect glass to get this difficult pour under control. (Search online for James Squire Craftware and look for this glass by name or the #3.)

4 ounces Guinness stout
4 ounces Champagne

Slowly and carefully pour together the Guinness and Champagne into a Pilsner beer glass.

BLACKBERRY JULEP*

This was my signature drink at Blackbird Bar and also the most popular. We used a marinated berry sauce over the baked Alaska for years at the Rainbow Room, and that sauce was the inspiration for this drink and also the garnish. I altered the original recipe for this drink by adding gin for a dry version.

- 1½ ounces Plymouth gin
- 1 ounce Marie Brizard No 21 blackberry liqueur
- 1 ounce fresh lemon juice
- ¼ ounce Simple Syrup (page 225)
- 1 tablespoon Mixed-Berry Marinade (recipe follows)

Shake all the ingredients (except the marinade) with ice and strain into a highball glass filled with crushed ice. Stir until the glass begins to frost. Garnish with the berry marinade. Serve with a teaspoon on the side so the guest can enjoy the berries!

MIXED-BERRY MARINADE
MAKES 3 PINTS

Wash and dry a pint each of blueberries, hulled and quartered strawberries, and a pint of mixed black and red raspberries and place them in a bowl. Cover with 1½ cups superfine sugar. After 3 hours add 1½ ounces brandy and 3 ounces Cointreau and gently stir the mixture. Set aside to macerate for an hour, stirring occasionally.

BLACKBERRY SAGE SMASH+

This recipe is from Sean Kenyon, owner of Williams & Graham bar in Denver, Colorado.

4 large blackberries
3 medium sage leaves
½ ounce Simple Syrup (page 225)
Dash of grenadine, homemade (page 224) or store-bought
¼ ounce fresh lemon juice
2 ounces Woody Creek bourbon

In a Boston shaker, muddle 3 blackberries and 2 sage leaves with the simple syrup, grenadine, and lemon juice. Add the bourbon and ice and shake. Fine strain over crushed or cracked ice into a double old-fashioned glass. Garnish with the remaining sage leaf pulled through the remaining blackberry. Run a bamboo cocktail pick through the center as well to hold the garnish upright.

BLACKTHORN

In his 1922 book *Cocktails: How to Mix Them*, Robert Vermeire credited nineteenth-century bartender Harry Johnson for this cocktail. The Black Thorn (two words) appeared in the 1900 edition of *Harry Johnson's New and Improved Illustrated Bartenders Manual* as an Irish whiskey drink. The *Café Royal Cocktail Book*'s recipe is made with sloe gin, and thanks to Gaz Regan, we have a modern version made with regular gin.

1 ounce Powers Irish whiskey
1 ounce Dolin dry vermouth
½ ounce Plymouth sloe gin
2 dashes of Angostura bitters
1 dash of Jade 1901 Absinthe Supérieure
Flamed lemon zest coin (see page 62), for garnish

Stir all the ingredients (except the garnish) with ice and strain into a chilled Nick & Nora glass. Garnish with the flamed lemon zest coin.

BLAZER

Jerry Thomas's famous flaming drink is challenging and can be dangerous. Use large double-walled stainless steel mugs (see The Crafty Bartender, page 228). Finally, make a small amount for each batch to avoid spillage. Practice outdoors to avoid any chance of fire. Indoors, prepare the drink over a nonflammable surface. Never attempt it at the table.

¼ ounce Simple Syrup (page 225)
Splash of fresh lemon juice
Boiling water
1½ ounces The Glenlivet Nàdurra single malt scotch whisky (60.3% ABV)
Lemon twist, for garnish

Add the simple syrup and lemon juice to a London dock glass. Warm two mugs with the boiling water. Leave about 2 ounces boiling water in one mug and add the scotch to it; immediately ignite the mixture. Pour the flaming mixture back and forth between the two mugs; the oxygen added by *carefully* pouring the flaming liquid back and forth will create a wonderful display. Smother the flame by holding one mug over the other for a moment, then pour the mixture into the prepared glass. Garnish with the lemon twist.

BLOOD AND SAND

At first glance, this unusual cocktail seemed a god-awful mix. But over time, I have noted that the recipe appears in some serious cocktail books, so I finally tried it. The taste convinced me to never judge a drink again without tasting it. The drink has inspired craft bartenders to come up with numerous variations on the theme.

¾ ounce The Famous Grouse blended scotch whisky
¾ ounce Heering cherry liqueur
¾ ounce Italian sweet vermouth
¾ ounce fresh orange juice
Flamed orange zest coin (see page 62), for garnish

Shake all the ingredients (except the garnish) well with ice and strain into a chilled cocktail glass. Garnish with the flamed orange zest coin.

BLOOD ORANGE COSMO+

This was created by Julie Reiner at her original Flatiron Lounge in New York City, which closed in 2018 after a long, successful run. Julie and her partner, Susan, now own Clover Club in Brooklyn, as well as a share of Pegu Club in Manhattan. They recently partnered with bartender Ivy Mix at Leyenda, an agave bar and restaurant also in Brooklyn.

1½ ounces Stolichnaya Ohranj vodka
½ ounce Cointreau
¼ ounce fresh lime juice
¼ ounce fresh blood orange juice
Splash of cranberry juice
Orange slice, for garnish

Shake the ingredients (except the garnish) well with ice and serve in a chilled cocktail glass. Garnish with the orange slice.

BLOODBATH IN THE BRONX

This recipe by Simon McGoram is related to the classic Bloodhound Cocktail. Simon spices the sweet vermouth with cinnamon and cardamom, but I choose Vya sweet vermouth for its unique spice profile.

1½ ounces Hendrick's Orbium gin
¾ ounce Martini Riserva Speciale Ambrato vermouth
¾ ounce Vya sweet vermouth
¾ ounce blood orange juice
Dash of Dale DeGroff's Pimento Aromatic Bitters
Half-wheel blood orange, for garnish (see Note)

Assemble all the ingredients (except the garnish) in a cocktail shaker and shake well with ice. Strain into a large chilled coupe glass and garnish with the half-wheel blood orange.

NOTE If blood oranges aren't available, use a regular orange.

BLOODHOUND COCKTAIL

David Solmonson, coauthor with his wife, Lesley, of *The 12 Bottle Bar*, listed this early twentieth-century nugget in his book. He didn't have room to tell the entire story, so I encourage you to visit 12bottlebar.com/2011/05 /bloodhound-cocktail to enjoy his marvelous treatise on the cocktail.

3 or 4 fresh strawberries
1½ ounces Hendrick's Orbium gin
¾ ounce Martini & Rossi sweet vermouth
¾ ounce Noilly Prat dry vermouth
Splash of maraschino liqueur

Mash the strawberries in the bottom of a cocktail shaker and build the remaining ingredients on top. Shake well with ice and strain into a chilled cocktail glass.

BLOODY MARY

The Bloody Mary is like barbecue sauce: everyone thinks their recipe is the best—and, of course, I'm no different. My rule at the bar has been to appeal to the widest possible audience with my Bloody Mary. First, don't destroy the heart of the drink: the sweetness of the tomato juice. Too much Worcestershire or hot sauce will make the drink muddy and too spicy, and the delicate balance of sweet and spicy may be lost. Testing one's tolerance for spice is not the objective. Lemon juice is a must with tomato juice, and so the Bloody Mary mix should always have a little squeeze of fresh lemon juice. I garnish the drink with another lemon wedge and a lime wedge on the side, and let the drinker decide which—if either—to add. Use organic tomato juice if you can easily source it, but if not, I recommend Sacramento.

The arrival of the first tins of tomato juice right after World War I made this drink possible. I worked with Michelin-starred chef Gérard Pangaud to create a house-made tomato juice as thick and tasty as Sacramento canned variety without success. Evidently, Frank Meier, head barman at the Ritz Bar in Paris, had been mixing his famous Tomato Juice Cocktail from fresh tomatoes for years, basically mashing them with spices and straining. But his recipe was missing one fundamental ingredient: booze! At Harry's New York Bar in Paris, barman Ferdinand "Pete" Petiot purportedly made vodka Bloody Marys, but somehow they never made it into any of the editions of Harry MacElhone's *ABC of Mixing Cocktails.* The name, according to a conversation I had with Duncan McElhone (Harry's grandson), came into being because of the continued appearance at the bar of a woman named Mary, who was regularly left waiting for her man, nursing one of Pete's tomato-and-vodka cocktails. The bartenders gave her the nickname Bloody Mary after Mary, Queen of Scots, pining in the tower. That story sounds suspect, but Pete Petiot did end up playing a major role in the Bloody Mary saga.

Pete emigrated to America and eventually joined the bar staff at the King Cole Bar at New York's St. Regis hotel. He introduced the drink to New Yorkers with gin, since vodka was not well-known in the United States, and he changed the name to the Red Snapper at the behest of the Astors, who found the Bloody Mary name offensive. In a 1964 *New Yorker* interview, Pete gave away the fact that he was the one who added the spices for the first time, but he was not the one who first paired tomato juice and vodka; that, it seems, was comedian George Jessel.

John Martin, grandson of Heublein founder Gilbert Heublein, used the drink as a vehicle to promote a new product, Smirnoff vodka, in the 1960s. This led to an almost exclusive use of vodka in the drink and helped to make it the de rigueur morning-after cocktail.

Natural Blonde Bloody Mary Mix has spices added (and I include another couple touches), and it makes a lively and natural addition to the Bloody Mary repertoire.

2 ounces vodka
Dash of Tabasco Sauce
4 ounces Natural Blonde
    Bloody Mary Mix (see page 231)
Freshly ground black pepper
Basil sprig, for garnish
Yellow bell pepper slice, for garnish

Combine all the ingredients (except the garnishes) in a mixing glass and roll back and forth between two mixing glasses to combine the ingredients. Strain into a goblet or pint glass over ice. Garnish with the basil sprig and yellow bell pepper slice.

BLOODY BULL

This recipe and the Bullshot (opposite) are the only Bloody variations that I shake. The beef broth lessens any unwanted frothing from the tomato juice.

1½ ounces vodka
Splash of fresh orange juice
4 dashes of Tabasco sauce
Freshly ground black pepper
3 ounces beef broth (see Note)
2 ounces tomato juice
Orange zest coin (see page 62),
   for garnish

Combine all the ingredients (except the garnish) in the glass portion of a Boston shaker and shake well. Strain into a goblet or pint glass over ice. Garnish with the orange zest.

NOTE I use Campbell's beef broth, and it works fine; just don't use additional salt.

BLOODY BUTRUM

This Bloody Caesar variation from my buddy Carl's kitchen, served at his infamous "Straight on 'til Morning" parties; prepared right after the late Chris Gillespie played "Rhapsody in Blue" just before the sunrise. Carl's recipe called for half vodka and half juice, though I don't recommend that version as a session drink.

> 2 ounces vodka
> 2 dashes of celery salt
> Pinch of dried dill
> Freshly ground black pepper
> 2 dashes of Tabasco sauce
> 3 dashes of Worcestershire sauce
> 4 ounces Clamato juice or 1 ounce clam juice
> 3 ounces tomato juice
> Lemon and lime wedges, for garnish

Build over ice in a mixing glass and roll all ingredients (except the garnish) between two mixing glasses. Strain into a goblet or pint glass over ice. Serve with lemon and lime wedges on the side.

BLOODY MARIA

Use the Bloody Mary/Red Snapper recipe (below) but substitute Sangrita (page 93) for the tomato juice, and tequila for the vodka. Serve with a lime wedge on the side.

BLOODY MARY/ RED SNAPPER

This is my recipe, so naturally it *really* is the best recipe; actually, what it is, is a template upon which you can improvise with garnishes and ingredients. A dash of celery salt is a nice touch, and New Yorkers traditionally add horseradish. Have fun.

> 1½ ounces vodka or gin
> 2 dashes of Worcestershire sauce
> 4 dashes of Tabasco sauce
> Pinch of salt and freshly ground black pepper
> 2 splashes of fresh lemon juice
> 4 to 6 ounces tomato juice
> Lemon and lime wedges, for garnish

Combine all the ingredients (except the garnish) in a mixing glass and roll it back and forth between two mixing glasses to combine the ingredients. Strain into a large goblet or pint glass filled three-quarters full with ice. Serve with lemon and lime wedges on a side plate for drinkers to garnish themselves.

BULLSHOT

Here's the ultimate steak-house drink and, yes, Campbell's beef broth is the way to make it. David Wondrich, our historical oracle, cites chapter and verse: Lester Gruber, owner of Detroit's Caucus Club, and John Hurley, account man from Batten, Barton, Durstine & Osborn (who managed the Campbell's soups account) decided the drink would be a superior ploy for moving the slow-selling beef broth. I like to write out the full name of BBDO—Batten, Barton, Durstine & Osborn. It reminds me of ad man Ron Holland's quip, that the whole name said out loud sounds like a suitcase falling down the stairs. Leave out salt; the beef broth is plenty salty enough.

> 1½ ounces vodka
> 4 dashes of Tabasco sauce
> Dash of orange juice
> Freshly ground black pepper
> 4 ounces Campbell's beef broth
> Orange zest coin (see page 62),
>   for ganish

Combine all the ingredients (except the garnish) in the glass portion of a Boston shaker and shake well. Strain into a goblet or pint glass over ice. Garnish with the orange zest coin.

DANISH MARY

Substitute aquavit for vodka in the original Bloody Mary/Red Snapper recipe (above). Serve with a lemon wedge, a lime wedge, and a giant caper berry on a side plate.

THE BLOODY MARY BUFFET

This is a wonderful brunch party idea, featuring a buffet for preparing self-service Bloody Marys, stocked with vegetables and shellfish for garnishes. The simple tomato juice is augmented with several homemade vegetable juices and a variety of spirits is available.

Build a double-sided display on a six-by-three-foot draped table with the different Bloody Mary juice mixes in carafes or pitchers. Create two garnish displays on either side, so guests can garnish at the same time. Place an ice bucket with tongs or an ice scoop on each end of the table. Provide a Boston shaker set so the drinks can be poured back and forth for mixing.

SPIRITS Vodka · Gin · Tequila · Aquavit

SHELLFISH Clams · Oysters · Shrimp (Presented on a platter piled with crushed ice and surrounded with lemon wedges, with tongs for serving.)

GLASSWARE Goblets · Pint glasses

CRUDITÉS STATION with raw and pickled garnishes. Provide small bread-and-butter plates. · Radishes · Scallions · Olives · Cocktail onions · Tomolives · Elephant caper berries · Endive · Daikon radish · Fresh peeled horseradish root and a vegetable grater, for grating into the drinks · Tall spears of crudités that can act as stirrers: celery, carrot, and cucumber · Decorative fresh, potted herb plants: dill, basil, and oregano · Peppermills and salt cellars · Citrus wedges in bowls · Bottled hot sauces, including Tabasco · Worcestershire sauce

Using the glass portion of the Boston shaker, the guest pours one jigger of their spirit of their choice, followed by the spices of their choice, then fills it to the two-thirds mark with the juice of their choice. Pour the mixture back and forth between the two parts of the shaker to mix well. Then pour the drink into a goblet or highball glass, fill it with ice cubes, and garnish.

THE JUICE RECIPES

CLAM AND TOMATO JUICE

MAKES 60 OUNCES

Use this in the Bloody Butrum cocktail (page 91).

14 ounces fresh chilled clam juice
46 ounces tomato juice, preferably Sacramento
Freshly ground black pepper

Combine all the ingredients and mix well. Chill.

RAINBOW V-7 JUICE

MAKES 60 OUNCES

Prepare this with a juicer.

40 ounces tomato juice, preferably Sacramento
4 ounces fresh celery juice
4 ounces fresh carrot juice
4 ounces fresh green bell pepper juice
4 ounces fresh red bell pepper juice
2 ounces fresh onion juice
2 ounces fresh fennel juice
Salt and freshly ground black pepper to taste

Combine all the ingredients and mix well. Chill.

SANGRITA

MAKES 60 OUNCES

¼ cup puréed stemmed and seeded jalapeño peppers
2½ ounces fresh lime juice
5 ounces fresh orange juice
1 ounce grenadine, homemade (page 224) or store-bought
4 ounces Simple Syrup (page 225)
46 ounces tomato juice, preferably Sacramento
¾ tablespoon kosher salt
¾ tablespoon ground white pepper

Combine all the ingredients and mix well. Chill. Adjust the seasonings, if needed, and serve with shots of tequila or as a Bloody Maria (page 91).

SPICY TOMATO JUICE

MAKES 50 OUNCES

2½ ounces fresh lemon juice
2 teaspoons Tabasco sauce
1 teaspoon Worcestershire sauce
46 ounces tomato juice, preferably Sacramento
Salt and freshly ground black pepper

Combine all the ingredients and mix well. Chill.

BLUE BAYOU*

Blue drinks are back . . . at least that's what my friend Jacob Briars claims. Mr. Briars is the worldwide ambassador to the bartending community for the Bacardi company, and he knows these things. And true or not, if one has enough visibility in the press, then statements like that become true. Blue sour-style drinks are hard to pull off because the acid in lemon and lime juices turns the blue in blue curaçao green. Here's a trick to overcome that problem.

> 1½ ounces Rutte gin
> ½ ounce blue curaçao
> ¼ ounce St-Germain elderflower liqueur
> ¾ ounce Lime Acid (page 224; see Note)
> Flamed orange zest coin (see page 62), for garnish
> Tiki bird tchotchke, for garnish (optional)

Combine all the ingredients (except the garnishes) in a shaker. Shake well with ice and strain into a chilled coupe glass. Flame the orange zest coin over the glass. Perch the tiki bird on the rim of the glass, if desired.

NOTE Lime acid is clear, so although it has the same acidity as fresh lime juice, it will not turn the blue curaçao green.

BLUE MONDAY

Blue Monday is an early vodka cocktail from *The Savoy Cocktail Book.* That is the most interesting thing about it. It calls for Cointreau and blue vegetable extract, but I have taken the liberty of replacing the extract with blue curaçao.

> 1½ ounces vodka
> ½ ounce Cointreau
> ¼ ounce Marie Brizard blue curaçao
> ¾ ounce Lime Acid (page 224; see Note, above)
> Flamed orange zest coin (see page 62), for garnish

Combine all the ingredients (except the garnish) in a shaker. Shake well with ice, then strain into a chilled cocktail glass. Flame the orange zest coin over the glass.

BOBBY BURNS

Frank Meier's version of this drink in *The Artistry of Mixing Drinks* (1936) calls for one part sweet vermouth and one part dry vermouth.

> 2 ounces blended or lighter-style malt scotch whisky
> 1 ounce Italian sweet vermouth
> ¼ ounce Bénédictine
> Shortbread cookie, for garnish

Stir all the ingredients (except the garnish) with ice in a mixing glass and strain into a chilled cocktail glass. Serve with the shortbread cookie on the side.

BOBBY BURNS, NAREN'S+

This variation on the theme was created by Naren Young for Saxon + Parole, New York City.

> 1 ounce Dewar's 12-year-old scotch
> 1 ounce Martini & Rossi sweet vermouth
> ¼ ounce Bénédictine
> 2 dashes of Dale DeGroff's Pimento Aromatic Bitters
> Shortbread cookie, for garnish

Stir all the ingredients (except the garnish) with ice in a mixing glass and strain into a chilled cocktail glass. Serve with the shortbread cookie on the side.

BOCCI BALL

> 1½ ounces Disaronna Originale amaretto
> 4 to 5 ounces fresh orange juice
> Half orange wheel, for garnish

Build the first two ingredients in a highball glass over ice. Garnish with the half orange wheel.

BOSOM CARESSER

This variation on a classic includes elements from the *The Savoy Cocktail Book* (1930) recipe and from George Kappeler's recipe in *Modern American Drinks* (1895).

1 ounce Rainwater Madeira
1½ ounces brandy
1 teaspoon raspberry syrup, such as Monin raspberry syrup
1½ ounces whole milk
¾ ounce emulsified whole egg (see page 204)
Freshly grated nutmeg, for garnish

Combine all the ingredients (except the garnish) in a shaker and add ice. Shake very well to completely integrate the egg. Strain into a chilled large coupe glass. Dust with the nutmeg.

BOULEVARDIER

We think this rye whiskey variation on the Negroni (page 175) was created by expat American Erskine Gwynne, the publisher of *Boulevardier*, a newsletter for expat Americans living in Paris in the 1930s. *Cocktails de Paris* (1929) lists the drink as a contest winner of the Grand Prix au Championnat des Barmen by barman Robert du Viel with the following recipe: "1p Dubonnet, 1p Rapheäl and ½p each of Campari and Cognac." Hmm. But I still prefer the following rye whiskey Negroni version over all the others.

1 ounce Bulleit rye whiskey
1 ounce Martini & Rossi sweet vermouth
1 ounce Campari
Orange zest coin (see page 62), for garnish

Combine the whiskey, vermouth, and Campari in a double old-fashioned glass over ice and stir. Garnish with the orange zest coin.

BRAMBLE+

Created in 1984 by Dick Bradsell, the godfather of the UK bar scene at Fred's Club, the Dean Street destination bar for a decade that Dick helped put on the map. Dick opened Dick's Bar behind a velvet rope in the Atlantic Bar and Grill that defined the bar scene in the 1990s.

1½ ounces gin
1 ounce fresh lime juice
¾ ounce Simple Syrup (page 225)
¾ ounce Giffard crème de mûre (blackberry liqueur)
Lime wheel, for garnish
Fresh raspberries, for garnish

Combine the gin, lime juice, and simple syrup with ice in a shaker and shake well. Strain into a double old-fashioned glass over crushed ice. Dribble the liqueur down through the ice, and garnish with the lime wheel and fresh raspberries.

BRANDY CRUSTA

Crustas were extra-fancy cocktails invented by Joseph Santina, who opened the Jewel of the South on Gravier Street in New Orleans in 1852. The name of the drink refers to the crusted sugar around the rim of the glass.

Sugar, for the rim
1½ ounces Cognac
2 dashes of Luxardo maraschino liqueur
2 dashes of lemon juice
4 dashes of Monin apple syrup (see Note)
Dash of Dale DeGroff's Pimento Aromatic Bitters
Lemon spiral, for garnish

Coat the top ½ inch of the rim of a small cocktail glass with sugar (see page 63). Set aside.

Combine the Cognac, liqueur, lemon juice, apple syrup, and bitters in a shaker. Add ice and shake well. Strain into the prepared cocktail glass. Garnish with a wide spiral lemon peel around the inside rim of the glass and extending above the rim.

NOTE The apple syrup is substituting for orchard syrup. The recipe for orchid syrup has a lot of drinks historians stumped.

BRANDY MILK PUNCH

To turn this into quick brandy eggnog by the glass, add a small egg and substitute heavy cream for one ounce of the milk. I found a delicious version in *The Flowing Bowl* by Edward Spencer, called Arctic Regions; it is made with four ounces whole milk, two ounces Pedro Ximénez sherry, and one ounce brandy. Shake it well with ice and serve over ice that's been dusted with cinnamon.

2 ounces Cognac
1 ounce rock candy syrup or Simple Syrup
    (page 225) with a drop of vanilla extract
4 ounces milk
Freshly grated nutmeg, for garnish

Combine the Cognac, syrup, and milk in a shaker. Add ice and shake. Strain and serve in a highball glass over ice. Dust with nutmeg.

BREAKFAST MARTINI+

Salvatore Calabrese—one of the true masters behind the bar—created this recipe in 1996 at London's Lanesborough hotel. *Burke's Complete Cocktail and Drinking Recipes* (1934) by Harman Burney Burke has a marmalade variation called the Miami Cocktail, made with gin as the base and sweet vermouth, orange juice, bitters, and marmalade.

1½ ounces Bombay Sapphire gin
½ ounce fresh lemon juice
½ ounce Cointreau
1 teaspoon light marmalade (without much rind)
1 small slice of buttered toast with marmalade,
    for garnish (my idea)

Shake all the ingredients (except the garnish) with ice and strain into a chilled cocktail glass. Garnish with the buttered toast and marmalade on the side.

BRILLIANTE COCKTAIL*

The Brilliante Cocktail is a morning-after variation on the iconic Negroni (page 175). I replaced the bitter ingredient, Campari, with brewed coffee. I start with medium-roast whole beans, I grind them with fennel seeds, and then prepare a pot of drip-brewed coffee; the fennel seeds add a slight spicy and vegetal note that the Campari usually provides.

1 ounce fennel-accented coffee (see Note)
1½ ounces Cynar
¾ ounce Hendrick's Orbium gin
Orange zest coin (see page 62), for garnish

Build the three ingredients in a double old-fashioned glass over ice cubes. Stir to chill and marry the three ingredients. Garnish with the orange zest coin.

NOTE To make the fennel-accented coffee, finely grind ½ cup medium-roast coffee beans with 1 teaspoon fennel seeds. Use 3 cups filtered water to drip-brew the coffee. Cool to room temperature for use. Coffee keeps in the refrigerator for up to 3 days.

BRONX COCKTAIL

When the Waldorf Astoria New York was just the Waldorf and it stood where the Empire State Building stands today, it was the home of the famous "Big Brass Rail," a watering hole for the robber barons of the late nineteenth and early twentieth centuries. It was also the home of Johnnie Solon, top barman of the day. Shortly after a trip to the newly opened Bronx Zoo, as popular cocktail lore has it, Johnnie invented the Bronx Cocktail for a guest, claiming it was impossible to discern any difference between the zoo and his bar.

1½ ounces Ransom Old Tom gin
¼ ounce Italian sweet vermouth
¼ ounce Noilly Prat Original dry vermouth
1 ounce fresh orange juice
Dash of Angostura bitters (optional)
Orange zest coin (see page 62), for garnish

Shake all the ingredients (except the garnish) with ice and strain into a large cocktail glass. Garnish with the orange zest coin.

BROWN DERBY COCKTAIL

This cocktail is from Hollywood's Vendome Club circa 1930 and is named after the famous hat-shaped restaurant on Wilshire Boulevard that opened in 1926. The restaurant was demolished in 1980, but the derby-shaped dome was saved and incorporated into the Brown Derby Plaza, a strip mall in the heart of Koreatown at Wilshire Boulevard between Normandie and Vermont Avenues.

2 ounces bourbon
1 ounce fresh grapefruit juice
¾ ounce Honey Syrup (page 224)

Shake all the ingredients well with ice and strain into a cocktail glass.

BUD HERRMANN HIGHBALL

When I started working at the Hotel Bel-Air, Bud Herrmann, a very talented piano player who did a short stint with the Benny Goodman Orchestra, presided over the lounge. He was a master of ceremonies and a matchmaker in business as well as affairs of the heart. A good friend of Bud's, who was a resident of the hotel, made a sizable fortune through an introduction made by Bud and awarded him with an apartment building in West Hollywood. Now that is a tip! Bud died in 1985, and the room changed. I took that as my cue to move on; six months later I went to work for Joe Baum in New York City. In 1987, I took over my perch on top of 30 Rock as head bartender of the Rainbow Room.

2 ounces Metaxa 5- or 7-star brandy
5 ounces club soda

Build in a highball glass over ice.

BULL'S BLOOD

¾ ounce Myers's dark rum
¾ ounce Marie Brizard orange curaçao
¾ ounce Cardenal Mendoza Spanish brandy
1 ounce fresh orange juice
Flamed orange zest coin (see page 62), for garnish

Shake all the ingredients (except the garnish) well with ice and strain into a cocktail glass. Garnish with the flamed orange zest coin.

CABLE CAR[+]

The Cable Car was created in 1996 as a signature cocktail for the Starlight Room, a stunning nightclub and cocktail lounge atop the historic Kimpton Sir Francis Drake hotel in San Francisco. The Sir Francis Drake is located along the world-famous Nob Hill cable car tracks. Its Starlight Room was affectionately referred to as the lounge that could be found between the stars and the cable cars.

"I was approached by the folks at Captain Morgan to come up with a new cocktail featuring their rum. I looked, as we all should, to the classics and discovered the Brandy Crusta. Using that drink as a template, a drink that has given us many now-classic riffs, I came up with what would become my best-known cocktail, the Cable Car!" —Tony Abou-Ganim, owner of Libertine Social in the Mandalay Bay Casino, Las Vegas

Cinnamon sugar, for the rim
1½ ounces Captain Morgan spiced rum
¾ ounce Marie Brizard orange curaçao
1½ ounces fresh lemon sour (see Note)
1 whole orange zest, cut into a long spiral (see page 62)

Frost the rim of a cocktail glass with cinnamon sugar (see page 63). Chill in the freezer until ready to use. In a mixing glass, combine the rum, curaçao, and lemon sour with ice. Shake until well chilled. Strain into the chilled frosted cocktail glass and garnish with a thin orange spiral.

NOTE Tony's recipe for fresh lemon sour is 2 parts filtered fresh-squeezed lemon juice with 1 part Simple Syrup (page 225).

BROTHER CLEVE SOUR⁺

Original cocktail by Brian Miller, a pioneer of the craft scene in New York, working in Flatiron Lounge, Pegu Club, and Death and Co. Brother Cleve is the godfather of the Boston cocktail scene. In the 1980s and 1990s, he traveled with Combustible Edison, a band promoted by Paddington drinks and Campari corporation, and then the band Del Fuegos, playing keyboards and composing.

1½ ounces Macchu Quebranta Pisco
½ ounce fresh lemon juice
½ ounce fresh lime juice
½ ounce fresh pineapple juice
¼ ounce Cinnamon Syrup (page 223)
Dash of Dale DeGroff's Pimento Aromatic Bitters
½ ounce emulsified egg white (see page 204)
Lemon, for garnish

Shake all the ingredients (except the garnish) well with 3 large ice cubes. Strain into a double old-fashioned glass over 3 more large ice cubes. Garnish with a lemon.

CAFÉ BRÛLOT

Café Brûlot was created at Antoine's Restaurant in New Orleans at the end of the nineteenth century by Jules Alciatore. Jules was the son of founder Antoine Alciatore, who opened this shrine of Louisiana Creole cuisine in 1840. The special Sheffield-silver-lined Café Brûlot apparatus needed to prepare this extravagant postprandial libation is available from Cocktail Kingdom. It is difficult to prepare without the proper apparatus and the special two-sided ladle.

MARINADE (MAKES 25 SERVINGS)

1 (750 ml) bottle VS Cognac brandy
12 ounces kirschwasser eau-de-vie
12 whole cloves
1 navel orange, zest only
1 lemon, zest only
6 Ceylon cinnamon sticks, broken

To make the marinade: In a 2-liter container, mix the Cognac, kirschwasser, cloves, orange zest, the lemon zest, and broken cinnamon sticks. Cover and, let stand for several hours or for overnight for better results.

CAFÉ BRÛLOT (MAKES 6)

9 ounces Marinade (above)
12 ounces French roast coffee, chicory, if available (search Café du Monde online)
9 ounces warmed Brown Sugar or Demerara Syrup (page 223)
1 whole orange peel, cut into a long spiral (see page 62)
8 cloves
1 ounce 151 overproof rum, for fuel

Prepare the spiral-cut orange by pushing the pointed end of the cloves through the peel like studs. Set the zest aside on a dinner plate for use in the preparation.

To make the café brûlot: Find a spot with high ceilings to prepare this dessert coffee. Be sure there are no heat sensors in the ceiling above the area, because the flaming bowl can flare up. Set the apparatus on a fireproof surface, such as a large ceramic tile, so that the copper bowl on the bottom of the apparatus that contains the fuel sits on top. Place the studded orange zests, two-sided ladle, the coffee kept hot in a thermal coffeepot, and carafe of warmed syrup next to the apparatus.

Put no more than 1 ounce of 151 overproof rum in the copper pan at the bottom of the apparatus. This will serve as the fuel to warm the bowl. *This is important to prevent the bowl from flaring too high.*

Measure and pour 9 ounces of the marinade into the bowl of the apparatus.

Light the overproof rum in the copper pan underneath and let it heat up for a minute. Meanwhile, thread one end of the clove-studded orange peel spiral through the tines of a serving fork and keep it on the dinner plate next to the apparatus.

Let the marinade warm for a minute, then fill half the special ladle and expose it to the flame under the bowl. When the marinade in the ladle catches fire, pour it back into the bowl to ignite the remaining marinade. Pick up the fork with the orange peel spiral and position it over the center of the bowl, with the spiral dangling into the marinade. Ladle the flaming marinade from the side that has the guard filled with small holes and slowly pour it through the top of the peel spiral. Do this several times and watch the oil cells in the zest provide a nice light show and the cloves begin to glow. Return the peel spiral and the fork to the dinner plate and then pour the coffee slowly into the bowl until the fire is extinguished: this will cause the mixture in the bowl to flare up so keep the coffeepot well above the bowl.

Sweeten the mixture to taste with the warmed syrup. Serve in demitasse cups.

Café Brûlot
apparatus

Flaming the clove-
studded orange
peel spiral

Adding the French
roast coffee

Serving the coffee in
specially designed
Café Brûlot cups

CAFÉ MAGUEY*

Ever since Dick Bradsell came up with the Espresso Vodka Cocktail (page 122), renamed the Espresso Martini by the craft community, bartenders have been riffing on his recipe. The Café Maguey is mine. The stunning layer of foam erected atop the drink by a hard shake is the only garnish needed.

> 1 ounce Don Julio reposado tequila
> 1 ounce Del Maguey Crema de Mezcal
> ½ ounce agave nectar
> 2 ounces cold espresso
> Grated chocolate, for garnish (optional)

Assemble all the ingredients (except for the garnish) in a Boston shaker glass with ice and shake well. Strain into a large coupe glass and garnish with the grated chocolate, if desired.

CAIPIRINHA

The Caipirinha and its variations are unique in the cocktail world because we retain the spent fruit and the ice used in muddling and shaking; after a hard shake, we pour the ice and the spent lime husks into the serving glass. The Caipirinha is essentially a sour, and we want to end up with a nice balance of sweet and sour, equal amounts of lime juice and simple syrup. The method in the recipes below will help insure that balance, but monitor the juiciness of the limes as you muddle them: They vary with the seasons. You can adjust by adding or subtracting the number of lime pieces while muddling.

> ½ lime, quartered
> ¾ ounce Simple Syrup (page 225; see Note)
> 2 ounces cachaça

Place the lime pieces in the bottom of a mixing glass, add the simple syrup, and muddle, extracting not just the juice but the oil from the skin of the lime. Add the cachaça to the mixing glass, then fill a rocks glass three-quarters full with ice and dump the ice into the mixing glass and shake well. Pour the entire contents of the mixing glass—the ice, liquid, and muddled limes—back into the rocks glass and serve.

NOTE In place of syrup, the Brazilian method uses granulated sugar, approximately one heaping teaspoon to half a lime. But that may vary depending on the limes you are using. Some are smaller or less juicy, while others are oversize and full of juice, so adapt as needed. I suggest you use Simple Syrup, as it is easier to control the balance.

CAIPIRINHA

The word *caipirinha* is a colloquial term that came from the countryside, and no online Portuguese translation gives an English version. But the word *caipira* translates on Google Translator as "hillbilly," which is comical but understandable: the drink seems to have been a favorite of farmers. Until recently, urban professionals required that their Caipirinhas be made with the fashionable spirit of the day—vodka—even making up a word to separate the two: Caipiroska. Only when the rest of the world discovered cachaça as a heritage spirit of Brazil did the upper-crust Brazilians embrace their little "country brandy."

CAIPIRINHA, CHERRY

½ lime, quartered
4 Bordeaux cherries
¾ ounce Brown Sugar or Demerara Syrup
   (page 223)
2 ounces cachaça

Place the lime pieces and cherries in the bottom of a mixing glass. Add the syrup and muddle, extracting the juice and the oil from the skin of the lime pieces. Add the cachaça to the mixture in the mixing glass and measure the ice by filling a rocks glass three-quarters full with ice. Add it to the mixing glass. Shake well, pour the entire contents of the mixing glass back into the rocks glass, and serve.

CAIPIRINHA DE UVA

½ lime, quartered
4 seedless green grapes
¾ ounce Simple Syrup (page 225)
2 ounces cachaça

Place the lime pieces and grapes in the bottom of a mixing glass, add the simple syrup, and muddle, extracting the juice and the oil from the skin of the lime. Add the cachaça to the mixture in the mixing glass. Measure the ice by filling a rocks glass three-quarters full with ice and adding it to the mixing glass. Shake well, pour the entire contents of the mixing glass back into the rocks glass, and serve.

CAIPIROSCKA

Here's a variation on the classic Brazilian Caipirinha (page 102).

½ lime, quartered
¾ ounce Simple Syrup (page 225)
2 ounces vodka

Place the lime pieces in the bottom of a mixing glass, add the simple syrup, and muddle, extracting the juice and the oil from the skin of the lime. Add the vodka, then fill a rocks glass three-quarters full with cracked ice and pour it into the mixing glass.

Shake well. Pour the entire contents back into the rocks glass and serve.

NOTE For a Caipirissima, substitute rum as the base and follow the same instructions.

CAPE COD

In the 1950s, the Ocean Spray Cooperative, which became the Ocean Spray Cranberries company, was looking for ways to sell cranberries year-round instead of only at Thanksgiving. They created the juice and approached the Seagram's spirits company. They promoted aggressively from 1964 to 1970, with a series of cocktails, one of which was called the Harpoon and was made with one ounce of gin or vodka, one ounce of cranberry juice, and a squeeze of fresh lime. It was served as a cocktail, and when it was turned into a highball with more vodka and more juice, it became a big hit, known as the Cape Cod, or Cape Codder, as many people ordered it.

1½ ounces vodka
4 to 5 ounces cranberry juice
Lime wedge, for garnish

Combine the vodka and cranberry juice in a highball glass filled with ice and stir. Garnish with the lime wedge.

CARICATURE COCKTAIL⁺

This was created by Gary and Mardee Regan for my wife, Jill, who loves to capture unsuspecting victims with her caricature pen. Most of the victims are delighted; this cocktail will appease those who are not. It's definitely inspired by the Negroni triad.

2 ounces Tanqueray No. Ten gin
½ ounce Martini & Rossi sweet vermouth
½ ounce Campari
1 ounce fresh grapefruit juice
¾ ounce Simple Syrup (page 225)
Flamed orange zest coin (see page 62), for garnish

Shake all the ingredients (except the garnish) with ice and strain into a very large chilled cocktail glass. Garnish with the flamed orange zest coin.

CAIPIRINHA, CHERRY

CARDINALE

My Florentine friend Luca Picchi, author of *Negroni Cocktail: An Italian Legend*, found the story of the Cardinale, the first variation on the Negroni (page 175) in 1950, during the Year of Jubilee of the Roman Catholic Church. Giovanni Raimondo, the bartender at the Hotel Excelsior, crafted this variation in an effort to re-create the favorite of a German cardinal who occasionally sought refreshment at the bar of the great hotel; the use of dry vermouth created a closer match to the cardinal's robes.

1 ounce Fords gin
1 ounce Campari
1 ounce Noilly Prat Original dry vermouth
Half orange wheel, for garnish

Build the gin, Campari, and vermouth over ice in an old-fashioned glass and stir. Garnish with the half orange wheel.

CELERY CUP NO. 1+

This recipe is from H. Joseph Ehrmann, owner of the Elixir Bar in San Francisco. Elixir opened in 1858, and "H," as he is known in the business, is the twelfth proprietor.

1-inch-long English cucumber piece, chopped
2 tablespoons cilantro leaves (no stems)
2 celery stalks, chopped
1 ounce lemon juice
1½ ounces Square One cucumber vodka
½ ounce Pimm's No. 1
¾ ounce agave nectar
1 celery stick, for garnish

In the bottom of a Boston shaker, muddle the cucumber, cilantro, celery, and lemon juice to a pulp. Add the vodka, Pimm's, and agave nectar and shake well with ice. Strain into a highball glass over ice and garnish with the celery stick.

CHAMPAGNE COCKTAIL

This classic recipe can be traced back to 1862 when it appeared in *How to Mix Drinks, or The Bon-Vivant's Companion* by Jerry Thomas. For a stronger drink, add a float of Cognac or Grand Marnier.

1 sugar cube soaked with Angostura bitters
Champagne
Lemon zest coin (see page 62), for garnish
  (optional)

Place the Angostura-soaked sugar cube in the bottom of a champagne flute and fill the glass with Champagne, pouring slowly to avoid any spillage. Garnish with the lemon zest coin, if desired.

VIRGIN CHAMPAGNE COCKTAIL*
(Nonalcoholic)

Prepare this in the same way as a regular Champagne Cocktail, with an Angostura-soaked sugar cube in a champagne flute, but substitute nonalcoholic Sutter Home Fre alcohol-removed sparkling Brut.

CHARENTES REVERSE MARTINI

Pineau des Charentes is made from eaux-de-vie of grapes grown in the Cognac region, but before aging, it is blended with grape juice from the current year's vintage. Afterward, the resulting blend is barrel aged for a minimum of eighteen months.

2 ounces A. de Fussigny Pineau des Charentes
1 ounce Hendrick's Orbium gin
Dash of Dale DeGroff's Pimento Aromatic Bitters
Flamed orange zest coin (see page 62), for garnish

Assemble the ingredients (except the garnish) in a mixing glass with ice and stir. Strain into a chilled cocktail glass and garnish with the flamed orange zest coin.

CHARLIE CHAPLIN COCKTAIL

Mary Pickford and Douglas Fairbanks, two of the partners in United Artists, were celebrated with drinks on the menus and in the bars' recipe books in Havana, Cuba, during Prohibition. The third partner, Charlie Chaplin, apparently was doing his drinking before Prohibition at the "Big Brass Rail" in the old Waldorf Hotel. He is celebrated with the Charlie Chaplin Cocktail on their menu and in the Old Waldorf bar book.

1 ounce Marie Brizard Apry liqueur
1 ounce Plymouth sloe gin
1 ounce fresh lime juice
Thin lime wheel, for garnish

Shake all the ingredients (except the garnish) with ice and strain into a chilled Nick & Nora glass. Garnish with the lime wheel.

CHERRY BLOSSOM

This is adapted from Harry Craddock's *The Savoy Cocktail Book*. Make this one in the summer, when fresh cherries are available. Try different varieties of cherries as they come into season; the sour cherries from upstate New York add lots of zing to the cocktail. Ile de Ré Cognac is singular, made from grapes grown on an island off the westernmost part of Cognac.

> 3 pitted fresh cherries
> ½ ounce Pierre Ferrand dry curaçao
> ½ ounce Heering cherry liqueur
> 1½ ounces Camus VSOP Ile de Ré Cognac
> ¾ ounce fresh lemon juice
> 1 fresh cherry, for garnish

In the bottom of a Boston shaker, muddle the pitted cherries with the liqueurs. Add the Cognac, lemon juice, and ice and shake well. Fine strain into a chilled cocktail glass. Garnish with the cherry.

CHI CHI

Make a Piña Colada (page 183) but substitute vodka for the rums.

CHOCOLATE PUNCH

William Schmidt was a prodigious experimenter and also quite the self-promoter. This is the ultimate dessert drink, and it is so rich that it must be shared. The recipe is found in Schmidt's 1891 cocktail book titled *The Flowing Bowl: When and What to Drink*.

> 1 ounce Cognac
> ½ ounce ruby port
> ½ ounce Tempus Fugit crème de cacao
> ½ ounce Simple Syrup (page 225)
> 1 ounce heavy cream
> Freshly grated nutmeg, for garnish

Shake all the ingredients (except the garnish) very well with ice and strain into a chilled cocktail glass. Sprinkle a little nutmeg on top.

CHRISTMAS WHISKEY COCKTAIL+

This is the original recipe of H. Joseph Ehrmann, owner of Elixir Bar in San Francisco for 15 years. The bar, at the corner of Mission and Guerrero in the Mission District, has been in continuous operation for 160 years.

> 2 orange zest coins (see page 62)
> Dash of Bitter Truth chocolate bitters
> Dash of Dale DeGroff's Pimento Aromatic Bitters
> ¾ ounce Sandeman Royal Ambrosante Pedro Ximénez 20-year-old sherry (see Note)
> 2 ounces Blanton's Single Barrel bourbon

Muddle 1 orange zest coin with both bitters and the sherry in the bottom of an old-fashioned glass. Add the bourbon and 4 large ice cubes and stir. Express the oil of the remaining orange zest coin over the top of the drink and drop it in.

NOTE This Sandeman sherry is a bit pricey, so feel free to use your favorite Pedro Ximénez–style sherry.

CLAREMONT (OLD-FASHIONED VARIATION)

The Claremont is a beautiful old hotel in the Berkeley Hills that opened in 1915 and was dry for the first twenty-two years through Prohibition, finally allowing alcoholic beverages in 1937. If you happen to stay in room 422, make sure to stop at the bar for a couple Claremont Old-Fashioned specials before returning to your room, as it is known to be haunted.

> 3 dashes of Angostura bitters
> ¾ ounce Pierre Ferrand dry curaçao
> 2 orange slices
> 2 Bordeaux cherries
> Splash of soda water
> 1½ ounces bourbon

In the bottom of an old-fashioned glass, carefully muddle the bitters, curaçao, 1 of the orange slices, and 1 of the cherries with a splash of soda. Remove the orange rind and add the bourbon and several ice cubes and stir. Garnish with the remaining orange slice and cherry.

CHOCOLATE PUNCH

CLARET LEMONADE

This lemonade recipe was popular in the last decade of the nineteenth century. The recipe in the 1900 edition of *Harry Johnson's New and Improved Illustrated Bartenders' Manual* couldn't be simpler: a tumbler with crushed ice, a little lemon juice, ¾ tablespoon of sugar, and water, shaken well, with a float of 2 ounces of claret wine. *Claret* was the English word for the wines of Bordeaux.

1 ounce fresh lemon juice
1 ounce Simple Syrup (page 225)
3 ounces water
2 ounces Bordeaux-style red wine blend
Lemon wheel, for garnish

Shake the lemon juice, simple syrup, and water together in a cocktail shaker. Strain into a goblet filled with crushed ice and float the wine on top. Garnish with the lemon wheel.

CLOVER CLUB

In his *Old Waldorf Bar Days* (1931), Albert Stevens Crockett credits this pre-Prohibition cocktail to the Bellevue-Stratford Hotel in Philadelphia, where an Algonquin Round Table sort of group—but a bit less literary—called the Clover Club lent its name to the drink. When raspberries are in season, omit the raspberry syrup, bump up the simple syrup to ¾ ounce, and muddle 6 fresh raspberries in the shaker with the syrup, then add the rest of the ingredients.

1½ ounces gin
¾ ounce Dolin dry vermouth
½ ounce Simple Syrup (page 225)
¾ ounce fresh lemon juice
½ ounce raspberry syrup
½ ounce emulsified egg white (see page 204)

Shake all the ingredients well with ice and strain into a chilled cocktail glass. If you're using fresh raspberries, fine strain using a small stainless-steel mesh strainer to remove the raspberry bits.

VARIATION To make the Clover Leaf, add a sprig of mint to the shaker before shaking.

CLUB COCKTAIL*

This is adapted from *Just Cocktails* by W. C. Whitfield, who produced a series of whimsical cocktail books with carved-wood covers in the 1930s.

2 ounces Gran Duque d'Alba Spanish brandy
½ ounce Luxardo maraschino liqueur
½ ounce pineapple juice
2 dashes of Peychaud's bitters
Lemon zest coin (see page 62), for garnish
Bordeaux cherry, for garnish

Shake all the ingredients (except the garnishes) well with ice and strain into a cocktail glass. Garnish with the lemon zest coin and cherry.

VARIATION Add ½ ounce orange curaçao and switch to Angostura bitters and you have a Rising Sun cocktail.

COCKTAIL JEREZ+

2 ounces Jameson Irish whiskey
¾ ounce Lustau dry oloroso sherry
¼ ounce Lustau Pedro Ximénez sherry
Dash of Dale DeGroff's Pimento Aromatic Bitters
Orange zest coin (see page 62), for garnish

Stir the whiskey, both sherries, and bitters with ice in a mixing glass and strain into a chilled cocktail glass. Garnish with the orange zest coin.

COCOWEE*

This was created originally as a vodka drink in Mexico City for a special bartender's event.

1 ripe kiwi
1 ounce coconut water
1½ ounces Cruzan Single Barrel rum
½ ounce fresh lime juice
½ ounce Coco López Cream of Coconut
½ ounce Agave Syrup (page 222)
Mint sprig with stem, for garnish
Thin lime wheel, for garnish

Scoop the kiwi flesh out of its skin, discarding the skin, and muddle the kiwi and the coconut water in the bottom of a cocktail shaker. Add the rum, lime juice, coconut cream, agave, and ice. Shake well and fine strain using a small stainless steel mesh cocktail strainer into a large coupe. Pull the stem of the mint leaf through the center of the lime wheel and float it on top of the drink.

COCTEL ALGERIA

This is an unusual pisco recipe from the menu of the famous Manhattan restaurant La Fonda del Sol, opened in 1960 by Joe Baum during his tenure as president of Restaurant Associates. Joe imported Demonio de los Andes pisco from Tacama, Peru, just for this restaurant. He was a visionary; he also imported tequila and mezcal for the beverage menu. I took a few liberties with the original recipe to bring it into the new millennium.

1½ ounces pisco
½ ounce Cointreau
½ ounce Marie Brizard Apry liqueur
1 ounce fresh orange juice
Dash of Bitter Truth orange bitters
Flamed orange zest coin (see page 62), for garnish

Shake all the ingredients (except the garnish) with ice and strain into a chilled cocktail glass. Garnish with the flamed orange zest coin.

COFFEE COCKTAIL

This nineteenth-century specialty drink is from the 1887 edition of Jerry Thomas's *The Bar-Tender's Guide, or How to Mix All Kinds of Plain and Fancy Drinks.* Thomas died in 1885, two years before this edition; the editors expanded the cocktail section from ten recipes in the 1862 edition to twenty in the 1887 edition. The editor added a disclaimer, noting that the drink did not contain coffee and went on to note that it did not contain bitters, either. Bitters was the ingredient that defined the cocktail category in the beginning, and that disclaimer noted a growing trend to include a wider group of mixed drinks in the cocktail category. The color and texture of the drink evokes coffee with cream and sugar.

1 ounce Courvoisier VSOP Cognac
1 ounce 10-year tawny port (see Note)
1 small egg
¾ ounce Simple Syrup (page 225)
Freshly grated nutmeg, for garnish

Shake all the ingredients (except the garnish) especially well with ice to emulsify the egg. Strain into a port glass. Dust with nutmeg.

NOTE I like tawny port, but it's a bit pricey. Your house ruby port will work just fine in this recipe.

COFFEE NUDGE

1 ounce Cardenal Mendoza Spanish brandy
½ ounce Tempus Fugit crème de cacao
½ ounce Tia Maria coffee liqueur
4 ounces hot coffee
Unsweetened Hand-Whipped Irish-Coffee Cream (page 225)

Build the brandy, liqueurs, and hot coffee in an Irish coffee glass and float the cream on top.

COGNAC AND SODA

This was Hemingway's favorite while perusing the Paris edition of the *New York Herald* in cafés on the West Bank. It was listed in Jerry Thomas's 1862 book *How to Mix Drinks, or The Bon-Vivant's Companion* as the Stone Wall. In England it was called the Peg (as in "one peg in your coffin"). A dash of Peychaud's bitters is a pleasant addition.

2 ounces Pierre Ferrand Ambre Cognac
3 to 4 ounces club soda

Pour the Cognac over ice in a highball glass and add the club soda.

COLONY ROOM COCKTAIL*

The Colony Room Club in London was known for many things, but cocktails were not one of them. A *Guardian* newspaper quote from longtime member Roddy Ashworth sums it up nicely: "If a member asks for a Piña Colada, he is likely to be served with little more than raised eyebrows and a large gin and tonic."

In 1998, while visiting London to judge a bartending contest, I ended up at the Colony Room, where I was surprised to discover that the most complex cocktail available was a screwdriver, although to get one, a member had to ask for a large vodka and orange. Cocktail names were frowned on as well, as was any fresh fruit or fresh juice—the orange came from a carton. Fresh fruit and eggs were allowed only on poetry days and that was for throwing purposes only. I made that bit up, but it fits perfectly with the profile. Faced with the prospect of drinking vodka and orange all night, I convinced proprietor Michael Wojas to allow me to get behind the bar and fashion my own special mix. The available ingredients were limited, but I did manage to concoct a drink worthy of the club's name. They liked the drink, and from that moment on, I was an official nonmember welcomed with all the privileges that encompasses, namely a drink when on visits to London and a game attitude when the members used the "Yank" for cannon fodder. Update: Sadly the Colony closed their doors in 2008, when Michael died. I think it may have been the last outpost of droll behavior as a competitive sport practiced while consuming large amounts of strong spirits.

Dash of absinthe
2 ounces gin
2 dashes of Noilly Prat Original dry vermouth
Dash of Dale DeGroff's Pimento Aromatic Bitters

Season a chilled cocktail glass by dashing it with absinthe and coating the inside, then pour out the excess. In a mixing glass, chill the gin, vermouth, and bitters by stirring with ice. Strain into the prepared cocktail glass. Garnish with wit touched with sarcasm; if these are unavailable, strike a pose and garnish with attitude.

COLORADO BULLDOG

This is your basic adult egg cream. Kahlúa subs for the Fox's U-bet syrup and . . . well, if you don't know what that is, google "NYC egg cream"; you'll be glad you did. This is a variation on the Smith and Kearns. The drink is way below the standards of a sophisticated cocktailian but try it as dessert and you won't be sorry.

1½ ounces Kahlúa
2 ounces cold milk
3 ounces Coca-Cola

Build the Kahlúa and milk in a highball glass over ice. Add the Coca-Cola last and gently stir with a long barspoon while pouring; let the foam recede, pour more, and stir again. Repeat until the glass is full, and the foam is the garnish.

COOPERSTOWN

In *Old Waldorf Bar Days* (1931), author Albert Stevens Crockett claims that this was created in the "Big Brass Rail" at the old Waldorf for some high rollers from Cooperstown, New York. The "Big Brass Rail" was a legendary bar in the old Waldorf Hotel, which was located in the footprint of today's Empire State Building. The clientele included everyone from Annie Oakley and Wild Bill Hickok to British royals and local gangsters and politicians, who were difficult to distinguish from one another.

2 fresh mint sprigs
½ ounce Dolin sweet vermouth
½ ounce Noilly Prat Original dry vermouth
2 ounces Bluecoat American dry gin

Muddle 1 of the mint sprigs and the vermouths in a mixing glass. Add the gin and ice, stir well, and strain into a cocktail glass. Garnish with the remaining mint sprig.

COPA VERDE*

This is a shot prepared in a blender as an accompaniment to small bites. I have made these shots for a barbecue at Cuervo's La Rojeña distillery in the town of Tequila and for the Sunday chef's party at the close of the Food & Wine Classic in Aspen, and they are crowd-pleasers. They are also food friendly. The recipe below is for one blender-full, which translates to fifteen to twenty shots.

> Chili powder, kosher salt, and lemon wedges, for frosting the glass rims (optional)
> 6 ounces Don Julio blanco tequila
> 4 ounces Triple Syrup (page 225)
> 3 ounces fresh lemon or lime juice
> ½ ripe but firm avocado, skinned and coarsely chopped
> 3 ounces spring water

To frost the rim of the shot glasses, if desired: Mix 1 part chili powder and 3 parts kosher salt in a small, shallow dish. Wet the outside rim of a 1½-ounce shot glass with a lemon wedge and then dip it into the chili-and-salt mixture. Set aside. Repeat with the remaining glasses.

In a blender, combine the tequila, triple syrup, lemon juice, avocado, and spring water. Blend without ice until completely smooth. Pour into a pitcher, cover, and refrigerate until ready to use.

To serve, stir the mixture and transfer 4 ounces of the mix into a cocktail shaker with cracked ice. Shake well to chill and add dilution. Strain into sixteen 1½-ounce shot glasses.

NOTE To serve a large party, prepare plenty of chopped avocado, juice, and Triple Syrup ahead of time and blend as needed. At the two events I described above, we would routinely go through a case of tequila and a case of avocados.

CORPSE REVIVER #2

Who cares what's in this cocktail; the name sold me when I read it in Harry Craddock's *The Savoy Cocktail Book* (1930). This is the best of the variations.

> ¾ ounce Tanqueray No. Ten gin
> ¾ ounce Cointreau
> ¾ ounce Lillet Blanc
> ¾ ounce fresh lemon juice
> Dash or a spritz of Jade Esprit Edouard Absinthe Supérieure

Shake the first four ingredients well with ice and strain into a chilled cocktail glass. Dash or spritz the surface of the drink with the absinthe.

CUBA LIBRE

Coca-Cola had been available in bottles for only four years when the Rough Riders brought it along with them to Cuba during the Spanish-American War. They mixed it with Cuban rum and lime and named it after their battle cry—"Cuba Libre," which was heard from the Rough Riders and their Cuban counterparts as they swept the Spanish out of Cuba.

> 2 ounces Cuban rum (May I suggest the 3-year-old Havana Club? Of course, that requires a sourcing trip to Cuba.)
> 4 ounces Coca-Cola (see Note)
> Lime wedge, for garnish
> Dash of Dale DeGroff's Pimento Aromatic Bitters (optional)

Pour the rum over ice in a highball glass and fill with Coca-Cola. Squeeze in a lime wedge for garnish. I add a dash of bitters for a touch of spice, but that's up to you.

NOTE Get the Coca-Cola in the little green bottle. It is sweetened with cane sugar and stevia, not corn syrup.

COBBLERS

Cobblers comprised a broad category in the nineteenth century, when they were made with wine or spirits, syrups, and fresh fruits. They were decorated with fresh fruit of the season, sweetened with sugar or syrup, and served over ice in large glasses. Frankly, they don't show up on menus but I had some tasty fun with the category and came up with the recipes below.

I was intrigued by the Whiskey Cobbler recipe in the 1862 *How to Mix Drinks* by Jerry Thomas. He was shaking orange slices in the shaker with the rest of the ingredients—that rocked my world. I expanded on the idea by muddling the fruits and then shaking them with the other ingredients as well.

I re-created cobblers at the Blackbird Bar in 1999, reviving the tradition of muddling and shaking the drink with the fruit. I garnished with slices of the same fruit that I muddled.

CHAMPAGNE COBBLER*

1 orange slice
1 lemon wedge
1 fresh pineapple wedge, peeled
½ ounce Simple Syrup (page 225)
½ ounce maraschino liqueur
4 ounces Champagne
Flamed orange zest coin (see page 62)

Muddle the fruits, simple syrup, and liqueur in
the bottom of a mixing glass. Add ice and pour
in the Champagne slowly. Stir gently so to retain
the bubbles and strain the drink carefully into a
champagne flute. Flame the orange zest coin over
the drink and discard.

JAPANESE COBBLER*

2 fresh pineapple wedges, 1 peeled
2 orange slices
2 lemon wedges
½ ounce maraschino liqueur
2 ounces daiginjo sake
2 ounces amazake (nonalcoholic
    rice-based drink from Japan)
Sprig of fresh mint, for garnish

In the bottom of a Boston shaker glass, muddle the
peeled pineapple wedge, 1 of the orange slices, and
1 of the lemon wedges with the maraschino liqueur.
Add the sake and the amazake and shake with ice.
Strain into a double old-fashioned glass filled with
crushed ice. Garnish with the sprig of mint and
the remaining pineapple wedge, orange wedge, and
lemon wedge.

PORT COBBLER*

2 fresh pineapple wedges, 1 peeled
2 orange slices
2 lemon wedges
1½ ounces Pierre Ferrand dry curaçao
1 ounce water
4 ounces Sandeman Founder's Reserve ruby port
½ ounce Simple Syrup (page 225; optional)

In the bottom of a Boston shaker glass, muddle the
peeled pineapple wedge, 1 of the orange slices, and
1 of the lemon wedges with the curaçao, simple
syrup, and water. Add the port, shake with ice, and
strain into a double old-fashioned glass filled with
crushed ice. Garnish with the remaining pineapple
wedge, orange slice, and lemon wedge.

SHERRY COBBLER*

2 fresh pineapple wedges, 1 peeled
2 orange slices
2 lemon wedges
1 ounce Lustau Pedro Ximénez sherry
3 ounces Lustau dry amontillado sherry
1 ounce pineapple juice

In the bottom of a Boston shaker glass, muddle
the peeled pineapple wedge, 1 of the orange
slices, and 1 of the lemon wedges with the Pedro
Ximénez sherry. Add the amontillado sherry and
the pineapple juice and shake well with ice. Strain
into a goblet filled with crushed ice. Garnish with
the remaining pineapple wedge, orange slice, and
lemon wedge.

WHISKEY COBBLER*

This drink works especially well paired with game meats
with a fruit sauce.

2 fresh pineapple wedges, 1 peeled
2 orange slices
2 lemon wedges
¾ ounce Marie Brizard orange curaçao
2 ounces Wild Turkey 101 bourbon

In the bottom of a Boston shaker glass, muddle the
peeled pineapple wedge, 1 of the orange slices, and
1 of the lemon wedges with the orange curaçao.
Add the bourbon and ice and shake well. Strain
into a double old-fashioned glass filled with crushed
ice. Garnish with the remaining pineapple wedge,
orange slice, and lemon wedge.

COSMOPOLITAN

1½ ounces Absolut Citron vodka
¾ ounce Cointreau
¼ ounce fresh lime juice
1 ounce cranberry juice
Flamed orange zest coin (see page 62),
　for garnish

Shake all the ingredients (except the garnish) with ice. Strain into a chilled cocktail glass. Garnish with the flamed orange zest coin.

COSMOPOLITAN DELIGHT

From *Recipes of American and Other Iced Drinks* by Charlie Paul (1902), this Cosmopolitan shares the name but not much else. It's a bit like a New York Sour with Cognac and a little orgeat tossed into the mix.

1½ ounces Pierre Ferrand Ambre Cognac
½ ounce Pierre Ferrand dry curaçao
¼ ounce Simple Syrup (page 225)
¾ ounce fresh lemon juice
¼ ounce orgeat
Splash of red wine
Seasonal fresh fruits, for garnish

Shake all the ingredients (except the red wine and the garnish), with ice, and strain over ice into an old-fashioned glass. Top with the splash of red wine and garnish with fruit. Don't be shy with the fruit garnishes; these early drinks looked like fruit salads—you may need to add a spoon.

DAIQUIRI

This Cuban classic gets its name from a town in what was the Oriente Province. Created by an American mining engineer named Jennings Cox and a Cuban engineer named Pagliuchi in the late nineteenth century, the talented barmen in Havana, especially Constantino Ribalaigua Vert of El Floridita, refined it.

Transported from Cuba by Admiral Lucius Johnson, the daiquiri made its first appearance in the United States at the Army and Navy Club in Washington, D.C.

2 ounces Mount Gay white rum
¾ ounce Simple Syrup (page 225)
¾ ounce fresh lime juice

Shake all the ingredients with ice and strain into a chilled cocktail glass.

DALE'S ABSOLUTELY GUARANTEED APHRODISIAC*

I created this for Tony Hendra's "Cocktail Challenge" article in *New York* magazine. The other challengers were chef Anne Rosenzweig, winemaker Alex Hargrave, and *Sex and the City* columnist Candace Bushnell. Anne made the final challenge of the afternoon, asking for an "absolutely guaranteed aphrodisiac" with "no fruit."

1 ounce Grand Marnier
1 ounce cachaça
¼ ounce Lemon Hart 151 overproof rum

Stir together the Grand Marnier and cachaça and pour over ice in a rocks glass. Float the rum. No fruit!

DALE'S RYE & CHERRY PUNCH*

MAKES ABOUT 1 GALLON

A colonial-style punch inspired by Martha Washington's Cherry Bounce.

1 liter Rittenhouse 100-proof straight rye whisky
8 ounces Blandy's Rainwater Madeira
18 ounces Heering cherry liqueur (absolutely no substitutes)
1 recipe Dale's Lemon and Orange Shrub (page 223)
1 liter spring water
Freshly grated nutmeg, for garnish

Combine the whiskey, Madeira, cherry liqueur, shrub, and spring water in a large batching container or punch bowl. Refrigerate until ready to use. Serve from a punch bowl or a pitcher, pouring it into white-wine glasses over ice cubes. Dust with the nutmeg.

DARK AND STORMY

2 ounces Goslings Black Seal Bermuda black rum
4 ounces Fever-Tree ginger beer
Lime wedge, for garnish

Pour the rum over ice in a highball glass and fill it with the ginger beer. Squeeze in the lime wedge.

D'ARTAGNAN

1 teaspoon Loubère Vieille Réserve Bas Armagnac or your favorite Armagnac
1 teaspoon Grand Marnier
½ ounce fresh orange juice
½ teaspoon Simple Syrup (page 225)
5 ounces chilled Champagne
1 whole orange peel, cut into a long spiral (see page 62), for garnish

Chill the first four ingredients over an ice cube in a mixing glass and strain into a champagne flute. Top with the Champagne. Hook the orange peel spiral over the rim of the glass so it extends the length of the inside of the glass.

DEBONAIRE COCKTAIL

Gary and Mardee Regan supplied me with orange bitters that they prepared in their kitchen during my last couple years at the Rainbow Room. Regan's Orange Bitters No. 6 is now commercially available. They prepared this drink from a recipe that appeared in the 1862 first edition of Jerry Thomas's *How to Mix Drinks*.

2½ ounces Highland malt scotch
½ ounce Barrow's Intense ginger liqueur (see Notes)

Stir both ingredients in a mixing glass with ice to chill and strain into a chilled cocktail glass.

NOTES The Barrow's liqueur is made from Peruvian ginger in Brooklyn, New York. This drink can also be served over ice in an old-fashioned glass with the liqueur floating on top, in the style of a Rusty Nail (page 198).

THE DEMOCRAT⁺

"I was reading David McCullough's Truman. Truman and his wife enjoyed bourbon in the evening on their porch in Missouri. I wanted to make a drink to honor him; he's an underrated president who faced impossible odds. So I started to think about great porch drinks, like sweet tea and lemonade, things one could sip while enjoying the Missouri evening. The Democrat is that drink, a boozy lemonade." —Jon Santer, owner of the Prizefighter (Emeryville, California) and Nommo (San Francisco)

   3 or 4 large mint leaves
   ½ ounce Honey Syrup (page 224)
   2 ounces Old Grand-Dad bourbon
   ¾ ounce fresh lemon juice
   ½ ounce peach liqueur (I suggest Marie Brizard No 11)
   Lemon wheel, for garnish
   Mint sprig, for garnish

Bruise the mint leaves in the bottom of a Boston shaker glass with the honey syrup. Add the bourbon, lemon juice, and liqueur and shake with ice cubes. Fine strain into a highball or goblet glass over crushed ice and stir well to frost the glass. Garnish with the lemon wheel and mint sprig.

DERBY COCKTAIL

The Derby a classic from *The Savoy Cocktail Book*, 1930, is listed by the International Bartenders Association as one of the unforgettables. I took the liberty of enriching the cocktail with a splash of liqueur.

   3 mint leaves
   ¼ ounce Marie Brizard No 11 peach liqueur
   Dash of Fee Brothers peach bitters
   2 ounces Plymouth gin
   Mint sprig, for garnish

In a mixing glass, gently bruise the mint leaves with the peach liqueur and peach bitters. Add the gin and ice and stir. Fine strain into an old-fashioned glass over crushed ice. Garnish with the mint sprig.

DIRTY MOTHER

   1½ ounces Bertoux brandy
   1 ounce Kahlúa

Pour the ingredients into a rocks glass over ice cubes and stir.

DIRTY WHITE MOTHER

   1½ ounces Bertoux brandy
   1 ounce Kahlúa
   1 ounce heavy cream

Shake all the ingredients with ice. Strain into a rocks glass over ice cubes.

D.O.M. COCKTAIL

This is modified from a recipe found in *The Artistry of Mixing Drinks* (1936) by Frank Meier of the Ritz Bar in Paris.

   2 ounces Hendrick's Orbium gin
   ¾ ounce fresh orange juice
   ½ ounce Bénédictine
   Flamed orange zest coin (see page 62), for garnish

Shake all the ingredients (except the garnish) with ice and strain into a chilled Nick & Nora glass. Garnish with the flamed orange zest coin.

THE DEMOCRAT

DOUBLE "D" COCKTAIL[+]

Original drink by Gaz Regan (see left).

2½ ounces Ketel One vodka
¼ ounce Belle de Brillet pear liqueur
Pear slice, for garnish

Stir the vodka and liqueur with ice in a mixing glass and strain into a chilled Nick & Nora glass. Garnish with the pear slice.

DOUGLAS FAIRBANKS

1½ ounces Dorothy Parker gin
1 ounce Marie Brizard Apry liqueur
½ ounce fresh lime juice
½ ounce emulsified egg white (see page 204)
Grated lime zest, for garnish

Shake all the ingredients (except the garnish) extra hard to completely emulsify the egg white, then strain into a chilled cocktail glass. Sprinkle a little freshly grated lime zest over the foam on top of the drink.

DUBLINER*

I created the Dubliner in Prague in 1995, at Molly Malone's Irish bar to prove to the Czech bartenders that the local cream whipped up just fine.

2 ounces Jameson Irish whiskey
1 ounce Irish Mist liqueur
Unsweetened Hand-Whipped Irish-Coffee Cream (page 225)

Pour the spirits into a mixing glass with ice and stir to chill. Strain into a Nick & Nora glass and top carefully with 1 inch of the lightly whipped cream.

DUBONNET COCKTAIL

In 2018, Lynette House collaborated with the tasting team at Heaven Hill in Bardstown, Kentucky, to redo the American version of Dubonnet Rouge to more closely align with the European version. They added a bit more quinine and replaced the corn syrup with cane sugar, among other changes. Americans are finally cozying up to this European bitter aperitif.

This cocktail is also known as the Zaza. Dubonnet and gin is featured in the Noël Coward song "I Went to a Marvelous Party."

1½ ounces Dubonnet Rouge
1½ ounces Hendrink's gin
Lemon zest coin (see page 62), for garnish

Pour the Dubonnet and gin together over ice in an old-fashioned glass and stir to chill. Strain into a cocktail glass. Express the oil of the lemon over the drink and drop it in.

A MARVELOUS PARTY

We knew the excitement was bound to begin

When Laura got blind on Dubonnet and gin

And scratched her veneer with a Cartier pin.
I couldn't have liked it more.

— "I Went to a Marvelous Party"
by Noël Coward

DUSTY ROSE*

1 ounce Heering cherry liqueur
½ ounce Marie Brizard white crème de cacao
1½ ounces heavy cream

Shake all the ingredients with ice and strain into a Nick & Nora glass.

EGGNOG, UNCLE ANGELO'S+

MAKES 72 OUNCES

This was my great-uncle Angelo Gencarelli's recipe, which he submitted to the Four Roses whiskey people in a contest many years ago and won. Uncle Angelo always had two bowls of eggnog at Christmas: one for the kids and one for the grown-ups. What made this recipe special was its lightness: there's twice as much milk as cream and the egg whites are whipped stiff and folded into the mix, so it was almost like clouds on top of the eggnog. If you're nervous about using raw eggs, see Faux Nog (page 123).

6 large eggs, separated
¾ cup sugar
1 quart milk
1 pint heavy cream
8 ounces Four Roses bourbon
6 ounces spiced rum
Freshly grated nutmeg, for garnish

In a large bowl, beat the egg yolks well until they turn light in color, adding ½ cup of the sugar as you beat. Add the milk, cream, and liquors and refrigerate until ready to serve. Just before serving, beat the egg whites with the remaining ¼ cup sugar until they hold stiff peaks. Fold the whites into the eggnog mixture. Serve cold with freshly grated nutmeg sprinkled over the drink.

EL PRESIDENTE

El Presidente was created in the 1920s at the Vista Alegre in Havana and named for Mario García Menocal, who was the president of Cuba from 1913 to 1921. Well maybe. We have the same issue that plagues so many of these claims—there's no documentation. Below is the Cafe La Trova version by Julio Cabrera. Cafe La Trova was opened by partners Julio Cabrera and renowned chef Michelle Bernstein, who re-created a bit of Havana, circa 1925, in Miami's Little Havana neighborhood. There is live music and dancing. The food—well, it is Michelle Bernstein.

1½ ounces Banks 7 Golden Age Blend rum
¾ ounce Pierre Ferrand dry curaçao
¾ ounce Dolin Blanc vermouth
1 barspoon grenadine, homemade (page 224)

Shake all the ingredients well with ice and strain into a chilled Nick & Nora glass.

ELK'S OWN

This is modified from a recipe in *The Artistry of Mixing Drinks* (1936) by Frank Meier of the Ritz Bar in Paris. Port was a popular ingredient in punches and cocktails, sometimes as a float and sometimes shaken into the drink.

1½ ounces Crown Royal blended Canadian whisky
1 ounce port
½ ounce fresh lemon juice
½ ounce Simple Syrup (page 225)
1 small emulsified egg white (see page 204)

Shake all ingredients with ice very well to totally emulsify the egg and strain into a chilled cocktail glass.

EMBASSY COCKTAIL

The brandy-and-rum combination was used often in nogs and holiday punches and occasionally in a cocktail like this one from Hollywood's Embassy Club, in 1930.

¾ ounce Camus IIe de Ré Fine Island Cognac
¾ ounce Joseph Cartron Curaçao Orange
¾ ounce Appleton Estate Jamaica rum
½ ounce fresh lime juice
Dash of Angostura bitters
Thin lime wheel, for garnish

Shake all ingredients (except the garnish) well with ice and strain into a chilled Nick & Nora glass. Garnish with the wheel lime.

VARIATION Add a dash of Simple Syrup (page 225) for a sweeter version.

ESPRESSO VODKA COCKTAIL (AKA ESPRESSO MARTINI)+

Dick Bradsell called the drink Vodka Espresso, and the rest of the world decided it should simply be called Espresso Martini. Dick would not approve; he was a purist when it came to the martini.

½ ounce Tia Maria coffee liqueur
½ ounce Kahlúa
1 ounce Ketel One vodka
1½ ounces cold espresso

Shake all the ingredients well with ice and strain into a cocktail glass. When properly shaken, the crema from the espresso rises again and will remain for the life of the drink.

EVEREST+

"In 2008 I was asked to join a bunch of bartenders to play with Beefeater 24 gin, which had not yet been released. On my way to the Pegu Club, where the research session took place, I sat on the train, mulling what I was going to do. Japanese sencha and Chinese green teas are among the botanicals in Beefeater 24, and tea made me think of India. India made me think of curry . . . [and] that's what led to this formula. The Everest was the name of an absolutely fabulous . . . hole-in-the-wall Indian restaurant in Blackpool, England, where I used to go for late night vindaloos in the early 1970s. That's where the name came from."
—Gaz Regan

2½ ounces Beefeater 24 gin
¾ ounce coconut curry paste (see Note)
½ ounce fresh lemon juice
Pinch of curry powder, for garnish

Combine the gin, curry paste, and lemon juice in a shaker. Add ice, shake, and strain into a chilled cocktail glass. Garnish with a pinch of curry powder and serve.

NOTE To make the coconut curry paste, mix 1 teaspoon curry powder with 1½ ounces Coco López Cream of Coconut. Store any leftovers in an airtight container in the refrigerator.

FAUX NOG*

Are you afraid of raw egg? Try this recipe as a substitute for eggnog. It's amazing how authentic it tastes.

1 ounce vodka
1 ounce Marie Brizard white crème de cacao
1½ ounces heavy cream
3 dashes of Angostura bitters
Freshly grated nutmeg, for garnish

Shake the ingredients (except the garnish) well with ice. Strain and serve over crushed ice in a large coupe glass. Dust with the nutmeg.

FERNET-BRANCA COCKTAIL

2 ounces Fords gin
¼ ounce Fernet-Branca amaro
¾ ounce Martini Riserva Speciale Rubino vermouth
Flamed lemon zest coin (see page 62), for garnish

In a mixing glass, stir the gin, amaro, and vermouth with ice to chill, Strain into a chilled cocktail glass. Flame the lemon zest coin over the drink and drop it in.

FISH HOUSE PUNCH, PHILADELPHIA

This recipe is based on the one from *How to Mix Drinks* by Jerry Thomas, with credit given to nineteenth-century writer Charles G. Leland, Esquire. Thomas was generous in his credit because Fish House Punch goes back more than one hundred years before Leland. It originated with the Schuylkill Fishing Club, an eating and drinking club for sportsmen founded in 1732. This recipe is one of many, so I took some liberties.

6 ripe, sweet Georgia peaches, washed, pitted, and sliced
8 whole lemon zests (very fresh firm lemons)
2 cups sugar
16 ounces fresh lemon juice
16 ounces VS Cognac
8 ounces peach brandy
1 liter Jamaican rum

To make an ice ring, fill a savarin ring mold three-quarters full with water and cover with plastic wrap; freeze until solid. Remove it carefully by turning the mold upside down on a clean surface and tapping the bottom of the mold.

In a large bowl, cover the peaches and the lemon zests with the sugar and set aside for a minimum of 3 hours. Stir the lemon juice into the slurry of peaches and sugar to dissolve the remaining sugar. Strain the mixture into a punch bowl. Discard the zests and fruit pulp. Add the Cognac, peach brandy, and rum to the punch bowl and stir. Serve with the ice ring.

FITZGERALD*

I came up with this one on the fly one busy night at the Rainbow Room Promenade Bar, when a customer who was bored with his regular summer libation (Gin and Tonic) asked me for a new gin drink for summer. The drink has appeared on craft bar menus around the world thanks to the Internet. We all have a love-hate relationship with the Internet; list this one under love.

1½ ounces Dorthy Parker gin (I couldn't resist this literary marriage, albeit only in a drink)
¾ ounce Simple Syrup (page 225)
¾ ounce fresh lemon juice
4 dashes of Angostura bitters
Thin lemon wheel, for garnish

Shake all the ingredients (except the garnish) with ice. Strain and serve in a rocks glass over ice cubes. Garnish with the lemon wheel.

FLAME OF LOVE

This variation on the martini is sometimes referred to as the Valencia Martini or the Spanish Martini. La Ina fino sherry may not be available in your area. Tio Pepe fino sherry is a good substitute. See page 212 for a bit of history about this drink.

¼ ounce La Ina fino sherry
2 flamed orange zest coins (see page 62), for garnish
2½ ounces Finlandia vodka

Coat the inside of a chilled cocktail glass with the sherry and toss the remainder into a cocktail shaker. Flame 1 of the orange zest coins into the cocktail glass and discard. Add the vodka with ice to the cocktail shaker. Strain into the seasoned cocktail glass. Flame the second orange zest and drop it into the drink.

FLAMINGO

This old gem is an easy-to-make, pleasant summertime feel-good drink. Translate the ratios and make a full pitcher, then serve them as you need them.

1½ ounces Myers's Platinum white rum
1½ ounces pineapple juice
¼ ounce fresh lime juice
¼ ounce grenadine, homemade (page 224) or store-bought

Shake all the ingredients well with ice and serve in a cocktail glass.

VARIATION For a sweeter drink, add ¼ ounce cane syrup or Simple Syrup (page 225).

FLEUR POWER⁺

"I am often asked what my favorite food is, and I always reply raspberries! So this garden-to-glass-inspired riff on the French 75 combines all my favorite things: raspberries, a very botanical gin, rosé Champagne, and flowers." —Kathy Casey

4 raspberries
1½ ounces Sipsmith gin
¼ ounce Monin rose syrup
¼ ounce Monin organic agave nectar
½ ounce fresh lemon juice
1½ ounces Moët & Chandon Rosé Impérial Champagne
MicroFlowers, for garnish (see Notes)

Place the raspberries in a cocktail shaker and gently press them with a cocktail muddler. Add the gin, rose syrup, agave, and lemon juice. Fill with ice and shake.

Place a flower-shaped ice cube, if desired, into a coupe glass and fine strain the cocktail into the glass. Top with the Champagne and garnish with flowers.

NOTES I recommend Fresh Origins (see page 230) for sourcing microgreens, edible flowers, and other culinary specialties.

Silicone flower-shaped ice molds are available online.

FLIP

The flip recipes from colonial times were hot drinks, with as many variations as there were inns on the Boston Post Road. Generally they involved a batter made from brown sugar, eggs, and sometimes cream that was added to a large mug of beer, then scalded with a hot loggerhead (a poker with a ball at the end). The loggerhead was heated in the fire and thrust into the mug, and rum, brandy, or applejack was added to fortify the drink. This is a cold variation.

COLD SHERRY FLIP

2 ounces Dry Sack sherry
1 ounce Simple Syrup (page 225)
1 ounce emulsified whole egg
 (see page 204)
Freshly grated nutmeg, for garnish

Shake all the ingredients (except the garnish) with ice very well to totally emulsify the egg. Strain into a London dock or port glass. Dust with nutmeg.

FOX FLIP

Recipe adapted from *The Hoffman House Bartender's Guide* by Charles S. Mahoney.

1½ ounces Old Forester Bourbon
¾ fresh lemon juice
½ ounce Simple Syrup (page 225)
1 medium emulsified egg (see page 204)
3 ounces Blenheim Ginger Ale

Fill a cocktail shaker half full with shaved ice and shake the first four ingredients very hard to emulsify the egg. Strain into a thin medium-size highball glass and top with the ginger ale.

THE FIZZ

The difference between a fizz and a collins is glass size and garnish. The collins goes in a tall, or collins, glass with a cherry and orange-slice garnish, and the fizz goes in an eight-ounce Delmonico or small highball glass without a garnish. The fizz drinks that contain eggs are served usually without ice. But a regular gin fizz with no egg is served with ice and no garnish. The 1862 edition of *How to Mix Drinks* by Jerry Thomas has no collins or fizz recipes, but it does list sours and the Gin Punch recipe #11 by Soyer, based on a pint of gin, with lemon juice, simple syrup, maraschino liqueur, and German seltzer water. The Tom Collins does show up in Jerry Thomas's *The Bar-Tender's Guide or How to Mix All Kinds of Plain and Fancy Drinks* (1887), along with six fizz recipes.

GIN FIZZ

This drink is just a Tom Collins on a short plan.

> **1½ ounces Fords gin**
> **¾ ounce fresh lemon juice**
> **¾ ounce Simple Syrup (page 225)**
> **2 ounces club soda**

Shake the gin, lemon juice, and simple syrup with ice and strain into a small highball glass filled with ice. Top with the club soda and stir.

GOLDEN FIZZ

There is a richer version of this drink called The Royal Fizz that uses a whole egg.

> **1½ ounces Fords gin**
> **¾ ounce fresh lemon juice**
> **1 ounce Simple Syrup (page 225)**
> **¾ ounce emulsified egg yolk (see page 204)**
> **2 ounces club soda**

Shake all the ingredients (except the club soda) with ice long and hard to completely emulsify the egg. Strain into a fizz or highball glass without ice, and top slowly with the club soda.

RAMOS OR
NEW ORLEANS FIZZ

1½ ounces Fords gin
½ ounce fresh lemon juice
½ ounce fresh lime juice
1¼ ounces Simple Syrup (page 225)
1½ ounces milk or cream
¾ ounce emulsified egg white
   (see page 204)
2 drops of orange-flower water
2 ounces club soda

Shake all the ingredients (except the club soda) with
ice and strain into a highball glass without ice. Top
slowly with the club soda.

SILVER FIZZ

1½ ounces Fords gin
¾ ounce fresh lemon juice
1 ounce Simple Syrup (page 225;
   see Note)
¾ ounce emulsified egg white
   (see page 204)
2 ounces club soda

Shake all the ingredients (except the club soda) with
ice long and hard to completely emulsify the egg.
Strain into a fizz or highball glass without ice and
top slowly with the club soda.

NOTE I find that a fizz with egg white needs
slightly more sweetener.

FLIRTINI*

This was the "it" drink for a minute in the 1990s. Lots of recipes are floating around; here's mine.

2 fresh pineapple wedges, peeled
½ ounce Cointreau
½ ounce Grey Goose vodka
1 ounce pineapple juice
3 ounces Champagne
Bordeaux cherry, for garnish

In the bottom of a mixing glass, muddle the pineapple pieces and the Cointreau. Add the vodka, pineapple juice, and ice and stir. Fine strain into a chilled cocktail glass and top slowly with the Champagne. Garnish with the cherry.

FLOR DE JEREZ+

"We may be living in the greatest time in history to be a bartender. The collective history, knowledge, and best practices have been codified, explained, dissected, and rigorously tested. But with all this abundance at our fingertips, we must never lose sight of what our profession is actually about: the person seated across the bar. Remember that real bartending doesn't happen on a drink rail; it happens across the bar with another person and with your coworkers. Never forget that hospitality is not optional in bartending, and your own legend will be burnished by those you serve."
—Joaquín Simó

½ ounce Appleton Estate Reserve Blend
   Jamaica rum
1½ ounces Lustau dry amontillado or dry
   oloroso sherry
½ ounce Marie Brizard Apry liqueur
¾ ounce fresh lemon juice
½ ounce Simple Syrup (page 225)
Dash of Angostura bitters

Shake all the ingredients with ice and strain into a large coupe glass.

FLORADORA

Named after the 1900 Broadway hit that introduced the Floradora Girls, who all were five feet four inches tall and weighed 130 pounds. The floral style of Hendrick's gin works very nicely in this recipe.

1½ ounces Hendrick's gin
½ ounce fresh lime juice
½ ounce framboise liqueur or raspberry syrup
3 ounces Fever-Tree ginger ale
Lime wheel, for garnish
Edible sweet violet or viola, for garnish (see Note)

Build the gin, lime juice, and framboise in a highball glass filled with ice. Top with the ginger ale. Garnish with the lime wheel and an edible violet.

NOTE I like flowers as garnish. Seek out food-grade edible flowers. Everything available in regular markets is covered with pesticides, but check with your local gourmet food shops. See *The Herb Garden Cookbook* by Lucinda Hutson (1998) for ideas on what is out there when it comes to edible flowers.

FOG

I prepared the Flaming Orange Gully for John Hodgman's Little Gray Book Lectures held at Galapagos bar in Williamsburg, Brooklyn. John's lectures led to a career as an author and an actor. John was a literary agent at that time and talked me into writing this book.

1½ ounces Stolichnaya Ohranj vodka
¾ ounce John D. Taylor's Velvet Falernum (see Note)
1 ounce fresh orange juice
½ ounce fresh lime juice
2 dashes of Regan's Orange Bitters No. 6
Flamed orange zest coin (see page 62)
Freshly grated nutmeg, for garnish

Shake all ingredients (except the garnishes) well with ice and strain into a chilled cocktail glass. Flame an orange zest coin over the drink and discard. Dust with grated nutmeg.

NOTE Velvet Falernum is available from Alpenz.com.

FOG CUTTER

After two of these the fog rolls in . . .

2 ounces Banks 7 Golden Age Blend rum
¾ ounce Camus Ile de Ré Fine Island Cognac
½ ounce Plymouth gin
1 ounce orgeat
1 ounce fresh orange juice
½ ounce fresh lemon juice
2 dashes of Pegu mix orange bitters (see Note)
¼ ounce Lustau Pedro Ximénez sherry
Orange zest coin (see page 62)
Freshly grated nutmeg, for garnish

Shake all ingredients (except the sherry, orange zest coin, and nutmeg) well with ice and pour into a double old-fashioned glass over ice cubes. Float the sherry on top of the drink and express the orange zest coin over the top and discard; dust with nutmeg.

NOTE I like to use Pegu Club's blend of 2 parts Regan's Orange Bitters No. 6 to 1 part Fee Brothers orange bitters.

FREDDIE FUDPUCKER

This is Harvey Wallbanger's Mexican cousin—and, yes, they're both fictitious!

1½ ounces Tequila Ocho plata tequila
5 ounces fresh orange juice
¾ ounce Float of Galliano

Build the tequila and orange juice in a highball glass over ice and top with Galliano.

FRENCH 75

The battle continues between the ranks of Cognac devotees and the gin traditionalists. In New Orleans, where the devotion to the French 75 is absolutely religious, expect to get the Cognac version. Don't fight it. I first enjoyed this cocktail at the Chanticleer Restaurant on Nantucket Island. It was their specialty at brunch, and it was served in a large goblet over ice and garnished extravagantly with fresh fruits.

1 ounce Cognac or gin
¾ ounce Simple Syrup (page 225)
¾ ounce fresh lemon juice
3 ounces Champagne

Shake the first three ingredients well with ice and strain into a goblet over ice or serve "up" in a flute. Top with the Champagne.

CAPTAIN HARRY S. TRUMAN AND THE FRENCH 75

During World War I, Captain Harry S. Truman once told his men, just minutes before their French seventy-five guns fired their 75-millimeter shells at the Germans (at a rate of thirty rounds per minute), "I'd rather be right here than be president of the United States!" This drink is named after that French artillery piece. The recipe originally called for gin, but it became more popular using Cognac brandy.

FRENCH 95

This drink actually calls for bourbon, but George Dickel makes an unusually pretty rye whiskey that will complement this drink beautifully.

¾ ounce George Dickel rye whisky
½ ounce Simple Syrup (page 225)
½ ounce fresh lemon juice
¾ ounce fresh orange juice, strained
3 ounces Champagne

Shake the first four ingredients with ice and strain into an ice-filled goblet. Top with the Champagne.

FRENCH CONNECTION

This is my erstwhile drinking companion Renee's nightcap or eye-opener—sometimes both.

1½ ounces Courvoisier
1 ounce Grand Marnier

Combine the ingredients in a warm brandy snifter at bedtime or over ice with a side of orange juice in the morning.

FRENCH FLAMINGO

I culled this one from the Sunday *New York Times* Styles section. It looked like my kind of recipe, so I changed it a bit to suit my taste.

1½ ounces Absolut Kurant vodka
¾ ounce Cointreau
½ ounce fresh lime juice
1 ounce Pom Wonderful pomegranate juice
Thin lime wheel, for garnish

Shake all the ingredients (except the garnish) well with ice and strain into a chilled cocktail glass. Garnish with the lime wheel.

FRENCH KISS ITALIAN-STYLE

1½ ounces Martini Riserva Speciale Rubino vermouth
1½ ounces Carpano dry vermouth
Lemon zest coin (see page 62), for garnish

Build in a wineglass over ice cubes and stir. Garnish with lemon zest coin.

FROZEN BLUE HAWAIIAN

This essentially is a blue Piña Colada (page 183).

1 ounce light rum, preferably Mount Gay Silver or Caña Brava
1 ounce Marie Brizard blue curaçao
1 ounce Coco López Cream of Coconut
2 ounces pineapple juice
1 cup cracked ice
Pineapple slice, for garnish
Pineapple leaf, for garnish

Blend all ingredients (except the garnishes). Pour into a copa grande glass. Garnish with the fresh pineapple slice and pineapple leaf.

FROZEN IGUANA*

It is *soo* cold that the iguanas are falling out of the trees! We need a drink.

1½ ounces Del Maguey Chichicapa mezcal
4 ounces Natural Blonde Bloody Mary Mix (see Note)
1 tablespoon Agave Syrup (page 222)
Dash of Dale DeGroff's Pimento Aromatic Bitters

Blend all the ingredients with a handful of ice and pour into a large goblet.

NOTE Natural blonde—no kidding. Made from yellow tomatoes, it's available at www.naturalblondebloodymary.com.

GALLERY GIMLET*

I created the Gallery Gimlet for the new Gallery Bars onboard Holland America Line ships. Founded in 1872, Holland America today is owned by Carnival Corporation. They remain the "adult" cruising brand, focused on fine food and drink served in elegant surroundings.

Black Hawaiian sea salt, for garnish
1½ ounces Plymouth gin
1 teaspoon yuzu juice
½ ounce fresh lime juice
¾ ounce Triple Syrup (page 225)
Thin lime wheel, for garnish

Frost the rim of a cocktail glass with black Hawaiian sea salt (see page 63) and chill. Assemble all the remaining ingredients (except the garnish) in a cocktail shaker with ice and shake well. Strain into the salted and chilled cocktail glass and garnish with the lime wheel.

GARNET*

1½ ounces Tanqueray No. Ten gin
½ ounce Pom Wonderful pomegranate juice
1 ounce fresh grapefruit juice
½ ounce St-Germain elderflower liqueur
Grapefruit zest coin (see page 62), for garnish

Assemble all the ingredients (except the garnish) in the glass half of a Boston shaker with ice and shake well. Strain into a chilled coupe glass and garnish with the grapefruit zest coin.

GENERAL HARRISON'S EGGNOG

The general was a teetotaler; the bourbon was my idea. This nog-in-a-glass is a simply delicious, perfect lactose-free nog for the holidays—or really anytime during cider season.

1½ ounces Bulleit bourbon
1 whole emulsified medium egg (see page 204)
1 ounce Simple Syrup (page 225)
4 ounces fresh apple cider
Freshly grated nutmeg, for garnish

Combine all ingredients (except the garnish) in a mixing glass with ice in the glass half of a Boston shaker and shake well to emulsify the egg. Strain into an eggnog cup or a mug. Garnish with nutmeg.

GILBERTO+

Created by Dushan Zaric as the signature drink for the opening of the restored Hotel Figueroa in Los Angeles, this is a fun, good-looking, and good-tasting drink.

1½ ounces BarSol Selecto Italia pisco
1 ounce Newton Chardonnay or any oaky Chardonnay
1 ounce Concord Grape Syrup (page 223)
¼ ounce Rich Simple Syrup (page 225)
1 ounce fresh lemon juice
5 dashes (¾ teaspoon) of Dale DeGroff's Pimento Aromatic Bitters
Cluster of frozen Champagne grapes, for garnish

Shake all the ingredients (except the garnish) vigorously with ice. Fine strain into a cocktail coupe and garnish with the frozen grapes clinging to the rim of the glass.

GIMLET

Be careful about switching fresh lime juice for Rose's lime juice in the Gimlet. *Real* Gimlet drinkers want the taste of the preserved lime juice. When the drink is made with fresh lime juice and sugar syrup, it's a Gin Sour, or as I have dubbed it, a California Gimlet.

2½ ounces Bluecoat American dry gin
½ ounce preserved lime juice, preferably Rose's or Angostura
Lime wedge

Shake gin, and lime juice well with ice and strain into a chilled cocktail glass or serve over ice in an old-fashioned glass. Squeeze the lime wedge over the drink, then discard.

GIN AND IT

The Gin and It is short for "Gin and Italian." I chose Old Duff genever because the whiskey-like mash-bill recipe of two-thirds rye and one-third malted barley makes it a good match for the "It," or Italian sweet vermouth. In the 1920s, Americans ordering martinis in European bars in Paris and London would order Gin and French or Gin and Italian chilled with ice. Gin and It was a drink separate from those and was usually imbibed without ice.

1½ ounces Old Duff genever
1½ ounces Martini Riserva Speciale Rubino vermouth

Stir the ingredients with ice in a mixing glass. Strain into a chilled cocktail glass like a Martini or over ice in a double old-fashioned glass like a Manhattan on the rocks. I include ice because warm gin drinks do not appeal to people these days.

THE GIBSON

For a Gibson, prepare the "Nick & Nora" Martini (page 165) but substitute a cocktail onion for the olive.

Celebrated illustrator Charles Dana Gibson gets the credit for the onion as a substitute for an olive. But there is a another story. Writing for the lifestyle website The Spruce Eats, Colleen Graham has unearthed some new information. *San Francisco Chronicle* reporter Charles McCabe spoke with Ms. Graham about an interview with Allan P. Gibson about his great-uncle Walter D. K. Gibson: "My grandfather and my father remembered D. K. well and the fact that it was he who invented the Gibson . . . . [Allen mentions later in the interview this was in the 1890s] He used to drink them until he died in 1938."

Ms. Graham found Allan Gibson's son, Charles Pollok Gibson, and he confirmed that the Gibson story was legitimate family history. Charles Gibson noted that his dad's great-uncle Walter complained to the bartender at the Bohemian Club that "he preferred them stirred, and made with Plymouth gin. He also believed that eating onions would prevent colds. Hence the onion."

The first written Gibson recipes were usually fifty-fifty (half gin and half vermouth), dry martinis, no onion. The first mention of the onion was late in the game, in bartender Bill Boothby's last book, in 1934.

MAKE IT A GIBSON, BARTENDER

Tony Abou-Ganim, noted bartender and drinks book author, always ordered his martini Gibson-style. One day I asked him why. He pointed to the ubiquitous garnish tray sitting on the bar and reasoned, "The standard bar garnish tray has six plastic inserts for the six most common garnishes: olives, twists, cherries, lemon wedges, lime wedges, and orange slices. And sadly, those garnishes sit out all shift long and get warm. There is no room for the cocktail onions, so guess where they are? Nice and cold in the bar fridge. . . ."

GIN GIN MULE+

This recipe is from Audrey Sanders, New York bartender and owner of Pegu Club, one of New York's premier cocktail bars. Pegu was the mother of the early craft bars, literally, and referred to as "the Harvard of mixology" by *The New York Times*. Bartenders trained by Audrey have gone on to open significant craft bars, including Death & Co. and PDT, among many others.

2 mint sprigs
¾ ounce fresh lime juice
1 ounce Simple Syrup (page 225)
1¾ ounces Tanqueray London dry gin
1 ounce ginger beer, homemade (page 222) or
  store-bought (see Note)
Lime wheel, for garnish
Candied ginger coin, for garnish

Gently muddle 1 of the mint sprigs with the lime juice and simple syrup in the bottom of a Boston shaker glass. Add the gin, ginger beer, and ice and shake well. Strain over ice in a 10-ounce highball glass. Garnish with the remaining mint sprig, the lime wheel, and candied ginger.

NOTE If you're using store-bought ginger beer, reduce the amount of Simple Syrup from 1 ounce to ½ ounce.

THE GIN THING

The Gin and Tonic is the traditional cocktail-hour standard for summer gatherings. Several years ago, a customer at the Rainbow Room Promenade Bar challenged me to create a new summer drink. I made a gin sour, but I spiced it up by adding Angostura bitters and called it The Gin Thing. It became quite the thing that summer, so I decided to put it on my cocktail menu, but one guest who enjoyed the drink, a fiction reader for *The New Yorker* magazine, insisted I give the drink a classier name. The Hemingway Daiquiri was on the menu at the time; she thought F. Scott Fitzgerald should get equal representation. (See the Fitzgerald, page 124.)

GIN SLING

This sling recipe is not at all historical. I made it up and served it for years at the Rainbow Room with great success. The ladies from the photo editing department of the Associated Press, which was next door, were especially fond of this recipe.

1½ ounces Plymouth gin
1 ounce Martini & Rossi sweet vermouth
¾ ounce fresh lemon juice
¾ ounce Simple Syrup (page 225)
Dash of Angostura bitters
1 ounce club soda
Lemon peel spiral (see page 62), for garnish

Shake all the ingredients (except the club soda and garnish) with ice and strain over ice into a highball glass. Top with the soda. Garnish with the spiral of lemon peel as in a Horse's Neck cocktail (page 143).

GIN TONIC AL FRESCO*

I made this one for Morandi Italian restaurant in Greenwich Village, but it never made the menu. Chef Jody Williams wanted only low-alcohol offerings, so for that version I dropped the gin and bumped up the Cynar.

1½ ounces Tanqueray No. Ten gin
¾ ounce Cynar
4 ounces Fever-Tree Mediterranean tonic water
2 dashes of Regan's Orange Bitters No. 6
Orange slice, for garnish

Build all the ingredients in a highball glass with ice and stir. Garnish with the orange slice.

GINGER & ORANGE HOLIDAY OLD-FASHIONED*

2 orange zests coins (see page 62)
2 dashes of Dale DeGroff's Pimento Aromatic
   Bitters
¼ ounce ginger syrup, homemade (page 224) or
   store-bought, preferably Monin brand
2½ ounces Maker's Mark 46 bourbon
1 barspoon orange marmalade
Flamed orange zest coin (see page 62),
   for garnish
Slice of candied ginger, for garnish

Muddle the oranges zest coins with the bitters and
the ginger syrup in the bottom of a Boston shaker
glass, then add the bourbon, marmalade, and ice
cubes. Shake well and fine strain through a fine-
mesh cocktail strainer into an old-fashioned glass
over ice cubes. Garnish with the flamed orange zest
coin and candied ginger.

GLOGG

SERVES 6

In 1946, Kenneth Hansen began a club in Los Angeles
called the Vikings of Scandia, which later became the
restaurant Scandia. Members included stars like Rita
Hayworth, Cornel Wilde, Marilyn Monroe, Gary
Cooper, and Marlene Dietrich. Scandia's Glogg, a
traditional holiday drink, was a favorite. I picked up
the custom and gave it away at the bar of the Rainbow
Room in small tastes during the two weeks around
Christmas.

1 (750 ml) bottle full-bodied red wine
⅓ cup dark raisins
⅓ cup blanched almond slices, plus more
   for garnish
Peel of 1 small orange (without pith)
5 crushed cardamom pods
5 whole cloves
1 cinnamon stick
4 ounces vodka or Cognac
3 ounces (or to taste) Simple Syrup (page 225)
Golden raisins, for garnish

In a container, combine the wine, raisins, almonds,
orange peel, and spices. Cover and let the mixture
stand at room temperature for 24 hours. Strain the
wine into a samovar, discarding the solids. Add the
vodka and simple syrup to taste. Serve hot from
the samovar in heat resistant stemware or in punch
cups. Garnish each serving with golden raisins and
blanched almonds.

GODFATHER/GODMOTHER

2 ounces Cutty Sark Prohibition Edition scotch
   or Smirnoff vodka
1 ounce amaretto

Pour both ingredients over ice in a rocks glass and
stir.

GOING BANANAS⁺

This original recipe is by Francesco Lafranconi, who
is an Italian classically trained in European four-star
hotel-style service. He relocated to Las Vegas and went
to work for Southern Glazer's Wine & Spirits, where
he put his training to good use developing the Academy
of Spirits and Fine Service. That program continues to
train young bartenders around the country in all aspects
of beverage service. Francesco opened Mr. Coco, his
piano bar with fine cocktails and small plates, in the
Palms Casino Resort early in 2019.

1 ounce Ron Botran Reserva rum
1 ounce Jameson Black Barrel Irish whiskey
¾ ounce Simple Syrup (page 225)
¾ ounce fresh lemon juice
2 dashes of Dale DeGroff's Pimento Aromatic
   Bitters
Dehydrated banana chips, for garnish

Shake all the ingredients (except the garnish) with
ice and strain into a chilled cocktail glass. Float the
banana chips on top of the drink.

GOLDEN CADILLAC

This was created at Poor Red's bar in El Dorado, California, where everything is golden.

1 ounce Galliano
1 ounce Tempus Fugit crème de cacao
1½ ounces heavy cream
Ground Ceylon cinnamon, for garnish

Shake all the ingredients (except the garnish) with ice and strain into a chilled cocktail glass. Dust with cinnamon.

GOLDEN DAWN

Created by bartender Tom Buttery of the Berkeley Hotel in London, this was winner of an international cocktail competition in 1930.

¾ ounce Dupont Vieille Reserve Calvados
¾ ounce Gordon's London dry gin
¾ ounce fresh orange juice
¾ ounce Marie Brizard Apry liqueur
Dash of grenadine, homemade (page 224)
  or store-bought
Bordeaux cherry, for garnish

Shake the first four ingredients well with ice and strain into a chilled cocktail glass. Pour the grenadine through the drink to the bottom to create the "golden dawn." Garnish with the cherry.

GOLDEN GIRL*

1½ ounces Bacardí Reserva Ocho rum
½ ounce Simple Syrup (page 225)
1 ounce unsweetened pineapple juice
¾ ounce Offley Porto 10-year tawny port or
  Sandemen Rainwater Madeira
¾ ounce emulsified whole egg (see page 204)
Grated orange zest, for garnish

Shake all the ingredients (except the garnish) well with ice and strain into a chilled cocktail glass. Garnish by sprinkling orange zest over the top of the drink.

GREEN DESTINY+

Brad Farran, created the Green Destiny for the Clover Club bar, and it's a winner. He says, "My craft cocktail experience has always been one of learning; I love the sense of discovery. Sharing it with others is why we keep pushing ourselves, learning and creating. I love it."

1½ ounces Beefeater 24 gin
¾ ounce Dolin dry vermouth
¾ ounce fresh grapefruit juice
½ ounce fresh lime juice
½ ounce Simple Syrup (page 225)
1 shiso leaf, to shake with the ingredients
1 shiso leaf, for garnish

Shake all the ingredients (except the garnish) well with ice and fine strain into a chilled cocktail glass. Float the shiso leaf on top.

GREEN DRAGON*

I originally intended this and several cocktails for Augustine restaurant in New York City.

1½ ounces Finlandia vodka
¾ ounce Momokawa Junmai Ginjo sake
¼ ounce green Chartreuse
½ ounce fresh lime juice
¾ ounce mixed Agave and Honey Syrup
  (see Note)
Rosemary sprig, for garnish
Lime wheel, for garnish
C. F. Berger Absinthe Supérieure, for misting

Shake all ingredients (except the garnish and absinthe) in a cocktail shaker with ice cubes. Fine strain into an old-fashioned glass with ice. Pull the rosemary sprig through the center of the lime wheel for the garnish. Mist with absinthe.

NOTE For this recipe, mix 3 parts Agave Syrup (page 222) with 1 part Honey Syrup (page 224). I developed this syrup for use in place of Simple Syrup to give additional flavor in specific cocktails and lend them a warmer, more floral flavor.

GRASSHOPPER

1 ounce Marie Brizard No 32 crème de menthe
1 ounce Tempus Fugit crème de cacao
1½ ounces heavy cream
Shaved chocolate, for garnish

Shake the ingredients (except the garnish) well
with ice and strain into a Nick & Nora glass. Shave
chocolate over the top of the drink.

GREEN DREAM*

ABOUT 18 (1½-OUNCE) SHOTS

I tweaked a Colin Cowie shooter called the Strepe Chepe, adding ginger, sake, and agave nectar to a vodka mint shot. I worked many parties with Colin, and there was always a moment after midnight when everyone spent the rest of the night on the dance floor. The cool minty shooter that went down in one gulp was the perfect fuel to make all those dancing fools happy!

   6 ounces Blue Shark vodka
   1 handful fresh mint leaves
   4 ounces Agave Syrup (page 222)
   2 ounces Triple Syrup (page 225)
   2 ounces ginger syrup, homemade (page 224) or
      store-bought, preferably Monin brand
   2 ounces sake
   4 ounces fresh lemon or lime juice
   1 cup cracked ice

In a blender, combine all the ingredients. Blend at high speed until the drink is completely liquefied with no mint bits. Serve in shot glasses.

GREEN TEA PUNCH

SERVES 6

Tea is playing a much larger role as a cocktail ingredient in the new millennium, but what is old will sometimes be new again. I adapted this fascinating recipe from *The Gentleman's Table Guide* by Edward Ricket, published in 1873.

   9 ounces red currant or guava jelly
   16 ounces hot green tea (see Note)
   4 ounces Martel VSOP Cognac
   4 ounces Appleton Estate Reserve Blend
      Jamaica rum
   3 ounces Joseph Cartron Curaçao triple sec
   2 ounces fresh lemon juice
   6 verbena leaves, for garnish

In a heatproof mixing glass, dissolve the jelly in the hot tea. Stir in the rest of the ingredients (except the garnishes). Strain and serve piping hot in mugs. Garnish with the verbena leaves.

NOTE More tea may be added for a less alcoholic version.

GREYHOUND TOO*

   1½ ounces Absolut vodka
   4 ounces fresh grapefruit juice
   Dash of Bitter Truth grapefruit bitters
   Splash of St-Germain elderflower liqueur

Build the vodka and grapefruit juice in a highball glass over ice. Brighten it up with a dash of bitters and a splash of elderflower liqueur.

GROG, NAVY

This is definitely not your grandmothers' cure for the sniffles.

   1 ounce Pusser's rum
   1 ounce El Dorado 3-year-old rum
   1 ounce Lemon Hart Original 1804 rum
   1 ounce Honey Syrup (page 224)
   ¼ ounce Cinnamon Syrup (page 223)
   ¾ ounce fresh lime juice
   ¾ ounce fresh grapefruit juice
   Dash of Angostura bitters
   Dash of Dale DeGroff's Pimento Aromatic Bitters
   Lime wheel, for garnish
   Mint sprig, for garnish

Assemble all the ingredients (except the garnishes) in a cocktail shaker and shake well with ice. Strain into a bucket glass or double old-fashioned glass over ice. Garnish with the lime wheel and mint.

GROG, TRADITIONAL

Strictly speaking, grog is either a hot or a cold drink of rum, sugar, molasses or honey, lemon juice, and water in the proportions given below. In William Schmidt's *The Flowing Bowl: When and What to Drink*, he substitutes hot tea for water.

1½ ounces rum
1 ounce Honey Syrup (page 224)
¾ ounce fresh lemon juice
4 ounces hot or cold water
Cinnamon stick or lemon wedge, for garnish

For a hot drink, mix all ingredients (except the garnish) in a mug and stir. Garnish with a cinnamon stick.

To serve cold, shake the ingredients (except the garnish) with ice and serve over ice in a rocks glass. Garnish with a lemon wedge.

HANKY PANKY

This three-ingredient drink by Ada Coleman, legendary head bartender of the Savoy Hotel, looked a lot like a shorthand version of the Martinez Cocktail (page 164), and that gave me the idea that it might work with a malty genever.

1½ ounces Old Duff single malt genever or
    Bols oude genever
1½ ounces Martini & Rossi sweet vermouth
Splash of Fernet-Branca amaro

In a mixing glass, stir the ingredients well with ice to chill and strain into a chilled Nick & Nora glass.

HARRY'S HARVEY'S PUNCH*

This cocktail was named after Harry Dwoskin, who, well into his nineties, had an elaborate birthday party for himself each year at the Rainbow Room. Harry was fastidious with his money; he claimed he had enough to cover the party through his 104th birthday. He liked the punch so much that we served it at every birthday party until his last one at age ninety-six.

2 ounces Harveys Bristol Cream sherry
½ ounce Luxardo maraschino liqueur
½ ounce fresh lemon juice
3 ounces fresh orange juice
Dash of Angostura bitters
7UP, club soda, or both (optional)
Sprig of fresh mint, for garnish
Orange slice, for garnish

Shake the first five ingredients with ice and strain into a large goblet. Top with sweet soda, club soda, or a combination of both, if desired. Garnish with the mint and orange slice.

HARVEST MOON PUNCH*

SERVES 20

For a nonalcoholic version of the drink, simply omit the bourbon.

1 gallon fresh apple cider
6 whole star anise
6 cinnamon sticks, plus more for garnish
6 whole cloves
8 ounces Brown Sugar or Demerara Syrup
   (page 223)
Zest of 1 whole orange with very little
   white pith
1½ (750 ml) bottles Bulleit bourbon

Combine the apple cider, star anise, cinnamon sticks, cloves, syrup, and orange zest in a large stainless steel pot and let simmer over low heat for 30 to 40 minutes. **Do not boil.** Add the bourbon and simmer another couple minutes just to warm the whiskey. Strain to remove all the spices and serve.

NOTES For a party, you can serve the punch in a hollowed-out pumpkin: Prepare the pumpkin by cutting a lid as you would for a jack-o'-lantern. Clean the lid piece by cutting away the pumpkin strands and seeds; save all the seeds (see below). Using a long-handled spoon, clean the inside of the pumpkin, being careful to leave a thick pumpkin wall to insure there are no punctures in the skin on the sides or the bottom. When the pumpkin is clean, rinse the inside with cool water, checking for leaks in the skin. Fill the pumpkin with the warm punch and replace the lid to retain the heat. Using a ladle, serve it in ceramic mugs and garnish with cinnamon sticks.

Clean and roast the pumpkin seeds and bake them on a greased cookie sheet in a preheated 350°F oven for 8 to 10 minutes, until crisp and golden. Remove from the oven and season to taste with salt, ground cumin, and ground allspice and serve with the punch.

HARVEY WALLBANGER

This 1960s drink is purportedly named after a surfer who drank so much he'd bump into the walls. My all-knowing friend Brian Rea (former 21 Club head bartender) tells me that the reason the surfer drank so many Wallbangers was to get the empty Galliano bottles—women really loved them.

1½ ounces Blue Shark vodka
4 ounces fresh orange juice
¾ ounce Galliano

Pour the vodka and orange juice together in a highball glass over ice and float the Galliano on top.

HAWAIIAN STONE SOUR*

I created this variation on the whiskey stone sour as a poolside drink for a regular guest at the Rainbow Room's Promenade Bar.

1½ ounces Old Forester 1897 bourbon
¾ ounce Simple Syrup (page 225)
¾ ounce fresh lemon juice
1 ounce pineapple juice
1 Bordeaux cherry, for garnish
1 skinless pineapple wedge, for garnish
Dale DeGroff's Pimento Aromatic Bitters

Shake the first four ingredients very well with ice and strain into a rocks glass over ice cubes. Garnish with the cherry and pineapple wedge. Place a couple drops of bitters on the pineapple foam.

HEMINGWAY DAIQUIRI (PAPA DOBLE)

In about 1921, the cocktail muse inspired the great Constantino Ribalaigua Vert of the El Floridita in Havana when he added fresh grapefruit juice and maraschino liqueur to the daiquiri. The result is ambrosia. The drink was frozen in a blender and named Daiquiri #3, or informally Papa Doble, ("Papa's Double") after Ernest Hemingway. The original recipe didn't call for any sugar, just a touch of the maraschino liqueur, and it is always reprinted that way out of respect to "Papa." But you can be sure that for the average customer at El Floridita, the sugar or simple syrup was part of the recipe.

1½ ounces Havana Club 3-year-old rum (or if a trip to Cuba is not in the stars for the near future, use your favorite rum)
¼ ounce maraschino liqueur
½ ounce fresh grapefruit juice
¾ ounce Simple Syrup (page 225)
¾ ounce fresh lime juice

Shake all the ingredients with ice and strain into a chilled cocktail glass.

VARIATION For a frozen version, increase the Simple Syrup to 1½ ounces and the lime juice by ¼ ounce and blend with ¾ cup of cracked ice.

HI HO COCKTAIL

2 ounces Plymouth gin
1 ounce Warre's Fine White port
4 dashes of Bitter Truth orange bitters
3 frozen white Thompson seedless table grapes, for garnish

Shake all the ingredients (except the garnish) with ice and strain into a chilled cocktail glass. Garnish with the frozen grapes.

HONEYMOON COCKTAIL

This is from the Brown Derby, Hollywood, circa 1930. I bumped up the Laird's Apple Brandy and lightened up on the Bénédictine to appeal to a move toward drier style drinks.

1½ ounces Laird's Straight Apple brandy (bonded)
½ ounce Bénédictine
1 splash Pierre Ferrand dry curaçao
½ ounce fresh lemon juice
Lemon zest coin (see page 62), for garnish

Shake all the ingredients (except the garnish) well with ice and strain into a chilled Nick & Nora glass. Garnish with the lemon zest coin.

HONOLULU COCKTAIL

Made at the Brown Derby bar and restaurant, in Hollywood, circa 1930.

Cinnamon sugar, for the rim
2 ounces Nikka Coffey gin (lemony, fruity gin; it suits the cocktail to a tee)
½ ounce pineapple juice
½ ounce fresh orange juice
¼ ounce fresh lemon juice
½ ounce Simple Syrup (page 225)
Dash of Pegu Club orange bitters mix (see Note)
2 dashes of Dale DeGroff's Pimento Aromatic Bitters
Orange zest coin (see page 62), for garnish

Frost the rim of a cocktail glass with cinnamon sugar (see page 63). Chill until ready to use. Shake the remaining ingredients (except the garnish) with ice and strain into the prepared glass. Garnish with the orange zest coin.

NOTE I like to use Pegu Club's blend of 2 parts Regan's Orange Bitters No. 6 to 1 part Fee Brothers orange bitters.

HORSE'S NECK

This drink takes its name from the distinctive garnish that resembles a horse's head and neck peeking over the rim of the glass. This drink was originally a nonalcoholic offering, so just omit the whiskey if you prefer. I find it to be a satisfying highball with your favorite American whiskey. Rum-cask-finished Angel's Envy rye makes this a very special whiskey highball.

Lemon peel spiral (see page 62), for garnish
1½ ounces Angel's Envy rum-finished
  rye whiskey
5 ounces Fever-Tree ginger ale
Dash of Dale DeGroff's Pimento Aromatic Bitters

Place the lemon peel spiral in a highball or collins glass, spiraling up from the bottom, with the curled end of the spiral hanging over the rim of the glass; this should resemble a stylized horse's neck and head. Put ice cubes down through the center of the spiral and then build the drink.

HOT BUTTERED RUM

Have fun and experiment with the variations of this recipe. Try using spiced rums or sweetening it with maple syrup or brown sugar.

- 1 ounce dark or spiced rum
- 1 ounce light rum
- 1 teaspoon Compound Butter (recipe follows)
- 1 ounce Brown Sugar or Demerara Syrup (page 223)
- 4 ounces hot water or cider
- Cinnamon stick, for garnish

Mix all the ingredients (except the garnish) in a heatproof goblet and stir a few times to melt the butter. Garnish with the cinnamon stick.

COMPOUND BUTTER

Add 1 pound softened butter to a stainless steel mixing bowl and mix in 1 teaspoon each of ground cinnamon, ground nutmeg, and ground allspice, and ½ teaspoon ground cloves. Add ¼ cup dark brown sugar and mix well. Line a cookie sheet with wax paper and spoon heaping teaspoons of the compound butter on the wax paper. Cover and store them in the refrigerator, removing 30 minutes before use.

IBÉRICO & BOURBON+

This is a Manhattan variation by Will Van Leuven for Herb & Wood restaurant in San Diego, and it is special. The fat-washing part is surprisingly easy.

- 2 ounces Ibérico Fat-Washed Bourbon (page 224)
- ¾ ounce Amaro Montenegro
- 2 dashes of R&D Bitters Aromatic #7 bitters (see Note)
- Flamed orange zest coin (see page 62), for garnish

Stir all the ingredients (except the garnish) with ice and strain into a chilled coupe glass. Express the oil of the flamed orange zest coin over the top and then drop it in.

NOTE These are available at Keg N Bottle (kegnbottle.com). In a pinch you can use Angostura bitters.

ICE HOUSE HIGHBALL

If edible flowers are not available, garnish this drink with fresh mint and lemon slices. I did a series of summer drinks for Absolut vodka and garnished them with edible flowers. This is one example. For information on edible flowers, see Lucinda Hutson's book *The Herb Garden Cookbook* (1998) for ideas, or google "edible flowers."

- 2 ounces Absolut Citron vodka
- 5 ounces fresh lemonade
- 2 dashes of Marie Brizard No 33 white crème de menthe
- Edible orchid or other edible flower, for garnish

Build the vodka and lemonade in a large pint glass filled with ice and top with the crème de menthe. Garnish with an edible orchid.

INTERNATIONAL STINGER

- 2 ounces Metaxa 7-star brandy
- ¾ ounce Galliano

Shake well with ice and strain over crushed ice in an old-fashioned glass.

IRISH BLOND*

- 2 ounces The Dead Rabbit Irish whiskey
- ¾ ounce Marie Brizard orange curaçao
- ¼ ounce Tio Pepe fino sherry
- Dash of Bitter Truth orange bitters
- Flamed orange zest coin (see page 62), for garnish

Stir all the ingredients (except the garnish) in a mixing glass with ice and then strain into a chilled Nick & Nora glass. Garnish with the flamed orange zest coin.

HURRICANE

This was made famous by Pat O'Brien's in New Orleans, but was it original to Pat O'Brien's? The Museum of the American Cocktail in New Orleans heard from the grandchildren of Andrew Kucharski, a Chicago resident.

In the 1930s, Mr. Kucharski opened the Webb Lake Hotel on Big Bear Lake in the northern woods of Wisconsin. Andrew's daughter Babe ran the hotel's Hurricane Bar, and she created a drink called the Hurricane. The Kucharski family has staked a claim on the Pat O'Brien's Hurricane recipe as their own. Their claim is that Pat O'Brien came to the resort in the 1930s and took their recipe to New Orleans.

1 ounce Myers's dark rum
1 ounce Angostura White Oak rum
½ ounce Galliano
¾ ounce fresh lime juice
1½ ounces sweetened passion fruit purée
1½ ounces fresh orange juice
1½ ounces pineapple juice
Dash of Angostura bitters
Pineapple leaf, for garnish
Orange slice, for garnish
Pineapple wedge, for garnish
Lime wheel, for garnish
Simple Syrup (page 225; optional)

Shake all the ingredients (except the garnishes and simple syrup) with ice and strain into a hurricane glass filled with cracked ice. Garnish with the fruits and pineapple leaf. Adjust the sweetness, if needed, with simple syrup.

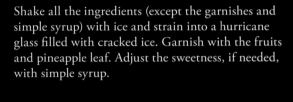

IRISH COFFEE

Joe Sheridan, a chef at the Old Ground Hotel Ennis, not far from Foynes Flying Boat & Maritime Musem (near Shannon International Airport) in Ireland, originally prepared this drink. Sheridan had a habit of greeting weary travelers sneaking into war-torn Europe on seaplanes from the United States with hot coffee laced with Irish whiskey and topped with lightly whipped Irish cream. Here are some hints to make Irish Coffee as good as Joe's:

- *Never use canned cream in an Irish Coffee. Hand-whip cream with a piano whip in a stainless steel bowl or pitcher that has been chilled in the fridge until it is very cold. Start with very cold heavy cream and whip or whisk it to just under stiff; the cream should have no bubbles, but it will pour slowly and float nicely on top. No sugar in the cream—the coffee is sweetened, not the cream.*
- *Sweeten the coffee with Brown Sugar or Demerara Syrup (page 223).*
- *Don't drown the drink in coffee—about 4 ounces is all you need.*
- *Find the classic stemmed Irish-coffee glasses; because of their size, they will force you to use the right amount of coffee.*

1½ ounces Irish whiskey
4 ounces hot coffee
1 ounce warm Brown Sugar or Demerara Syrup (page 223, see Note)
Unsweetened Hand-Whipped Irish-Coffee Cream (page 225)

Combine the whiskey, coffee, and syrup in a preheated Irish-coffee glass. Gently ladle 1 inch of the hand-whipped cream on top.

NOTE: Keep the syrup warm on the stove and heat the glasses with hot water before assembling the drink.

IRISH COFFEE VARIATIONS
Café Amore: amaretto and brandy
Calypso Coffee: rum and Kahlúa
Jamaican Coffee: rum and Tia Maria
Mexican Coffee: tequila and Kahlúa
Spanish Coffee: Spanish brandy and Kahlúa
Royale: Cognac and sugar
Kioke Coffee: California brandy and Kahlúa

JACK ROSE

Albert Stevens Crockett, author of *Old Waldorf Bar Days* (1931), loved to set the world straight on cocktail names. He assures us that the Jack Rose was not named after a murdered gangster, but was, in fact, inspired by a pink rose called the Jacquemot rose. If you look deep enough, the Jack Rose story gets really murky. I suggest you make yourself one before you embark on your research.

1½ ounces Laird's Straight Apple brandy (bonded)
¼ ounce fresh lime juice
¾ ounce fresh lemon juice
½ ounce Simple Syrup (page 225)
½ ounce Stirrings Authentic Grenadine or homemade (page 224)
Apple slice, for garnish
Bordeaux cherry, for garnish

Shake all the ingredients (except the garnish) with ice and strain into a cocktail glass. Garnish with the apple slice and cherry.

JAPANESE COCKTAIL

The Japanese Cocktail was one of the very few cocktails listed in Jerry Thomas's 1862 edition of *How to Mix Drinks, or The Bon-Vivant's Companion*. He called for stirring the drink with a couple of peels of lemon in the bar glass.

2 ounces Martel VSOP Cognac
½ ounce orgeat
3 dashes of Bitter Truth Bogart's Bitters
Lemon zest coin (see page 62), for garnish

Assemble the ingredients (except the garnish) in an old-fashioned glass with ice and stir well. Express the oil of the lemon zest coin over the drink and drop it in.

NOTE Always use tender, young sprigs of mint for juleps. They last longer and look better in the glass. Spearmint has small leaves with good structure that don't wilt quickly. Pick about three inches off the top of the mint stalk and use the bottom leaves for bruising, saving the well-formed sprigs on top for the garnish.

JULEPS

The juleps were the first American drinks to attract international attention. Everyone thinks bourbon when they think julep, but actually the first juleps were made with Cognac and peach brandy. They garnered quite a bit of attention internationally, especially in England, but it was the hot American summers that made them so desirable: served icy cold, filled with shaved ice, and crusted with ice on the outside.

DALE'S PEACH JULEP*

4 or 5 mint leaves
2 sweet Georgia peach slices
½ ounce Marie Brizard No 11 peach liqueur
2 ounces Rieger's Kansas City whiskey
2 tender fresh mint sprigs, for garnish

In the bottom of a julep cup or serving glass, muddle the mint leaves and 1 of the peach slices with the peach liqueur. Add the whiskey and fill with crushed ice. Swirl with a barspoon until the outside of the cup frosts. Top up with crushed ice. Garnish generously with the mint sprigs and the remaining peach slice.

MINT JULEP

4 or 5 mint leaves
½ ounce Simple Syrup (page 225)
2 ounces Wild Turkey 101 bourbon
2 tender fresh mint sprigs, for garnish

In the bottom of a julep cup or serving glass, muddle the mint leaves with the simple syrup. Fill the cup with crushed ice and add the bourbon. Swirl with a barspoon until the outside of the cup frosts. Top up with more ice and garnish with the mint sprigs.

PRESCRIPTION JULEP

4 or 5 mint leaves
¾ ounce Simple Syrup (page 225)
2 ounces Martel VSOP Cognac
Splash of Smith & Cross Jamaica rum
2 tender fresh mint sprigs, for garnish

In the bottom of a julep cup or serving glass, add the mint leaves and simple syrup and gently bruise the mint leaves. Add the Cognac and fill with crushed ice. Swirl the drink with a barspoon until the outside of the cup frosts. Top up the ice and splash the rum on top. Garnish generously with mint sprigs.

KANSAS CITY MANHATTAN⁺

This original recipe is from Steve Olson of Del Maguey mezcal. Steve is an expert on agave spirits and a partner with myself and four others in Beverage Alcohol Resource, a company dedicated to bartender education.

2½ ounces Rieger's Kansas City whiskey
½ ounce Pedro Ximénez Sherry
½ ounce Cocchi Barolo Chinato
2 dashes of Dale DeGroff's Pimento Aromatic Bitters
Orange zest coin (see page 62)
Luxardo maraschino cherry, for garnish

Stir all the ingredients (except the orange zest and garnish) with ice and strain into a chilled glass. Express the orange zest coin over the drink and discard. Garnish with the cherry.

KARAKUCHI 50/50⁺

This was created by Masahiro Urushido at Katana Kitten in New York City.

1½ ounces iichiko Saiten shochu (Japanese 100 percent barley shochu)
1¼ ounces Noilly Prat extra dry vermouth
¼ ounce amazake (nonalcoholic rice beverage)
3 dashes of Scrappy's Bitters grapefruit bitters
Grapefruit zest coin (see page 62), for garnish

Combine all the ingredients (except the garnish) in a mixing glass. Stir with ice and strain into a frozen Nick & Nora glass. Express the grapefruit zest coin over the drink and drop it in.

KEMPINSKY FIZZ

I found this drink in John J. Poister's 1989 *The New American Bartender's Guide*. I must assume it was submitted by the Kempinsky luxury hotel group. My version is a bit more lavish with Polish luxury vodka and Champagne in place of the club soda.

1½ ounces Belvedere Lake Bartezek single estate rye vodka
½ ounce Merlet crème de cassis
½ ounce lemon juice
3 ounces Champagne
Lemon zest
Bordeaux cherry, for garnish

Build the first three ingredients in a highball glass with two-thirds ice and stir. Add the Champagne and stir again gently. Express the lemon zest over the drink and discard. Garnish with the Bordeaux cherry.

KENTUCKY CHRISTMAS⁺

The original recipe for this drink comes from Cody Goodwin of Single Shot and Tom Douglas restaurants in Seattle, Washington. The vermouth is produced in Italy by world-renowned bartender Giancarlo Mancino.

2½ ounces Woodford Reserve bourbon
1 ounce Mancino Vermouth Chinato (see Note)
¼ ounce Luxardo marschino liqueur
2 dashes of Dale DeGroff's Pimento Aromatic Bitters
Bordeaux cherry, for garnish

In a mixing glass, stir all the ingredients (except the garnish) with ice and strain into a chilled cocktail glass. Garnish with the cherry.

NOTE If the Mancino Vermouth Chinato is hard to source, try using Cocchi Barolo Chinato instead.

KENTUCKY COLONEL

This was the house drink for years at the Hotel Bel-Air, in Stone Canyon. Jim Beam bourbon produced a special Hotel-Bel-Air-labeled bottle for the hotel to use as their house bourbon. I tended bar at the Hotel Bel-Air for five years and I wanted to pay tribute to that collaboration with another special Beam bourbon.

2½ ounces Jim Beam Black extra-aged bourbon
½ ounce Bénédictine
Dash of Angostura bitters
Dash of Peychaud's Bitters

Assemble all the ingredients in an old-fashioned glass over ice cubes and stir.

KIR

Dijon is the official home of the black-currant liqueur cassis, and the Kir was a drink named to honor Canon Félix Kir, a catholic priest in Dijon who was active in the French Resistance during World War II and elected mayor in 1945. Some believe that the local drink *blanc-cassis* was renamed in honor of Kir because he created the drink in response to the German theft of all the good red wines of the region by mixing the liqueur made with black currants with white wine.

¼ to ½ ounce cassis
5 ounces white wine (I suggest French Chardonnay)
Lemon zest coin (see page 62), for garnish (optional)

Pour the cassis into a white-wine glass and add the white wine. Garnish with the lemon zest coin, if desired.

KIR ROYALE

½ ounce cassis
4 ounces Champagne
Lemon zest coin (see page 62), for garnish (optional, as it's not usually welcomed by our French brothers and sisters)

Pour the liqueur into the bottom of a wineglass or champagne flute and fill with the Champagne. Garnish with the lemon zest coin, if using.

VARIATION To make a Kir Impérial, substitute ½ ounce framboise (raspberry) liqueur for the cassis.

KNICKERBOCKER

Adapted from Jerry Thomas's *How to Mix Drinks* (1862), this can also be served over crushed ice with berries as a garnish.

2 ounces Appleton Estate Reserve Blend Jamaica rum
½ ounce Joseph Cartron Curaçao Orange
½ ounce Monin raspberry syrup
¾ ounce fresh lemon juice
Thin lemon wheel, for garnish

Shake all the ingredients (except the garnish) with ice. Strain into a chilled cocktail glass. Garnish with the lemon wheel.

VARIATION In raspberry season, omit the raspberry syrup and muddle 6 to 8 fresh raspberries with the lemon juice, ½ ounce Simple Syrup, and the curaçao in the bottom of a Boston shaker glass. Add the remaining ingredients and shake well with ice. Fine strain into a chilled cocktail glass. Float the lemon wheel on the surface of the drink.

LA VIDA BUENA⁺

Steve Olson has a passion for all things agave, augmented by a deep well of knowledge. Del Maguey mezcal's founder Ron Cooper embraced that expertise, and together with Ron's other associates, they have nurtured a company that brought not just the liquid in the bottle but the lives of the makers and their families to the public.

1½ ounces Del Maguey Vida de San Luis del Rio mezcal
¾ ounce Carpano Antica Formula sweet vermouth
¾ ounce Aperol
3 dashes of Regan's Orange Bitters No. 6
Orange zest coin (see page 62), for garnish

Assemble all the ingredients (except the garnish) in a tall mixing glass with ice and stir thoroughly to chill. Strain into a double old-fashioned glass over 1 large 2 x 2-inch ice cube. Garnish with the orange zest coin.

LAST WORD

I combed through *Bottoms Up* by Ted Saucier when I was preparing the first cocktail menu for the Rainbow Room. But I passed over this drink with the appealing name. It was 1987 and I didn't think I could get away with too many gin-based drinks; I had eight gin concoctions out of the twenty-four drinks on that first menu. Today Last Word is back, and gin drinks are like wildflowers in the spring. The Detroit Athletic Club served it first, and they credit a vaudevillian named Frank Fogarty with introducing them to the drink.

¾ ounce Fords gin
¾ ounce Luxardo maraschino liqueur
¾ ounce green Chartreuse
¾ ounce fresh lime juice

Shake all the ingredients with ice and strain into a chilled Nick & Nora glass.

LATIN LOVE+

Just surrender to this drink—but only drink one if you want to keep that hard body that attracts your Latin love. This drink by Aldo Zegarelli won the first annual Most Sensual Cocktail contest sponsored by *Penthouse* magazine.

Grenadine, homemade (page 224) or
    store-bought, for frosting the glass
Shredded coconut, for frosting the glass
1 ounce Cruzan Coconut rum
1 ounce Cruzan Banana rum
3 ounces pineapple juice
1 ounce Coco López Cream of Coconut
1 ounce raspberry syrup
1 ounce heavy cream

Wet a hurricane glass with grenadine and dip it in shredded coconut (see page 63). Set aside.

Combine all the remaining ingredients in a blender and add a scoop of ice. Blend to a smooth consistency. Pour the mixture into the hurricane glass.

LE PERROQUET

Splash of Campari
Splash of Fords gin
1½ ounces fresh orange juice
4 ounces chilled Champagne
Orange zest coin (see page 62), for garnish

Pour the Campari, gin, and orange juice into a champagne flute. Top with the Champagne and garnish with the orange zest coin.

LEMON DROP COCKTAIL

Sugar, for frosting the glass
2 ounces Absolut Citron vodka
¾ ounce fresh lemon juice
1 ounce Cointreau
Lemon wheel, for garnish

Frost the rim of a cocktail glass with sugar (see page 63). Refrigerate until ready to serve.

Shake all the remaining ingredients (except the garnish) well with ice and strain into the chilled cocktail glass. Float the lemon on top of the drink.

VARIATION To serve as an appealing shot: Use the recipe above and strain into three 1½-ounce shot glasses. Cover the mouth of each shot glass with a lemon wheel that has been dusted with sugar.

LEMON MERINGUE

If you want to get fancy, make a frosting for the rim of the glass out of crushed graham crackers (see page 63 for instructions).

2 ounces Absolut Citron vodka
¾ ounce limoncello (Italian lemon liqueur)
½ ounce white crème de cacao
¾ ounce emulsified egg white (see page 204)

Shake all the ingredients well with ice to fully emulsify the egg and strain into a large coupe glass.

THE PERFECT GENTLEMAN

One day at the Hotel Bel-Air, an elderly couple came in and sat at a corner table for lunch. They were alone in the lounge, seated at the one table that was out of view of the bar. In the middle of the lounge was a Steinway baby grand piano, The lock that secures the fallboard over the keys was broken, and Bud Herrmann, the long-time personality at the piano, asked me to keep an eye out to make sure that nobody played it while the lock was broken. Right after lunch, this slightly built, elderly man began to motor toward the piano, but by the time I noticed, he was seated and raising the fallboard. Just before his fingers hit the keys, I got to the piano and said, "Excuse me, sir. I'm sorry, but the regular piano player, Bud Herrmann, would prefer that people not play piano during the day when he's not here."

The gentleman was very understanding and went back to his table. He paid his check with a credit card, and as I was processing it, I noticed his name: Vladimir Horowitz. I called the desk, hoping against hope that this was a different Vladimir Horowitz. But this was the Hotel Bel-Air, and Mr. Horowitz was in town for a concert. I apologized and tried to rescind my edict. Mr. Horowitz was immovable, however, commenting that he actually had his own instrument shipped to wherever he was appearing. He was a perfect gentleman, bowing to Bud's wish not touch the piano, and I was devastated.

LIME IN DE COCONUT*

1 ounce Absolut Lime vodka
1 ounce Absolut vodka
1 ounce Ginger Syrup, homemade (page 224)
    or store-bought, preferably Monin
1 ounce fresh lime juice
2 ounces coconut water
½ ounce Coco López Cream of Coconut
Thin lime wheel, for garnish
Long slice of unpeeled English cucumber,
    for garnish

Shake all the ingredients (except the garnishes) with ice. Strain into a highball glass over ice cubes. Garnish with the lime wheel and cucumber slice.

LION OF BALTIMORE+

This was invented by author Phil Greene on the shores of Bodkin Creek, Maryland, after a day of sailing with his dad on Chesapeake Bay in the summer of 2013. The *Lion of Baltimore* was a vessel built by the United States to wreak havoc on British shipping during the War of 1812. The *Lion* was kept hidden on Bodkin Creek, where Phil and his dad moor their sloop.

2 ounces Appleton Estate Reserve Blend
    Jamaica rum
1 ounce Martini & Rossi sweet vermouth
¾ ounce fresh lime juice
¼ ounce orgeat
2 dashes of Dale DeGroff's Pimento Aromatic
    Bitters

Shake all the ingredients well with ice and strain into a chilled cocktail glass.

LITTLE GEM

"When I first started writing about drinks, back at the very end of 1999, I shook *everything*. Margarita? Shake it. Mai tai? Shake it. Martini? Shake it. Manhattan, Negroni, Presidente? Shake 'em—shake 'em all. In part, that was what I saw everyone doing, at least at the sorts of bars I was used to—rock-and-roll joints and dives, for the most part. Sure, there was the occasional geezer holding down the bar at a place like Musso & Frank's in Hollywood or the Bemelmans Bar in New York who would waltz the ice around with a spoon when I asked him for a dry Tanqueray Martini, but they were rare, and when I tried it at home, it came out as a slam dance, not a waltz.

"But then I met Dale, and he showed me how to properly stir a cocktail. It still took me a couple of years to get it down to the point where my stir wasn't embarrassing. It was worth the effort: to this day, the ability to stir a cocktail more or less properly is a skill that makes me ridiculously happy, considering how picayune it seems. But it is the essence of craft bartending: something fundamentally simple that nonetheless requires knowledge and experience to get it just right and results in a drink that is incrementally changed but transcendently better; that is alive in the glass.

"The Little Gem is a slightly odd but I think very tasty drink laid out on classic lines. It's a little sweet, but when stirred right, it's also velvety and delightful."
—David Wondrich, author

THE LITTLE GEM⁺

If made properly, this drink should have the crisp green color of Little Gem lettuce. If it doesn't, adjust the curaçao accordingly for the next round.

1 ounce blanco tequila (I suggest Siete Leguas)
1 ounce Carpano Bianco vermouth

¾ ounce Plantation Stiggins' Fancy Pineapple rum
¼ ounce Marie Brizard blue curaçao
2 dashes of Regan's Orange Bitters No. 6
Lemon peel

Assemble all the ingredients (except the lemon) in a mixing glass and stir *well* with cracked ice. Strain into chilled cocktail glass, twist the lemon peel over the top, and discard.

LITTLE ITALY⁺

"Dale, Rob Oppenheimer (general manager of Pegu Club), and I were sitting at the bar at Raoul's one night having steak frites for dinner, and we were drinking Manhattans. We were also talking about Cynar, and Dale mentioned that he really liked it. Since we were sipping on Manhattans, I wondered how it would taste with Cynar, and the Little Italy is the end result." —Audrey Saunders

2 ounces Rittenhouse 100-proof straight rye whisky
½ ounce Cynar
¾ ounce Martini & Rossi sweet vermouth
2 Luxardo maraschino cherries, skewered on a pick, for garnish

In a mixing glass, stir the whisky, Cynar, and vermouth well with ice. Strain into a chilled Nick & Nora glass. Garnish with the skewered cherries.

LOS ANGELES COCKTAIL

From the Hi Ho Club, Hollywood, circa 1930.

2 ounces Jim Beam Black extra-aged bourbon
½ ounce Martini & Rossi sweet vermouth
1 ounce Simple Syrup (page 225)
1 medium emulsified whole egg (see page 204)
¾ ounce fresh lemon juice
Freshly grated nutmeg, for garnish

Combine all the ingredients (except the garnish) in a shaker with ice and shake very well to emulsify the egg. Strain into a chilled port glass. Dust with the nutmeg.

LONG ISLAND ICED TEA

Credit for this incredibly successful frat-house drink is attributed to Robert C. Butt. When made properly, the drink tastes great and doesn't have to be an evening-ender. The key is to have all the spirits present but in small amounts. In the recipe here, the total alcohol content is 2½ ounces. It is a well-balanced, good-tasting drink, in large part because of the fresh lemon juice and simple syrup. Besides the Long Island version, there are a few other regional variations.

LONDON ICED TEA

¾ ounce Fords gin
¾ ounce Myers's Platinum white rum
½ ounce Disaronno Originale
  amaretto
½ ounce Simple Syrup (page 225)
¾ ounce fresh lemon juice
3 to 4 ounces Coca-Cola (see Note)
Lemon wedge, for garnish

Shake all the ingredients (except the Coca-Cola and lemon wedge) with ice and strain into an iced tea or collins glass filled three-quarters full with ice. Top with the Coca-Cola and stir. Garnish with the lemon wedge.

NOTE: Get the Coca-Cola in the little green bottles, which is sweetened with cane sugar and stevia, not corn syrup.

LONG ISLAND ICED TEA

½ ounce Blue Shark vodka
½ ounce Fords gin
½ ounce Bacardí Superior rum
½ ounce Jose Cuervo Especial gold
  tequila
½ ounce Marie Brizard triple sec
¾ ounce fresh lemon juice
½ ounce Simple Syrup (page 225)
3 to 4 ounces Coca-Cola (see Note)
Lemon wedge, for garnish

Shake all the ingredients (except the Coca-Cola and garnish) with ice and strain into an iced-tea or collins glass filled three-quarters full with ice. Top with the Coca-Cola and stir. Garnish with the lemon wedge.

LYNCHBURG LEMONADE

Here's my version of this whiskey lemonade drink.

2 ounces Jack Daniel's whiskey
¾ ounce Joseph Cartron Curaçao Orange
¾ ounce fresh lemon juice
1½ ounces 7UP
1½ ounces club soda
Lemon wedge, for garnish

Shake the first three ingredients with ice and strain into an ice-filled highball glass. Top with the 7UP and the club soda. Garnish with the lemon wedge.

MADISON AVENUE COCKTAIL

Created by Eddie Woelke at the Weylin Hotel bar in the years before Prohibition. After Prohibition, Woelke ended up at the Sevilla Hotel in Havana, Cuba, which is where he created a Cuban classic cocktail, the El Presidente.

1½ ounces Bacardí Superior rum
¾ ounce Cointreau
½ ounce fresh lime juice
Dash of Bitter Truth orange bitters
3 mint leaves
Fresh mint sprig, for garnish
Thin lime wheel, for garnish

Shake all the ingredients (except the garnishes) with ice and fine strain into a rocks glass filled with ice. Garnish with the mint sprig and lime slice.

MAHOGANY HALL GIMLET*

I made this one for the Gallery Bars aboard Holland America Line.

1½ ounces Beefeater gin
½ ounce fresh lime juice
½ ounce fresh grapefruit juice
½ ounce Triple Syrup (page 225)
2 dashes of Dale DeGroff's Pimento Aromatic Bitters
Thin lime wheel, for garnish

Shake all the ingredients (except the garnish) well with ice. Fine strain into a chilled cocktail glass and garnish with the lime wheel.

MAI TAI

2 ounces Appleton Estate Signature Blend Jamaica rum
¾ ounce Joseph Cartron Curaçao Orange
¾ ounce fresh lime juice
½ ounce orgeat
¾ ounce Lemon Hart 151 overproof rum
2 fresh mint sprigs, for garnish

Shake the ingredients (except the garnish) well with ice and strain into a mai tai or double old-fashioned glass filled with ice. Garnish with the mint sprigs.

NAMING THE MAI TAI

The Mai Tai was created in 1944 by Victor Bergeron at his famed bar, Trader Vic's, in Emeryville, California, to take advantage of some good sixteen-year-old Jamaican rum he had around. Victor often said it was one of the finest drinks he'd ever concocted. When he made the drink the first time, he served it to his friends from Tahiti, Ham and Carrie Guild. After tasting the drink, Carrie raised her glass and said, *"Mai tai roa ae,"* which means "out of this world" or "the best" in Tahitian. "That's the name of the drink," replied Bergeron.

MALIBU BAY BREEZE

1½ ounces Malibu rum
3 ounces pineapple juice
2 ounces cranberry juice
Lime wedge, for garnish

Build in a highball glass over ice and garnish with the lime wedge.

THE MANHATTAN

The Manhattan is the quintessential rye cocktail—except in Minnesota and Wisconsin, where they prefer brandy Manhattans. The craft community has embraced rye Manhattans again, and that is where my story begins. I produce an allspice-based aromatic bitters with my partner Ted Breaux, an absinthe maker of the first order. I wanted to promote our bitters in the Manhattan, but I didn't want to be too heavy-handed about it so I put together a Manhattan tasting with five different aromatic bitters and included mine. Try the tasting with friends and turn your cocktail hour into a Manhattan party.

CLASSIC MANHATTAN

2 ounces Rittenhouse 100-Proof straight rye whisky
1 ounce Italian sweet vermouth
2 dashes of Angostura bitters
Bordeaux cherry, for garnish

Stir all the ingredients (except the garnish) with ice in a mixing glass. Strain into a chilled cocktail glass. Garnish with the cherry.

A MANHATTAN PARTY

Make a batch of Manhattans without bitters, following the recipe below. Try the Manhattan with the four bitters listed below; the results are dramatic, ranging from a sweet Manhattan to the driest by simply changing the dash of bitters.

2 parts Bulleit rye whiskey
¾ part Dolin or Martini & Rossi sweet vermouth
½ part Dolin or Noilly Prat dry vermouth

Combine all the ingredients in a pitcher. Stir your batched Manhattan with ice to properly dilute for the tasting and then strain off the ice. Serve half portions (1½ ounces) for the tasting with the four bitters. Serve the half portions without ice and without garnish.

VARIATIONS For a dry Manhattan, use dry vermouth and garnish with a lemon peel. A Manhattan made with brandy is called a Harvard, and one made with applejack is called a Star Cocktail.

THE BITTERS FOR THE TASTING: Angostura aromatic bitters, Bitter Truth Bogart's Bitters, Dale DeGroff's Pimento Aromatic Bitters, and Fee Brothers Whiskey Barrel-Aged Bitters.

APPLE MANHATTAN+

This delicious combination comes from master bartender David Marsden when he worked in a classy little spot called First on First in New York City in the 1990s. The Berentzen apple liqueur is the key, so no substitutes.

2 ounces Maker's Mark bourbon
1 ounce Berentzen apple liqueur
Dash of Dale DeGroff's Pimento Aromatic Bitters
Thin slice of Granny Smith apple,
   for garnish

Stir the bourbon, liqueur, and bitters in a mixing glass with ice and strain into a chilled cocktail glass. Garnish with the apple slice.

EASTERN MANHATTAN*

I created this for the Inagiku Japanese restaurant in the Waldorf Astoria. Today the Waldorf is owned by the Chinese, and that Japanese restaurant is just a memory. The irony of the story: My son did cocktails for the Chinese restaurant that opened on the other side of the lobby, with shochu and baijiu drinks. The Waldorf is currently closed for a major renovation. The Chinese needed to upgrade all the tech capabilities for their guests (wink, wink).

3 dashes (½ teaspoon) of daiginjo sake
2½ ounces Suntory Toki blended whisky
½ ounce Martini & Rossi sweet vermouth
½ ounce Noilly Prat dry vermouth
Orange zest coin (see page 62),
   for garnish

Fill a cocktail glass with crushed ice, then discard the ice. Dash the sake into the glass, swirl, then toss out. Assemble the remaining ingredients (except the garnish) in a cocktail mixing glass with ice and stir to chill. Strain into the prepared cocktail glass. Garnish with the orange zest coin.

RED MANHATTAN*

Of course this is not a proper Manhattan. First of all, the base is vodka. I'm just having a bit of fun with "Phil Ward's potato head" system of substitution to create cocktail variations, in this case for the whiskey and the vermouth.

2½ ounces Absolut Kurant vodka
¾ ounce St Raphaël Rouge
2 dashes of Bitter Truth orange bitters
Orange zest coin (see page 62),
   for garnish

Stir the vodka, St Raphaël, and bitters in a mixing glass with ice to chill and then strain it into a chilled cocktail glass. Express the orange oil over the drink and drop the orange zest coin into the drink.

REVERSE MANHATTAN

I came up with this "perfect" reverse Manhattan for a fundraiser for the Jacques Pépin Foundation; it was Jacques's special request. In fact, it has real historical roots. The recipe appears in O. H. Byron's *Modern Bartenders' Guide* (1884) under Manhattan, where a two-to-one vermouth-to-whiskey recipe is the first of two Manhattans listed.

1 ounce Dolin sweet vermouth
1 ounce Dolin dry vermouth
1 ounce Bulleit bourbon
Dash of Dale DeGroff's Pimento Aromatic Bitters
Orange zest coin (see page 62),
   for garnish
Bordeaux cherry, for garnish

Stir the vermouths, bourbon, and bitters in a mixing glass with ice to chill and strain into a chilled cocktail glass. Garnish with the orange zest coin and cherry.

2 ounces Pusser's Gunpowder Proof British Navy rum
½ ounce Heering cherry liqueur
¼ ounce Rainwater Madeira (I suggest Broadbent, but there are lots of good ones out there)
¼ ounce Bittermens Hiver Amer cinnamon liqueur, or 4 dashes of Fee Brothers Whiskey Barrel-Aged Bitters
2 dashes of Dale DeGroff's Pimento Aromatic Bitters
2 lemon peels

Stir all the ingredients (except the lemon peels) with ice and strain into a chilled cocktail glass. Express the oil of 1 of the lemon peels over the top of the drink and discard, then garnish with the other lemon peel.

MARAGATO

This was an early recipe from the famous El Floridita bar in Havana, Cuba.

1 ounce Havana Club 3-year-old rum
½ ounce sweet vermouth
½ ounce dry vermouth
¾ ounce fresh orange juice
½ ounce fresh lime juice
Dash of Luxardo maraschino liqueur
Flamed orange zest coin (see page 62), for garnish

Shake all the ingredients (except the garnish) well with ice and strain into a chilled cocktail glass. Garnish with the flamed orange zest coin (this is my touch).

MARITIMER COCKTAIL+

Jon Smolensky is a first-class bartender from Vancouver who started his own distribution business for all his favorite cocktail ingredients. Some are long-tail market spirits for cocktail geeks only—for the present. But geeky ingredients may have a future as the market comes to them; my bitters is part of his portfolio in Canada.

MARK TWAIN COCKTAIL

As described to his wife in a letter from London, 1874.

1½ ounces scotch whisky
¾ ounce fresh lemon juice
¾ ounce Simple Syrup (page 225)
2 dashes of Angostura bitters

Shake all the ingredients with ice and strain into a chilled cocktail glass.

THE MARY PICKFORD

Created at the Hotel Nacional de Cuba during Prohibition to celebrate their famous guest Mary Pickford, actress and cofounder of United Artists, with her second husband, Douglas Fairbanks.

2 ounces white rum
1½ ounces pineapple juice
Splash grenadine, homemade (page 224) or store-bought
¼ ounce Luxardo maraschino liqueur
Bordeaux cherry, for garnish

Shake all the ingredients (except the garnish) with ice and strain into a chilled Nick & Nora glass. Garnish with the cherry.

MARGARITA

Lime wedge, for frosting the glass
Coarse salt, for frosting the glass
1½ ounces El Tesoro blanco tequila
1 ounce Cointreau
¾ ounce fresh lime juice
Splash of Agave Syrup (page 222; see Note;
   optional)

Frost half the rim of an old-fashioned or
cocktail glass with the lime and
salt (see page 63). Chill
the cocktail glass,
if using.

Shake all the remaining ingredients
well with ice. Serve over ice
in the old-fashioned or
"up" in the chilled
cocktail glass.

CADILLAC MARGARITA

Lime wedge, for frosting the glass
Coarse salt, for frosting the glass
1½ ounces El Tesoro añejo tequila
1 ounce Grand Marnier
¾ ounce fresh lime juice

Frost half the rim of an old-fashioned or a cocktail glass with the lime and salt (see page 63). Chill the cocktail glass, if using.

Shake the remaining ingredients well with ice and serve over ice in the old-fashioned or "up" in the chilled cocktail glass.

NOTE Extra sweetener (Agave Syrup) is needed with frozen drinks because the cracked ice increases dilution.

FROZEN MARGARITA

Lime wedge, for frosting the glass
Kosher salt or sea salt, for frosting the glass
2 ounces Cuervo Tradicional tequila
1 ounce Marie Brizard triple sec
1 ounce fresh lime juice
1½ ounces Agave Syrup (page 222)
1 cup cracked ice
1 lime wedge, for garnish

Frost half the rim of a large goblet with lime and salt (see page 63).

Combine all the remaining ingredients (except the garnish) in a blender. Blend and pour into the frosted goblet. Garnish with the lime wedge.

SMOKY MARGARITA

Lime wedge, for frosting the glass
Coarse salt, for frosting the glass
2 ounces El Tesoro blanco tequila
¾ ounce Agave Syrup (page 222)
¾ ounce fresh lime juice
Splash of Del Maguey Chichicapa mezcal

Frost half the rim of an old-fashioned or a cocktail glass with the lime and salt (see page 63). Chill the cocktail glass, if using.

Shake the tequila, agave syrup, and lime juice with ice and serve over ice in the old-fashioned or "up" in the chilled cocktail glass. Float the mezcal on top.

THE "UNDRINKABLE" MARGARITA

My mentor Joe Baum liked many different drinks: the Margarita, Whiskey Sour, Bloody Mary, Pisco Sour, and his session drink, the Glenlivet over ice. Joe would order the same cocktail three times in a row until he tasted one that pleased him. It wasn't an easy process—then again, nothing was easy with Joe. When he didn't like a drink, there was no explanation: it was simply wrong and needed fixing. I would work to improve it.

My first week as head bartender of Aurora, a fine-dining French concept that Joe opened with Gérard Pangaud, the youngest chef to win two Michelin stars. Joe brought Chef Pangaud to the bar for margaritas. After a sip, Gérard announced that he had just won the margarita contest in Paris and he said, "This is sheet"—hey, nice to meet you, too, chef, was my unspoken reply.

After several of those undrinkable margaritas, I tried to cut them off because they were both gone-jobs, to use the vernacular. Joe just snarled at me that he owned the joint and ordered another one—and another; no one was driving and I liked my new job. Later that evening, Joe slipped and fell on the stoop of his apartment and suffered a cut to his head. Joe arrived to work bandaged up nicely; I didn't say a word. But, unfortunately, it took a dozen or so stitches to prove that I had finally won him over with my margaritas.

EVOLUTION OF THE MARTINI

Like all royalty, the Martini cocktail has lineage. In Jerry Thomas's *How to Mix Drinks* (1862), a drink called the Fancy Gin Cocktail paired genever with curaçao, dashes of absinthe, gum syrup, and bitters. At the time the Fancy Gin Cocktail became popular, vermouth was not widely available in this country, but you can see that the architecture of the Martini was evolving: a gin base with modifying ingredients of curaçao, gum, and bitters, served "up" in a cocktail glass.

FANCY GIN COCKTAIL

**2 ounces Old Duff single malt
   genever**
Dash of Pierre Ferrand dry curaçao
**Splash of Monin gomme syrup or (in
   a pinch) Simple Syrup (page 225)**
**2 dashes of Bitter Truth Bogart's
   Bitters**
Lemon wedge
**Lemon zest coin (see page 62),
   for garnish**

Fill a shaker one-third full with cracked ice, add the genever, curaçao, syrup, and bitters and shake well. Moisten the edge of a fancy coupe glass with the lemon wedge and strain the cocktail into the glass. Express the oil of the lemon zest coin over the drink and drop it in.

FANCY GIN COCKTAIL

MARTINEZ COCKTAIL

1 ounce of Ransom Old Tom gin
2 ounces of Martini & Rossi sweet vermouth
2 dashes of Luxardo maraschino liqueur
Dash of Monin gomme syrup or Simple
   Syrup (page 225)
Dash of Bitter Truth Bogart's Bitters
Lemon zest coin (see page 62), for garnish

Shake the ingredients (except the garnish) well with ice and strain into a large cocktail glass. Express the oil of the lemon zest coin over the drink and drop it in the glass.

THE VERMOUTH

The first shipments of the French Noilly Prat dry vermouth arrived in New Orleans in 1851, and shortly after in San Francisco, but it remained largely unknown in the rest of the country. It was consumed as wine and didn't make the cocktail scene until the 1890s.

When Italian vermouth became widely available by the 1870s, the use of curaçao and maraschino as sweeteners or flavor additive in cocktails waned, and vermouth took its place. The vermouth cocktail was an ice cube and a lemon zest—not very sexy. But the stage was set for the two most iconic of all cocktails, the Manhattan and the Martini. Italian vermouth stepped into the spotlight in two Manhattan recipes found in *The Modern Bartenders' Guide* (1884). Below the Manhattan recipes in that book there was a note that said, "For the Martinez Cocktail substitute gin for whiskey," so the Manhattan came first and the Martini was . . . well, just an afterthought!

MARTINI COCKTAIL 1888

This is Harry Johnson's martini recipe from his 1888 *Bartender's Manual*, where he retained the curaçao, the gum, and the bitters from the Fancy Gin Cocktail (page 162) and added vermouth in equal parts with the gin. The gin is Old Tom gin, not dry gin. And we must assume Johnson used Italian sweet vermouth because he listed simply vermouth in his inventory earlier in the book.

Fill a large bar glass with ice.

1 ounce Ransom Old Tom gin (see Note)
1 ounce sweet vermouth
Splash of gomme syrup (careful—not too much;
   I suggest Monin gomme syrup)
2 or 3 dashes of Bitter Truth Bogart's
   Bitters
Dash of Pierre Ferrand dry curaçao or absinthe
   (optional)
Bordeaux cherry or a medium pitted Spanish
   olive, for garnish (Johnson offers both
   options)
Lemon zest coin (see page 62), for garnish

In a mixing glass, stir all the ingredients (except the garnishes) with ice well with a spoon. Strain into a cocktail glass; garnish with a cherry or olive and squeeze a lemon zest coin on top.

NOTE The slight color comes from a short time in French wine barrels. There are six very classic gin botanicals in Ransom, but the real character comes from the whiskey-inspired mash-bill recipe of corn and malted barley with a small amount of unmalted barley. Ransom Old Tom was a collaboration between distiller and owner Tad Seestedt and drinks writer and bon vivant David Wondrich. It is not sweetened, so it makes sense for these old recipes that are kinda sweet.

DRY MARTINI (1905)

Martini di Arma di Taggia, the principal bartender at one of the grandest bars in New York, which was housed in Colonel John Jacob Astor's Knickerbocker Hotel, gets the credit for the dry martini. In 1912, he married dry Plymouth gin with Noilly Prat dry vermouth and orange bitters for the first time—or was it the first time? Charles Mahoney, principal bartender at the Hoffman House Hotel and author of the *Hoffman House Bartender's Guide* (1905), lists three drinks: one named after himself and the other two after people whom we must presume were regular guests. The Mahoney Cocktail is equal parts of Nicholson London dry gin and French vermouth, with a dash of orange bitters. The second is called the J. P. C. Cocktail with equal parts of Nicholson gin and French vermouth but no bitters—very modern—and essentially a dry martini. Both of these were served up in a cocktail glass, but both were shaken, not stirred. Score one for

James Bond! A third drink in Mr. Mahoney's book, the Nutting Cocktail, is two-thirds Plymouth gin and one-third French vermouth, this time served with a dash of orange bitters . . . like the J. P. C. Cocktail pairing of dry gin and dry vermouth, but moving the dry gin into a leading role.

THE "NICK & NORA" MARTINI (POST-PROHIBITION)

During Prohibition, the gin tasted so bad that everything imaginable was added to it to mask the flavor. The Martini waned in popularity. After Prohibition, Nick and Nora Charles (of *The Thin Man* movies) and President Franklin Roosevelt helped put the Martini back on the map. America got wetter and the Martini got drier: I styled this version as the "Nick & Nora" Martini recipe, three parts gin to one part dry vermouth, and skipped the orange bitters. This ratio reigned through the 1930s and '40s.

> 1½ ounces Beefeater gin (or for Nick and Nora, it would have been Gordon's or Gilbey's)
> ½ ounce Noilly Prat Original dry vermouth
> Pitted Manzanilla cocktail olive, for garnish

Fill a mixing glass with ice, add the gin and vermouth, and stir well. Strain into a chilled . . . well, Nick & Nora glass, of course. Garnish with the olive.

EXTRA-DRY
& DIRTY MARTINI

Franklin D. Roosevelt was the first person to popularize this odd drink. The brine in a gallon jar of olives can get really funky after daily withdrawals, not all of which are executed using a spoon. I don't think many bartenders would drink the Dirty Martini. But since the craft movement began, several brands of gourmet olive brine have come on the market, catering to this now popular Martini variation.

> **Dash of Noilly Prat Original or extra dry vermouth**
> **2½ ounces gin or vodka**
> **¼ ounce olive brine (I suggest the Dirty Sue or Filthy Foods version)**
> **Pitted Manzanilla cocktail olive (no pimento), for garnish**

Stir all the ingredients (except the garnish) with ice in a mixing glass. Strain into a chilled cocktail glass. Garnish with the olive.

EXTRA-DRY MARTINI
(COLD-WAR ERA)

After World War II, gin was still king, but the amount of vermouth in a Martini began to diminish dramatically. By the Kennedy years and the 1960s, the Cold War was getting more nerve wracking, and the Martini was getting stronger: a lethal twelve parts gin to one part vermouth.

> **3 drops of Noilly Prat Original or extra dry vermouth**
> **3 ounces gin**
> **Pitted Manzanilla cocktail olive (no pimento), for garnish**

Stir the vermouth and gin with ice in a mixing glass—50 times if using large ice cubes, 30 times if using small cubes. Strain into a chilled cocktail glass. Garnish with the olive.

EXTRA-EXTRA DRY:
ROUND 1 WITH AUTHOR
MARC CONNELLY

It was March 8, 1971, day of the much-hyped "Fight of the Century": Muhammad Ali's first fight after a three-year, government-imposed layoff. Ali was fighting Joe Frazier for the world heavyweight championship at Madison Square Garden. The advertising agency I worked for bought a block of tickets to the Waldorf Astoria's closed-circuit broadcast, and I got one in exchange for bartending in a suite upstairs at the Waldorf. I lied; I had never tended bar. The match was close, but everyone thought Ali was easily ahead on points. After Frazier won with a late-round knockdown, they took him to the hospital because Ali had done a pretty good job rearranging his face. Famous ad man George Lois said later in the suite, "Where I grew up in the Bronx, the guy who went to the hospital was the loser!" Eighty-one-year-old Marc Connelly, author and one of the original members of the Algonquin Round Table, was a guest. After the fight he came to the bar and ordered a dry martini. I grabbed a bottle of vermouth and started to make what I have since dubbed an "Irish Martini." With a pained look on his face, Marc's surprisingly steely grip closed around my wrist as he forced the vermouth bottle back down to the bar, saying, "It is only necessary to grip the vermouth bottle tightly and quietly enunciate the word *vermouth* while looking at the glass."

VODKATINI: THE SILVER BULLET

In 1967, John Martin succeeded in putting his Smirnoff vodka bottle in front of all the right people, and vodka actually surpassed gin as the white spirit of choice in the Martini. And as for the vermouth? Hold an open bottle of vermouth in front of a fan across the room.

With the reader's indulgence, the following recipes are not proper Martinis but cocktails. It was the 1990s, and martini menus were all the rage—the word *martini* was accompanied by a descriptor to ease the irritation of the classic Martini drinker, and apple was the favorite modifier at the time.

UPSIDE-DOWN MARTINI

Proceed only on doctor's orders!

2 ounces Noilly Prat Original dry vermouth
1 ounce Beefeater gin
Lemon zest coin (see page 62),
    for garnish

Assemble the vermouth and gin in a mixing glass filled with ice and stir. Strain into a chilled cocktail glass and garnish with the lemon zest coin.

SOUR APPLE MARTINI* (MY VERSION)

I made this for singer Natalie Cole and her manager on the occasion of Rupert Murdoch's seventieth birthday party. I had the cocktail gig, it was a surprise party, and she was the surprise entertainment. Rupert loved her, and she loved my Sour Apple Martinis. I gave the recipe to her manager, who loved them as well.

1½ ounces Absolut Citron vodka
½ ounce DeKuyper Sour Apple Pucker
½ ounce Cointreau
¾ ounce fresh lemon juice
Thin slice of Granny Smith apple,
    for garnish

Assemble all the ingredients (except the garnish) in a cocktail shaker and shake well with ice. Strain into a chilled cocktail glass and garnish with the apple slice.

MY FIRST BAR GIG

If there was one pivotal day in my life that determined my future, it was when I volunteered to fill in for a bartender who failed to show up for a party that Charley O's was catering at Gracie Mansion, the home of New York City's mayor. None of the regular bartenders wanted to work a thankless, tipless job, but I lied and said I was a bartender and so I got the gig. In what seemed like seconds later, I was behind the bar. Mayor Abe Beame was presenting the keys of the city to Rupert Murdoch. All the top people in the Beame administration and a number of other prominent New Yorkers were attending. I was center stage with a captive audience.

It was a makeshift, poorly stocked bar, and I never really had to make anything that fancy, but there was something about being behind the bar that felt just right. I don't know how Muhammad Ali felt the first time he climbed into a ring, or how Louis Armstrong felt the first time he picked up a trumpet, but for me, I knew I was standing in a very familiar and cozy place. I was home.

FRENCH MARTINI

This drink is one of the sparks that got the cocktail-as-martini craze started. We put it on the menu at Pravda and never took it off.

2 ounces Blue Shark vodka
¾ ounce Chambord
1½ ounces pineapple juice

Shake all the ingredients with ice and strain into a chilled cocktail glass. Skip the garnish.

SECOND CHANCE MARTINI*

This drink is a variation on the famous Vesper Martini from *Casino Royale*, James Bond's original Martini, named for the love interest in the movie, Vesper Lynd. This recipe is James Bond's second chance to make a proper Martini, by stirring not shaking, and maybe a second chance at finding love.

1½ ounces Hendrick's gin
1½ ounces Reyka vodka
½ ounce Martini Riserva Speciale Ambrato vermouth
4 dashes of Dale DeGroff's Pimento Aromatic Bitters
Freshly cut thin round of English cucumber, for garnish

Assemble the ingredients (except the garnish) in a mixing glass or martini beaker, fill with ice, and stir. Strain into a large, chilled cocktail glass and garnish with the cucumber slice.

SMOKY MARTINI #2*

Hendrick's Orbium is the first variation on the original Hendrick's gin. Hendrick's captured a new audience for the traditional juniper-driven spirit by pushing the juniper character to the background and putting the floral and vegetal flavor and aroma in the foreground. Hendrick's Orbium is a nod to a drinker's love affair with all things bitter, achieved with the addition of two classic bittering agents—quinine and wormwood—and a floral note from lotus blossom essence. The result is a gin that is at home at the heart of a Martini cocktail. But I decided to place it at the heart of a Martini variation called the Smoky Martini #2.

2 ounces Hendrick's Orbium gin
1 ounce Reyka vodka
1 ounce Martini Riserva Speciale Ambrato vermouth
1 teaspoon Monkey Shoulder blended malt scotch whisky
4 dashes of Dale DeGroff's Pimento Aromatic Bitters

Assemble all the ingredients in a mixing glass with ice. Stir to chill and strain into a chilled cocktail glass.

MARTINI, VALENCIA-STYLE

This is the Martini that Joe Drown, the original owner of the Hotel Bel-Air, enjoyed nightly at the hotel bar.

½ ounce La Ina fino sherry
2½ ounces Bombay dry gin (white label)
2 flamed orange zest coins (see page 62)

Coat the inside of a cocktail glass with the fino sherry and pour the excess into a mixing glass with ice. Pour the gin into the mixing glass and stir to chill. Flame 1 orange zest coin into the empty cocktail glass to further season and discard. Strain the chilled gin into the seasoned glass. Garnish with the remaining flamed orange zest coin.

SECOND CHANCE
MARTINI

MCEWAN COCKTAIL+

Original cocktail created by noted San Francisco craft bartender Jacques Bezuidenhout.

2 ounces Auchentoshan Three Wood single malt scotch
½ ounce fresh lemon juice
¼ ounce poire William eau-de-vie
½ ounce Spiced Simple Syrup (page 225)
1 teaspoon emusified egg white (see page 204)
2 dashes of Dale Degroff's Pimento Aromatic Bitters
Freshly grated nutmeg, for garnish

Shake all the ingredients (except the garnish) well with ice and strain into an old-fashioned glass over ice cubes. Dust with freshly grated nutmeg.

MELONCHOLY BABY*

One of my most memorable experiences as a bartender was in the Rainbow Room: I created a special drink, on the spot, for a woman who had just ended a love affair and was really, really down in the dumps. It had flaming lemon peels and ended up becoming the drink of the night.

1½ ounces Absolut Citron vodka
¾ ounce fresh lemon juice
2 ounces Simple Syrup (page 225)
½ cup chopped cantaloupe
2 ounces Sutter Home Fre alcohol-removed Moscato wine
2 drops of saline solution
Lemon zest coin (see page 62), for garnish

Blend all the ingredients (except the garnish) in a blender with cracked ice until smooth and serve in a copa grande glass. Garnish with the lemon zest coin.

MERRY WIDOW

Adapted from *The Savoy Cocktail Book*, by Harry Craddock (1930).

Dash of Jade Nouvelle Orléans Absinthe Supérieure
2 ounces Tanqueray London dry gin
½ ounce Noilly Prat Original dry vermouth
Dash of Angostura bitters
Dash of Bénédictine
Flamed lemon zest coin (see page 62), for garnish

Season a chilled cocktail glass with the absinthe and set it aside. Stir the remaining ingredients (except the garnish) with ice in a mixing glass and strain into the chilled cocktail glass. Garnish with the flamed lemon zest coin.

METROPOLITAN+

Created by Mike Hewett at Marion's Bar in New York City, late 1980s.

1½ ounces Absolut Kurant vodka
1½ ounces cranberry juice
½ ounce Rose's lime juice
¾ teaspoon fresh lime juice
Thin lime wheel, for garnish

Shake the ingredients (except the garnish) with ice and strain into a chilled cocktail glass. Garnish with the lime wheel.

MIAMI BEACH SPRITZ[+]

"It was the saltwater and sun of the beach that brought me to the Sicilian Castelvetrano olive as the perfect garnish." —"Soho" Phil Halpern

The Miami Beach Spritz is based on the Italian classic the Aperol Spritz, a genius of a low-alcohol refresher.

3 ounces Conegliano Valdobbiadene DOCG dry prosecco
2 ounces soda water
1½ ounces Aperol
½ ounce Giffard or Combier crème de pamplemousse rose (pink grapefruit liqueur)
Grapefruit zest coin (see page 62)
3 pitted Sicilian Castelvetrano olives, for garnish (no substitution)
Orange slice, for garnish

Build the first four ingredients in a tall glass over ice and stir. Express the oil of the grapefruit zest coin and discard. Garnish with the Castelvetrano olives and the orange slice.

MICHELADA

½ ounce fresh lime juice
Dash of Tabasco sauce
Dash of soy sauce
Dash of Worcestershire sauce
Pinch of freshly ground black pepper
½ ounce Maggi Seasoning
2 ounces tomato juice
1 (12-ounce) beer of choice (I prefer Bohemia
    from Mexico)

Mix all the ingredients except the beer in a beer glass. Fill the glass three-quarters with ice and add beer.

MILLENNIUM COCKTAIL*

I was commissioned to create a cocktail with the Millennium release by Courvoisier. I did a riff on the East India Cocktail; it helped to stave off Y2K.

1½ ounces Courvoisier Millennium 2000 Cognac
1 ounce pineapple juice
1 ounce Joseph Cartron Curaçao Orange
Dash of Angostura bitters
Flamed orange zest coin (see page 62), for garnish
Freshly grated nutmeg, for garnish

Shake all the ingredients (except the garnishes) with ice to raise an attractive pineapple foam. Strain into a chilled cocktail glass and garnish with the flamed orange zest coin and a dusting of nutmeg.

MILLION-DOLLAR COCKTAIL

The original was created by Ngiam Tong Boon of Raffles Hotel in Singapore, circa 1910. A recipe by George Kaiho switched out the grenadine for Peter Heerings cherry liqueur—I liked that—but he left out vermouth, and I didn't like that.

2 ounces Plymouth gin
½ ounce sweet vermouth
½ ounce pineapple juice
½ ounce emulsified egg white (see page 204)
1 teaspoon Heering cherry liqueur

Shake all the ingredients with ice and strain into a cocktail glass.

MIMOSA

This drink was also known as a Buck's Fizz, a similar drink by Pat McGarry at the Buck's Club in London. Buck's recipe was four ounces of Champagne to two ounces of orange juice. Frank Meier of the Ritz Bar in Paris had an appealing alternate recipe called the Valencia, with orange juice, apricot liqueur, and Champagne. A float of Cointreau is a very pleasant addition.

3 ounces fresh orange juice
3 ounces Champagne

Pour the orange juice into a champagne flute and fill with the Champagne.

MOJITO

La Bodeguita is credited with popularizing the minty Mojito, but there's a lot of controversy about the drink's origin. Some believe Constantino Ribalaigua Vert of El Floridita made the first Mojito. Maybe the Cuban *cantineros* (bartenders) were riffing on the American julep; the origin is cloudy. Ice and club soda are critical to the modern Mojito, and the first shipments of ice arrived in Cuba from New England in the 1850s. Ice must have had a profound impact on drinks production on steamy Havana evenings.

5 fresh spearmint leaves
¾ ounce Simple Syrup (page 225)
¾ ounce fresh lime juice
1½ ounces Havana Club 3-year-old rum or your
    favorite white rum
2 dashes of Angostura bitters (optional)
1 ounce club soda
2 fresh tender spearmint sprigs

Muddle the spearmint leaves with the simple syrup and the lime juice in the bottom of a Boston shaker glass. Add the rum, bitters, if desired, and ice and shake. Strain into a highball glass filled with cracked ice, top with the club soda, and garnish with the mint sprigs.

MONKEY GLAND

Harry MacElhone takes credit for this cocktail in his *ABC of Mixing Cocktails* (1930) and claims he named it after Dr. Serge Voronoff's experiments in rejuvenation. We have no reason to doubt that he did just that.

Splash of Jade 1901 Absinthe Supérieure
2 ounces Beefeater gin
1 ounce fresh orange juice
Splash of grenadine, homemade (page 224)
  or store-bought
Flamed orange zest coin (see page 62),
  for garnish

Splash the absinthe in a cocktail shaker and follow with the remaining ingredients (except the garnish). Shake with ice and strain into a Nick & Nora glass. Garnish with the flamed orange zest coin.

MOSCOW MULE

Finally, one of the few drinks that is actually well documented. John Martin used this drink to promote his new product, Smirnoff vodka, after World War II. He did promotions with the owner of the Cock'n Bull, Jack Morgan, and a Russian immigrant named Sophie Berezinski, whose father owned the Moscow Copper Company. The Cock'n Bull was near many Beverly Hills mansions and attracted a sizable contingent of movie folk. Martin and Morgan came up with the recipe featuring Smirnoff and ginger beer (a weird English soda that Jack Morgan was having difficulty moving) and served it in the copper mugs that Sophie's dad was trying to sell in the United States. Eventually, two kicking mules were engraved on the mugs. The thing caught on with the movie crowd, and Morgan engraved stars' names on their mugs and hung them over the bar for their personal use only. They were still hanging above the bar in 1978 when the Cock'n Bull became my after-work hang.

1½ ounces Smirnoff vodka
4 to 5 ounces ginger beer, homemade (page 222)
  or store-bought
Lime wedge, for garnish

Combine the vodka and ginger beer in a glass over ice cubes and stir. Garnish with the lime wedge.

MUD AND BLOOD* (NONALCOHOLIC)

This is another drink from *New York* magazine's 1996 article by Tony Hendra. I had to create a drink à la minute from the least favorite liquid of each of several guests, and Alex Hargrave of Hargrave Vineyard chose a nonalcoholic drink with carrot juice. Add two ounces of pepper vodka, and you have a pleasant drink.

2 ounces carrot juice
2 ounces beef broth
2 ounces fresh orange juice
Dash of Tabasco sauce
Dash of Worcestershire sauce

Shake the ingredients with ice and strain into a glass.

MUD SLIDE

Rod Stewart stopped by the Rainbow Room with a group occasionally, but they never met the dress code. During their first visit, the problem was solved when Bismark Irving, who ran the Rainbow Room's cabaret, led the group through the back of the house to a stairway leading to the old observation deck, which was closed when we operated the Rainbow Room. I supplied pitchers of Mud Slides, and they loved it up there, unmolested and left to their own devices. Use your imagination.

1 ounce Blue Shark vodka
1 ounce Kahlúa
1 ounce Baileys Irish cream
1 ounce heavy cream

Shake all the ingredients with ice and serve over ice in a rocks glass.

VARIATIONS The Mud Slide can also be served as a frozen drink. Blend the ingredients with ¾ cup ice and serve in a large goblet. Switch amaretto for the vodka and it is called an Orgasm. Add vodka to an Orgasm and it becomes a Screaming Orgasm.

MUSK WE (NONALCOHOLIC)*

This drink was created for Rosemary Clooney's band members. Rosemary called me at the front bar one night and requested emphatically that I refrain from serving alcoholic beverages to her band members between the first and second shows. Tenor sax player Scott Hamilton acquiesced but Clooney's cornet player Warren Vache went down fighting and only fell in line when Scott reminded him that Rosemary invited the band to play on her next album.

½ cup chilled and chopped cantaloupe
¼ cup chilled and chopped honeydew melon
3 ounces Sutter Home Fre alcohol-removed white Zinfandel
2 ounces Simple Syrup (page 225)
½ ounce fresh lemon juice
½ ounce fresh lime juice
½ cup cracked ice

In a blender, blend the ingredients until smooth. Serve in a specialty glass or large goblet.

NAPOLEON'S COMPLEX+

This was created by absinthe maker and owner of Jade Liqueurs, Ted Breaux, and bartender Evan Baldwin. Ted is my partner in the bitters business, and he also makes the Jade Liqueurs absinthe line. Here's an unusual take on the Amaretto Sour.

1 ounce amaretto
½ ounce Jade 1901 Absinthe Supérieure
½ ounce fresh lemon juice
Dash of Simple Syrup (page 225)
2 or 3 dashes of Dale DeGroff's Pimento Aromatic Bitters

Shake all the ingredients with ice and strain into a chilled coupe glass.

DALE DEGROFF'S PIMENTO AROMATIC BITTERS

Early in my tenure at the Rainbow Room in New York City, I discovered Wray & Nephew pimento dram liqueur. I loved intense allspice flavor. I used it like bitters, dashing it into drinks, and it delivered multiple layers of flavor. It disappeared from the market and when I queried my distributor, he informed me that the Rainbow Room and one other bar, in Los Angeles, were the only accounts left in the whole United States. Many years later, in 2009, Ted Breaux (absinthe producer and founder of Lucid Absinthe) and I decided it was time to create a concentrated bitters version of my old favorite pimento dram. Dale DeGroff's Pimento Aromatic Bitters is handcrafted by infusing high proof alcohol with a blend of select whole botanicals. Not only do I use it in numerous cocktails, I also dash it liberally over many foods, from gumbo to baked clams and oysters Rockefeller to sweet potatoes.

NEGRITA

The name of this means "pretty little dark one" in Spanish. The recipe below is for one shooter.

½ ounce pisco
½ ounce coffee liqueur
½ ounce cold espresso

Combine all the ingredients in a mixing glass with 1 large ice cube and stir to chill. Strain into a shot glass.

NEGRONI

The Negroni was created during the 1920s at the Casoni Café in Florence, Italy, when customer Count Camillo Negroni asked the barman to add gin to his Americano Highball (page 77). The bitter finish was a challenge for the American palate, and European bartenders would emphasize the gin and vermouth over the Campari. Those times have changed. The culinary revolution has created a huge audience for strong, bitter, and smoky flavors, and today the Negroni is one of the hottest cocktails on the block.

1 ounce Campari
1 ounce Martini & Rossi sweet vermouth
1 ounce Fords gin
Half orange wheel, for garnish

Combine all the ingredients (except the garnish) in an old-fashioned glass filled with ice and stir. Garnish with the orange wheel.

NIEUW AMSTERDAM FIZZ*

This drink is inspired by the fruit-forward Old Duff genever.

¾ ounce Old Duff genever
¼ ounce Simple Syrup (page 225)
½ ounce fresh lemon juice
1 ounce pineapple juice
Splash of Perfect Purée of Napa Valley mango purée
Dash of Dale DeGroff's Pimento Aromatic Bitters
2 ounces Champagne
Fresh spearmint leaf, for garnish

Assemble the genever, simple syrup, both juices, mango purée, and bitters in a cocktail shaker with ice and shake well. Strain into a chilled cocktail glass and top with the Champagne. Garnish with a single spearmint leaf.

OAXACA OLD-FASHIONED

A groundbreaking drink by Phil Ward, an alumnus of both Death & Co. and Pegu Club, two New York City bars that have defined the recent craft cocktail movement.

2 orange zest coins (see page 62)
1 teaspoon agave nectar
2 dashes of Angostura bitters
2 ounces El Tesoro reposado tequila
½ ounce Del Maguey Vida de San Luis del Rio mezcal or your favorite

Add 1 orange zest coin to the bottom of an old-fashioned glass with the agave nectar and the bitters; muddle to extract the orange oil. Add the tequila and an oversize ice cube. Stir well and top with the mezcal. Garnish by flaming the remaining orange zest coin (see page 62) over the top of the drink and discard.

O'CALLA MOVES EAST⁺

This recipe is from Del Pedro, partner in Tooker Alley on Washington Street in Brooklyn, just around the corner from the Brooklyn Museum. Some of the ingredients below will take some work to source, but with the Internet it's not that much work. In the end it will be worth it.

1 ounce Dimmi Liquore di Milano
1 ounce Yuzuri yuzu liqueur (see Note)
2 teaspoons Suntory Roku gin
4 teaspoons Blume Marillen apricot eau-de-vie (see Note)
2 dried apricots frozen on a skewer, for garnish

Stir the ingredients (except the garnish) with cracked ice in a mixing glass. Strain into a coupe glass. Garnish with the skewered frozen dried apricots.

NOTE The yuzu liqueur is available at Cask Cartel Premium Spirits (www.caskcartel.com). The apricot eau-de-vie is at Astor Wines & Spirits (www.astorwines.com).

OLD-FASHIONED

The Old-Fashioned was created at the Pendennis Club in Louisville, Kentucky. There are two warring camps of Old-Fashioned drinkers: those who muddle the fruit and those who don't. I belong to the first camp; muddled Old-Fashioneds are a holiday thing in our household. But I have had customers throughout my career who would have thrown the glass at me if I put fruit in their Old-Fashioned. There is passion on both sides. For the classic Old-Fashioned, just muddle the sugar cube with a splash of water or soda and the bitters before adding the whiskey and the ice; for the muddled fruit version, see below.

1 teaspoon granulated sugar or sugar cube
  (or 2 per taste)
2 dashes of Angostura bitters
2 half-orange wheels
2 Bordeaux cherries
Splash of water or club soda
2 ounces Wild Turkey 101 bourbon

In the bottom of an old-fashioned glass, carefully muddle the sugar, bitters, 1 of the half-orange wheels, 1 of the cherries, and a splash of water. Remove the orange rind and add the bourbon and ice and stir. Garnish with the remaining orange wheel and cherry.

VARIATION For the alternate version, simply muddle an orange zest coin (see page 62), a sugar cube, the bitters, and a splash of water in the glass. Add ice and the bourbon and stir to finish. Garnish with a second orange zest coin.

OLD FLAME*
(AKA FANCY NANCY)

The Old Flame is a variation on the Negroni (page 175). I was doing cocktail dinners on my book tour for the first edition of *The Craft of the Cocktail* and paired the Negroni with the canapés. In Texas the bitter finish of the Negroni left the writer and photographer less than enthusiastic. I pulled their two drinks and retooled the recipe on the fly, adding a sweet note—Cointreau—and some orange juice. Nancy, the photographer, was very enthusiastic with the results. I renamed the drink the Fancy Nancy in her honor. I won first prize in the Fancy Cocktail category at the 2001 Martini & Rossi Grand Prix in Málaga, Spain, with this cocktail under another name, the Old Flame.

1 ounce Bombay dry gin (white label)
½ ounce Martini & Rossi sweet vermouth
½ ounce Campari
½ ounce Cointreau
1 ounce fresh orange juice
Flamed orange zest coin (see page 62),
    for garnish

Shake all the ingredients (except the garnish) well with ice to chill and strain into a chilled cocktail glass. Garnish with the flamed orange zest coin.

OLD-FASHIONED, FRENCH+

This variation on the classic Old Fashioned is Pete Volkmar's of Gourmet Galley Catering, North Stonington, CT. Pete attended Gaz Regan's Cocktails in the Country and it changed his life.

¼ ounce green Chartreuse
2 dashes of Regan's Orange Bitters No. 6
2 dashes of Dale DeGroff's Pimento Aromatic Bitters
2 large orange zest coins (see page 62)
2 ounces Michter's Kentucky Straight rye whiskey

In the bottom of an old-fashioned glass, carefully muddle the Chartreuse and both of the bitters with 1 of the orange zest coins. Add the whiskey and ice cubes. Stir well and garnish with the remaining orange zest coin.

ORANGE BLOSSOM

David A. Embury, author of *The Fine Art of Mixing Drinks*, refers to this cocktail as the "spawn of the Prohibition toad." But he does reluctantly offer his recipe: two parts gin to one part orange to a half part simple syrup. Modern tastes lean toward a lighter drink, so I altered the recipe and added Cointreau instead of simple syrup to bring a bit of flavor along with sweetness.

1½ ounces gin
1½ ounces fresh orange juice
½ ounce Cointreau
Flamed orange zest coin (see page 62), for garnish

Shake all the ingredients (except the garnish) with ice and strain into a chilled cocktail glass. Garnish with the flamed orange zest coin.

OYSTER SHOOTER*

MAKES 3 SHOOTERS

I created this one out of pure selfishness in 1999 at Blackbird, a short-lived bar and restaurant that I ran for eleven months. I ordered it almost daily for lunch.

3 oysters, preferably a small variety like Olympia
1½ ounces pepper or lemon vodka
3 ounces Oyster Shooter Tomato Mix (recipe follows)
3 oyster shells
3 lemon wedges
3 giant capers, with stems

Drop 1 oyster in each of 3 shot glasses. To each add ½ ounce vodka and 1 ounce of the tomato mix. Bury the shot glasses in a plate of crushed ice and garnish the ice next to each shot glass with an oyster shell, a lemon wedge, and a giant caper. The procedure is to suck on the lemon wedge, then take the shooter bottoms up, then bite into the caper.

OYSTER SHOOTER TOMATO MIX
MAKES ABOUT 1 QUART, OR ENOUGH FOR 30 OYSTER SHOOTERS

2 leaves of pineapple sage
26 ounces tomato juice
2 ounces balsamic vinegar
2 ounces fresh lemon juice
¼ teaspoon each freshly ground black pepper and salt
2 teaspoons Tabasco sauce
1 tablespoon freshly grated horseradish root

Bruise the sage leaves in the bottom of a pitcher and add the remaining ingredients. Stir and let stand covered in the refrigerator for a couple of hours. Strain and use in the shooters as directed.

PARADISE COCKTAIL

This recipe has been on the back of the Marie Brizard Apry (apricot liqueur) bottle for years. I just touched it up a bit.

2 ounces gin
¾ ounce Marie Brizard Apry liqueur
¾ ounce fresh orange juice
2 dashes of Bitter Truth orange bitters
Flamed orange zest coin (see page 62), for garnish

Combine all the ingredients (except the garnish) in a shaker. Shake with ice and strain into a chilled cocktail glass. Garnish with the flamed orange zest coin.

PAINKILLER

My son and I were cruising on a small ocean liner, working cocktail hours for a hedge fund manager, who was celebrating his fiftieth birthday. It was a good gig; we were guests, really, except at cocktail hour. The vessel was small enough to pull into the shallow harbor at White Bay, Jost Van Dyke, in the British Virgin Islands. The ship's launch dropped us about fifteen feet from shore in order to avoid getting into too shallow water. We found ourselves at the Soggy Dollar Bar, where I enjoyed my first (through my fourth) Painkiller. Our folded money, like everyone else's, was wet from jumping into the water and the bartender/owner hung it on the clothesline running from one end of the back bar to the other.

2 ounces Pusser's rum
1 ounce coconut cream (I suggest Coco López)
2 ounces fresh or unsweetened pineapple juice
1 ounce fresh orange juice
Freshly grated nutmeg, for garnish

Shake all the ingredients (except the garnish) well with ice and strain into a highball glass over ice. Dust with freshly grated nutmeg.

VARIATION For Dale's spicy Sundeck Special, add 2 dashes of Dale DeGroff's Pimento Aromatic Bitters to the drink when shaking.

PARADISI⁺

This original drink was created by Leo DeGroff and Tyler Kitzman at Sweet Liberty bar, Miami.

1 ounce reposado tequila
1 ounce Campari
1 ounce fresh lime juice
1 ounce Agave Syrup (page 222)
2½ ounces Stiegl Radler or Schöfferhofer
grapefruit beer
Flamed orange zest coin (see page 62)
Half grapefruit wheel, for garnish

Shake the first four ingredients well with ice. Strain into a pilsner glass over ice and top with the grapefruit beer. Flame the orange zest over the drink and discard. Garnish with the grapefruit.

PARIS†

This is from the celebrated bartender Colin Field at the Hemingway Bar in the Ritz Hotel in Paris. While you're there, don't forget to try Colin's legendary Bloody Mary. Here, Colin creates a variation on the original Parisian by Frank Meier.

1 ounce Plymouth gin
1 ounce Dolin dry vermouth (French, of course)
1 ounce Marie Brizard Cassis de Bourdeaux
Flamed lemon zest coin (page 62), for garnish

Shake all the ingredients (except the garnish) well with ice and strain into a chilled cocktail glass. Garnish with the flamed lemon zest coin.

PEGU COCKTAIL

This was created at the Pegu Club in Burma when the sun didn't set on the British Empire. The Pegu goes very well with a fish course.

2 ounces gin
¾ ounce fresh lime juice
¾ ounce Joseph Cartron Curaçao Orange
2 dashes of Angostura bitters
Lime peel, for garnish

Shake all the ingredients (except the garnish) well with ice. Strain into a chilled cocktail glass. Garnish with the lime peel.

PENICILLIN†

Australian bartender Sam Ross successfully created one of a rare breed of cocktails: a cocktail based on malt scotch. The cocktail is fast becoming a modern classic. No surprise since Sam is an alumnus of Sasha Petraske's original Milk & Honey bar in New York City.

2 quarter-size slices of fresh ginger
¾ ounce Honey Syrup (page 224)
1½ ounces Dewar's blended scotch
¾ ounce fresh lemon juice
¼ ounce Laphroaig Islay single malt scotch whisky
Slice of candied ginger, for garnish

Muddle the fresh ginger pieces in a cocktail shaker glass with the honey syrup. Add the blended scotch and lemon juice. Fill with ice and shake to chill. Fine strain into a double old-fashioned glass filled three-quarters full with ice. Float the Islay whisky on top of the drink and garnish with the candied ginger.

PILGRIM COCKTAIL*

I prepared this at the Rainbow Room for our Thanksgiving celebrations.

¾ ounce Myers's dark rum
¾ ounce Banks 7 Golden Age Blend rum
¾ ounce Joseph Cartron Curaçao Orange
2 ounces fresh orange juice
½ ounce fresh lime juice
¼ ounce Bitter Truth pimento dram liqueur
Dash of Dale DeGroff's Pimento Aromatic Bitters

Shake all the ingredients with ice and strain into a large chilled cocktail glass over ice cubes.

PIMM'S CUP

The traditional recipe is Pimm's mixed with English lemonade—our lemon-lime soda—but I prefer fresh lemonade with club soda.

1½ ounces Pimm's No. 1
3 ounces fresh lemonade
1½ ounces club soda or 7UP
English cucumber spear, for garnish
Granny Smith apple slice, for garnish

Combine all the ingredients (except the garnishes) in a highball glass filled with ice. Stir and garnish with the cucumber and apple.

VARIATION For a Pimm's Royale, substitute Champagne for the club soda.

PIMM'S ITALIANO*

Wheel of English cucumber
½ ounce Cynar
1½ ounces Pimm's No. 1
4 ounces Fever-Tree tonic water
Long English cucumber spear, for garnish
Lemon wedge, for garnish

Muddle the cucumber wheel and the Cynar in
the bottom of a highball glass. Add ice cubes and
build the drink in the glass and stir. Then add the
cucumber spear and the lemon wedge.

PIÑA COLADA

In the 1950s in Puerto Rico, Don Ramón López-Irizarry came up with a delicious homogenized cream made from coconut. The product is known as Coco López Cream of Coconut, still used for tropical dishes and desserts. In 1957, Ramón Marrero, a bartender at Puerto Rico's Caribe Hilton, combined coconut cream with rum, pineapple juice, and ice in a blender to create this famous drink. The trick is to use both light rum and dark rum, a dash of bitters, and a little heavy cream.

1½ ounces Appleton Estate white rum
1 ounce Myers's dark rum or Gosling's Black Seal Bermuda black rum
2 ounces Coco López Cream of Coconut
1 ounce heavy cream
4 ounces pineapple juice
Dash of Angostura bitters
1 cup crushed ice
Pineapple leaf, for garnish
Pineapple wedge, for garnish

Add all the ingredients (except the garnishes) to a blender and blend for 15 seconds. Pour into a specialty glass like a copa grande glass and garnish with the pineapple leaf and pineapple wedge.

PINEAPPLE CHAMPAGNE COCKTAIL*

SERVES 6 TO 8

Adapted from a recipe served at the Embassy Club in Hollywood in the 1930s.

1 cup fresh ripe pineapple cubes
1 cup fresh ripe pitted cherries
12 ounces maraschino liqueur
2 ounces fresh lemon juice
1 (750 ml) bottle brut Champagne
6 to 8 flamed lemon zest coins (see page 62), for garnish

In a medium bowl, bruise the pineapple cubes and cherries and macerate them in the maraschino liqueur and lemon juice for 2 hours. Chill overnight. Strain the mixture, reserving the liquid and discarding the fruit. Add 2 ounces of the liquid to 6 to 8 chilled cocktail glasses and top each with Champagne. Garnish each with a flamed lemon zest coin.

PINK GIN

In 1978, I served this old recipe at the Hotel Bel-Air with orange bitters. After going through two bottles of orange bitters, I spoke to the steward about ordering more. He informed me that the brand was no longer produced and had not been available for more than twenty years; I switched to Angostura bitters. There are now many orange bitters to choose from, and I recommend Regan's Orange Bitters No. 6, Bitter Truth orange bitters, or Audrey Saunders's mix from Pegu Club in New York City.

Originally this drink was served without ice, but these days you won't find many takers for warm gin.

2 ounces gin
Dash of Audrey's mix orange bitters (see Note)
Dash of Angostura bitters
Lemon peel, for garnish

Combine the ingredients (except the garnish) in an old-fashioned glass over ice. Stir. Garnish with the lemon peel.

NOTE Audrey mixes half Regan's Orange Bitters No. 6 and half Fee Brothers orange bitters.

PINK LADY

1½ ounces gin
¼ ounce grenadine, homemade (page 224) or store-bought
¾ ounce Simple Syrup (page 225)
1 ounce heavy cream

Shake all the ingredients with ice and strain into a small cocktail glass.

PINK SQUIRREL

Crème de noyaux is an almond-flavored liqueur.

¾ ounce crème de noyaux
¾ ounce Tempus Fugit crème de cacao
1½ ounces heavy cream
Pinch of ground cacao nibs, for garnish

Shake all the ingredients (except the garnish) with ice and strain into a small cocktail glass. Dust with ground cacao nibs.

PISCO OLD-FASHIONED*

My variation on the classic that I prepared for road trips on behalf of the Trade Board of Peru 2019.

Dash of Bitter Truth Bogart's Bitters
1 orange zest coins (see page 62)
Dash of Barrow's Intense ginger liqueur (see Note)
½ ounce Brown Sugar or Demerara Syrup (page 223)
2 ounces Pisco 1615 Mosto Verde Italia
Splash of Ancho Reyes ancho chile liqueur
Flamed orange zest (see page 62), for garnish

Muddle the bitters, 1 orange zest coin, the Barrow's, and the syrup in the bottom of an old-fashioned glass. Add the pisco, chile liqueur, and ice.

Stir to chill. Garnish with a flamed orange zest coin over the top of the drink and drop it in.

NOTE The Barrow's liqueur is made from Peruvian ginger in Brooklyn, New York.

PINK GIN AND TONIC*

My variation on the classic Gin and Tonic.

2 sage leaves
1½ ounces Fords gin
2 dashes of Peychaud's bitters
5 ounces Fever-Tree tonic water
2 lime wedges, for garnish

Drop the sage leaves in the bottom of a highball glass. Add the gin and the bitters and muddle gently, then remove the sage leaves. Fill the glass three-quarters full with ice cubes. Top with tonic, stir, and garnish with two lime wedges.

PISCO SOUR, BLUEBERRY*

1½ ounces BarSol Primero Quebranta pisco
1½ ounces Blueberry Shrub (page 222)
½ ounce fresh lime juice
¾ ounce emulsified egg white (see page 204)
Angostura bitters

Shake all the ingredients (except the bitters) with ice well to fully emulsify the egg and strain into a small cocktail glass. Place several drops of the bitters on top of the foam.

PISCO PUNCH

111 OUNCES OR UNDER 1 GALLON

Duncan Nicol, the last owner of the Bank Exchange Saloon, died in 1926 and took with him the secret recipe for the legendary Pisco Punch. Here's my stab at the recipe.

1 batch Dale's Lemon and Orange Shrub (page 223)
1 (750 ml) bottle BarSol Pisco Mosto Verde Italia or your favorite pisco puro
10 ounces Sandeman Rainwater Madeira
15 ounces unsweetened pineapple juice (fresh, if you can get it)
1 liter spring water
Fresh lemon juice (optional)
Simple Syrup (page 225; optional)
Dash of Dale DeGroff's Pimento Aromatic Bitters
Freshly grated nutmeg, for garnish

Once you have prepared the shrub, the assembly is the easy part. Use a punch bowl or any large container that holds at least 1 gallon. Pour in the shrub, the pisco, the Rainwater Madeira, pineapple juice, and water and stir. Taste for sweetness; it should be perfect but adjust to your taste with more lemon juice or simple syrup, if desired. Serve over ice in a medium-size goblet or white wineglass with a dash of bitters and dust with freshly grated nutmeg.

PISCO SOUR

Pisco is a grape brandy that has been made for more than four hundred years in Peru and Chile, beginning when they were part of a Spanish colony called the Viceroyalty of Peru.

2 ounces BarSol Primero Quebranta pisco
¾ ounce fresh lime juice
¾ ounce Simple Syrup (page 225)
¾ ounce emulsified egg white (see page 204)
Angostura bitters

Shake all the ingredients (except the bitters) with ice well to fully emulsify the egg and strain into a small cocktail glass. Place several drops of the bitters on top of the foam and swirl with a cocktail pick.

PLANTER'S PUNCH*

My recipe from the Rainbow Plantation.

1 ounce Myers's dark rum
1 ounce Flor de Caña Extra Seco 4-year rum
½ ounce Joseph Cartron Curaçao Orange
2 ounces fresh orange juice
2 ounces pineapple juice
½ ounce Simple Syrup (page 225)
¼ ounce fresh lime juice
Dash of grenadine, homemade (page 224) or store-bought
Dash of Dale DeGroff's Pimento Aromatic Bitters
Orange slice, for garnish
Bordeaux cherry, for garnish

Shake all the ingredients (except the garnishes) with ice and strain into a collins glass filled three-quarters full with ice. Garnish with the orange slice and cherry.

POUSSE-CAFÉ

There is a section in Jerry Thomas's 1862 edition of *How to Mix Drinks* called "Fancy Drinks" that begins with three pousse-café recipes. The first is from an early nineteenth-century saloon owner in New Orleans named Joseph Santina, whom Thomas credits with improving the whole category of cocktails with his Brandy Crusta (page 96). Santina's Pousse-Café is made with Cognac, maraschino liqueur, and curaçao. Thomas's instructions say to "mix well"—not what I expected to find in what I have always known was a layered drink.

¼ ounce grenadine, homemade (page 224) or store-bought
¼ ounce crème de cacao
¼ ounce Luxardo maraschino liqueur
¼ ounce Joseph Cartron Curaçao Orange
¼ ounce Marie Brizard No 32 crème de menthe
½ ounce Martel VSOP Cognac

In the order they are listed, beginning with the grenadine, carefully pour each liqueur down the inside of a pousse-café glass over the back of a teaspoon positioned downward at an angle against the inside of the glass; each layer should float on top of the previous layer (see page 188).

PREAKNESS COCKTAIL

I found this in *International Cocktail Specialties from Madison Avenue to Malaya* (1962) by James Mayabb. The Preakness Stakes, the second leg of the Triple Crown, was well served for some years by this tasty whiskey cocktail, and it is time to return to it. But there is bigger change in the wind for the Preakness. Rumor has it that Pimlico Race Course, only active for the Triple Crown, will close sometime after 2020, and the Preakness will move to a new as-yet-unnamed track.

2 ounces Angel's Envy rye whiskey
1 ounce Martini & Rossi sweet vermouth
¼ ounce Bénédictine
Dash of Dale DeGroff's Pimento Aromatic Bitters
Orange zest coin (see page 62), for garnish

Stir the ingredients (except the garnish) with ice and strain into a chilled cocktail glass. Garnish with the orange zest coin.

PRESBYTERIAN

This was my mom's favorite drink. There is no satisfactory explanation for the name, but it seems to have been attached to the drink for more than a hundred years. My pal David Wondrich discovered that it works with scotch whisky as well. David also notes that Presbyterianism is part of the reform movement that was particularly associated with Scotland and so he experiments with scotch as the base. I am not an avid highball drinker so I haven't gotten around to tasting David's variation, but I shall when my tolerance for strong spirits starts to wane.

2 ounces Angel's Envy bourbon
2 ounces club soda
2 ounces Fever-Tree ginger ale
Lemon zest coin (see page 62), for garnish

Build all the ingredients (except the garnish) in a highball glass filled with ice and stir. Garnish with the lemon zest coin.

PRESTIGE COCKTAIL*

I served this at the release party for the original *The Craft of the Cocktail* along with seven other cocktails made by good friends Jerri Banks, Albert Trummer, Julie Reiner, Jeff Becker, David Marsden, Audrey Saunders, Angus Winchester, and George Delgado.

1 ounce Bacardí Reserva Ocho rum
¼ ounce Martini & Rossi dry vermouth
¾ ounce John D. Taylor's Velvet Falernum
¼ ounce fresh lime juice
1 ounce pineapple juice
Pineapple wedge, for garnish
Thin lime wheel, for garnish

Shake all the ingredients (except the garnishes) with ice and strain into a double old-fashioned glass. Garnish with the pineapple wedge and lime wheel.

PSYCHO KILLER⁺

"This drink was inspired by a Boulevardier cocktail with Redbreast 12 as the base instead of rye whiskey. This was originally included in our Volume 3 menu for 2014/2015. This menu won World's Best Cocktail Menu from Tales of the Cocktail in 2015.

"Redbreast, which has notes of dried fruit, banana, and baking spices and a rich texture, was complemented by cacao and banana liqueurs. Absinthe was the last touch to tie everything together and contrast the sweeter and fruited flavors."
—Jillian Vose, cocktail director at Dead Rabbit

The name is still a mystery to me, but I think it has something to do with the Rabbit character in the Dead Rabbit menus.

2 ounces Redbreast 12-year Irish whiskey
¾ ounce Campari
½ ounce Giffard white crème de cacao
½ ounce Giffard crème de banane (banana liqueur)
2 dashes of absinthe

Stir all the ingredients with ice and strain into a Nick & Nora glass.

PUNCH ROYALE

YIELDS 3½ QUARTS

This is a variation on a David Wondrich recipe for the Punch Royale, the yield just over 3 liters.

1 liter Jameson Irish whiskey
½ (750 ml) bottle Leacock's Rainwater Madeira
1 ounce Dale DeGroff's Pimento Aromatic Bitters
Dale's Lemon and Orange Shrub (page 223)
1 liter spring water
Freshly grated nutmeg, for garnish

Assemble the whiskey, Madeira, bitters, and shrub in a punch bowl; add the spring water and stir. Chill with block ice or large ice cubes added just before serving. Serve in goblets over cubed ice and dusted with fresh grated nutmeg.

RAINBOW PUNCH (NONALCOHOLIC)*

3 ounces fresh orange juice
½ ounce fresh lime juice
3 ounces pineapple juice
1 ounce Simple Syrup (page 225)
¼ ounce grenadine, homemade (page 224) or store-bought
2 dashes of Angostura bitters
1 ounce club soda
Bordeaux cherry, for garnish
Orange slice, for garnish

Shake all the ingredients (except the club soda and garnishes) and strain into an iced-tea glass filled with ice. Top with club soda and garnish with the cherry and orange slice.

RAINBOW SOUR*

Pineau des Charentes is a mistelle, a combination of raw grape juice and brandy—or, in the case of Pineau des Charentes, Cognac. The lore is that a Cognac producer thought he was blending two Cognacs when he topped up a barrel in his cellar, but one of the barrels contained raw grape juice. He was sure he had destroyed a batch of good Cognac and put it aside and left it. A couple of years later, his cellar master tasted it while checking barrels, and it had matured in an interesting way.

1½ ounces Pineau des Charentes
½ ounce Marie Brizard Apry liqueur
1 ounce fresh lemon juice
½ ounce Simple Syrup (page 225; optional)
Bordeaux cherry, for garnish
Orange slice, for garnish

Shake all the ingredients (except the garnishes) with ice and strain into an old-fashioned glass over ice cubes. Garnish with the cherry and orange slice.

RED BEER

This is a really popular country style of beer drinking, especially in the Catskills. The flavor is quite pleasant and it works nicely with beer nuts and pickled hard-boiled eggs.

2 ounces chilled tomato juice
1 (12-ounce) bottle Yuengling lager beer

Mix the tomato juice into a glass of beer. Serve with pickled eggs.

RED LION

Grand Marnier reached back to the 1930s for this drink. It was originally promoted by Booth's dry gin after it won first place in a 1933 cocktail competition, where it was served in a sugar-rimmed glass.

1 ounce Grand Marnier
1 ounce dry gin
½ ounce fresh orange juice
½ ounce fresh lemon juice
Flamed orange zest coin (see page 62),
   for garnish

Shake the ingredients (except the garnish) well with ice and strain into a chilled cocktail glass. Garnish with the flamed orange zest coin.

REGGAE*

I worked for a time creating cocktails for Colin Cowie–designed events, and the Reggae was created for a wedding in Mexico's Cabo San Lucas.

1½ ounces Mount Gay rum
½ ounce Pierre Ferrand dry curaçao
1½ ounces pineapple juice
2 dashes of Angostura bitters
Freshly grated nutmeg, for garnish

Shake all the ingredients (except the garnish) with ice and strain into a chilled cocktail glass. Garnish with freshly grated nutmeg.

RICARD TOMATE

A popular way to serve Ricard in France, this recipe sounds awful, but it is surprisingly drinkable. With this drink, it is important that the ice be added last to prevent an unpleasant film or scaling effect on the surface of the drink. Spirits like Ricard and absinthe are made with essential oils from fresh botanicals that bond with the alcohol molecule. Those bonds break as the ABV diminishes; if it happens slowly, the liquid will louche—turn cloudy—as the oil separates from the alcohol. If you shock the spirit by dumping ice water and ice cubes wholesale into it, the bond breaks rapidly and the oil molecules cling together and form a scaly scum on the surface.

2 ounces Ricard
¼ ounce grenadine, homemade (page 224)
   or store-bought
4 ounces room-temperature water

Pour the Ricard and grenadine into a highball glass and then slowly add the room temperature water. Finally, add ice cubes.

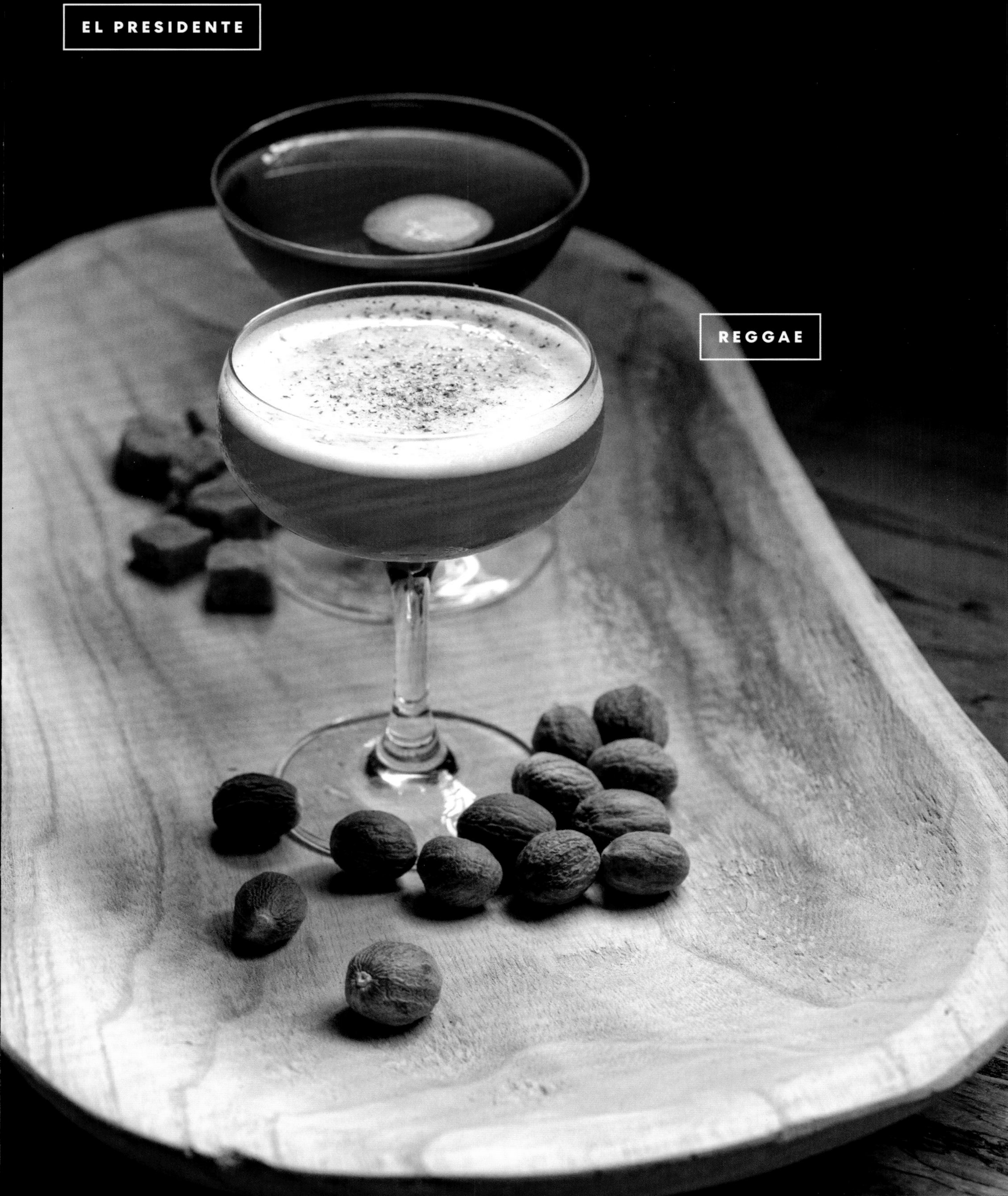
EL PRESIDENTE
REGGAE

RICKEYS

Rickeys are traditionally dry drinks, but syrup or sugar can be added—hey, it's cocktails, not watchmaking, so we can fool around a bit. Lore has it that the Rickey took its name from "Colonel Joe" Rickey, a Washington lobbyist in the late nineteenth century who regularly drank with members of Congress in Shoomaker's bar. Joe actually drank whiskey, which is not to say that he couldn't drop a lime in his whiskey. But, in fact, there is no evidence he had anything to do with the drink, it is just hard to overlook the eponymous evidence. Derek Brown, Washington, D.C., bar owner and author, tells the tale with all its twists and turns in his wonderful tome *Spirits, Sugar, Water, Bitters: How the Cocktail Conquered the World*. Early recipes for brandy, Canadian whisky, and gin rickeys appeared in George Kappeler's *Modern American Drinks* in 1895, and they are exactly the same as our contemporary recipes.

GIN RICKEY

**1½ ounces gin or base spirit of
   your choice**
½ ounce fresh lime juice
4 ounces club soda
Lime wedge, for garnish

Mix all the ingredients (except the garnish) in a highball glass with ice. Garnish with the lime wedge.

LIME RICKEY (NONALCOHOLIC)*

This is the drinking man's nonalcoholic drink that was popular at the Promenade Bar in the Rainbow Room.

¾ ounce fresh lime juice
¾ ounce Simple Syrup (page 225)
4 dashes of Angostura bitters
Club soda
Lime wedge, for garnish

Build all the ingredients (except the soda and garnish) in a highball glass, top with soda, and stir. Squeeze the lime wedge over and drop it into the drink.

LIME RICKEY

RIO BLANCO*

My margarita variation was created for the owner of GO RIO San Antonio River Cruises, who donated $10,000 to support children's charities at the San Antonio Cocktail Conference. It appeared on the menu at Bohanan's steak house, and it may still be listed there.

- 2 ounces Forteleza tequila blanco
- ¾ ounce French Sauternes (no substitutes)
- ½ ounce fresh lemon juice
- 2 dashes of Dale DeGroff's Pimento Aromatic Bitters
- 2 very thin slices of jalapeño pepper skin (no flesh or seeds)

Shake the tequila, Sauternes, lemon juice, bitters, and 1 of the jalapeño skin slices well with ice in a cocktail shaker. Strain into a coupe glass and slide the remaining jalapeño skin slice into the glass.

RITZ COCKTAIL*

This is my tribute to the Ritz cocktails of Paris and Madrid.

- 1 ounce Courvoisier VSOP Cognac
- ½ ounce Cointreau
- ¼ ounce Luxardo maraschino liqueur
- ¼ ounce fresh lemon juice
- 2 ounces Champagne
- Flamed orange zest coin (see page 62), for garnish

Shake the first four ingredients in a cocktail shaker with ice. Strain into a cocktail glass and fill with the Champagne. Garnish with the flamed orange zest coin.

ROASTED PINEAPPLE COCKTAIL*

SERVES 15

This is adapted from a 1930s recipe from the Embassy Club in Hollywood. For a drier version, use a fino sherry.

- ½ pineapple, skinned, cut into chunks, and roasted (see Note)
- 1 (750 ml) bottle dry white wine (without oak character)
- 10 ounces medium sherry, preferably Dry Sack
- 3 ounces Pedro Ximénez sherry
- 8 ounces pineapple juice
- 2 ounces fresh lemon juice
- 15 thin slices of pineapple wedge, for garnish

Bruise the pineapple chunks and macerate them in the white wine for 2 hours at room temperature. Add the remaining ingredients (except the garnish), cover, and chill overnight. The following day, strain the liquid from the pineapple chunks and discard the pineapple. For each individual serving, pour 3½ to 4 ounces of the mixture into a cocktail shaker and shake with ice. Strain into a chilled cocktail glass and garnish with a thin slice of pineapple wedge.

NOTE For a quick roast, use a kitchen torch, or prepare in advance under the broiler.

ROB ROY

Bill Grimes, in his wonderful book *Straight Up or On the Rocks* (2002), reveals the origin of the name of this scotch Manhattan: a Broadway show called *Rob Roy*. In the original *The Savoy Cocktail Book* (1930), Harry Craddock calls for equal parts of scotch, sweet vermouth, and dry vermouth, a tad sweet for today's drinker. Make it "perfect" with sweet and dry vermouth, and it is also called the Affinity cocktail. I think Peychaud's is a good match with scotch whisky.

- 2 ounces scotch
- 1 ounce Italian sweet vermouth
- Dash of Peychaud's bitters
- Lemon zest coin (see page 62), for garnish

Stir all the ingredients (except the garnish) in a mixing glass with ice and strain into a chilled cocktail glass. Express the lemon zest coin over the drink and drop it in.

VARIATION Substitute a dash of orange bitters and a dash of Cointreau for the Peychaud's bitters to make a Green Briar.

ROSARITA SUNRISE*

2 ounces Don Julio blanco tequila
½ ounce fresh lime juice
2 ounces fresh orange juice
¾ ounce Trenel Crème de Cassis de Bourgogne
1 whole orange peel, cut into a long spiral (see page 62), for garnish

Build the first three ingredients over ice cubes in a highball glass. Slowly pour the cassis down through the center of the drink. Garnish with the peel and add an orange spiral for decoration.

ROSETTA+

Las Vegas legend Tony Abou-Ganim and I were on a cocktail safari when we stumbled into Daddy-O's bar in Greenwich Village. Bartender Tony Debok invented this special cocktail just for us, but then I'll bet he says that to all the tourists.

1½ ounces Stolichnaya Ohranj vodka
½ ounce Cointreau
¾ ounce Campari
1 ounce fresh orange juice
Flamed orange zest coin (see page 62), for garnish

Shake all the ingredients (except the garnish) well with ice and strain into a chilled cocktail glass. Garnish with the flamed orange zest coin.

ROYAL FLUSH*

This from the *DeGroff Collection*, a small pamphlet produced in 1993 by Angostura bitters and Bacardí.

2 ounces Bacardí Gran Reserva Diez rum
1 ounce orgeat
½ ounce fresh lime juice
2 ounces pineapple juice
2 dashes of Angostura bitters
Edible Karma or Sonia orchid flower
   (see Notes, page 201), for garnish

Shake the ingredients (except the garnish) well with ice and strain into a double old-fashioned glass over ice. Garnish with an orchid.

ROYAL HAWAIIAN

This drink was a long time favorite at the legendary Royal Hawaiian hotel in Honolulu. Today the hotel is surrounded by ugly skyscrapers shaped like boxes— hotels with no charm. And sadly the 1950s signature cocktail has disappeared from the Royal Hawaiian.

1½ ounces gin
½ ounce fresh lemon juice
1 ounce pineapple juice
¾ ounce orgeat

Shake all the ingredients with ice and strain into a small cocktail glass.

ROYAL ROMANCE

I found this recipe in the *Café Royal Cocktail Book* by W. J. Tarling. It won the 1934 British Empire Cocktail Competition for its inventor, John Perosino. Really sexy for 1934!

1½ ounces Aviation American gin
½ ounce Grand Marnier
1 ounce sweetened passion fruit juice or nectar
2 dashes of grenadine, homemade (page 224) or
   store-bought
Flamed orange zest coin (see page 62), for garnish

Shake all the ingredients (except the garnish) with ice and strain into a chilled cocktail glass. Garnish with the flamed orange zest coin.

RUM RUNNER

I have no idea how an actual rumrunner found the time or had the inclination to assemble this edifice.

1 lime wedge
1 pineapple wedge, peeled
1 ounce Mount Gay white rum
1 ounce Appleton Estate Reserve Blend
   Jamaica rum
2 ounces pineapple juice
½ ounce fresh lime juice
1 ounce Simple Syrup (page 225)
¾ ounce emulsified egg white (see page 204)
Dash of Peychaud's bitters
Dash of Angostura bitters
Thin lime wheel, for garnish
Bordeaux cherry, for garnish
Pineapple wedge and pineapple leaf, for garnish

Bruise the lime and peeled pineapple wedge in the bottom of a Boston shaker glass, add the remaining ingredients (except the garnishes), and shake well with ice. Strain and serve over ice in a tall collins glass. Garnish the top with the lime wheel, cherry, and pineapple wedge and leaf.

ROYAL COCKTAIL

Adapted from a recipe of the Embassy Club, a
Hollywood boîte in the 1930s

1½ ounces Hendrick's Orbium gin
¾ ounce Noilly Prat Original dry vermouth
½ ounce Heering cherry liqueur
Flamed lemon zest coin (see page 62), for garnish

Stir all the ingredients (except the garnish) with ice
and strain into a chilled Nick & Nora glass. Garnish
with the flamed lemon zest coin.

RUSSIAN SPRING PUNCH+

Created at ZanZibar in London in the 1980s by the legendary London bartender Dick Bradsell.

1 ounce Stolichnaya vodka
¾ ounce fresh lemon juice
½ ounce crème de framboise
¼ ounce Trenel Crème de Cassis de Bourgogne
¼ ounce Monin raspberry syrup
¼ ounce Simple Syrup (page 225)
3 ounces Champagne
7 raspberries, for garnish

Build the first six ingredients in a large collins glass over crushed ice. Stir and top with the Champagne and the raspberries. Serve with long straws.

RUSTY NAIL

The Rusty Nail had its heyday in the 21 Club in the 1960s, and previously in the Little Club at 70 East Fifty-Fifth Street in the 1950s. Ted Saucier listed it in *Bottoms Up* (1951) as the Little Club #2.

2 ounces scotch
¾ ounce Drambuie

Pour the scotch over ice in a rocks glass and float the Drambuie on top. Stir with your index finger if you wanna be a real Rat Packer.

RYE CLUB MIST*

I created this for Fritz Maytag's malted rye whiskey Old Potrero. I served it "mist style" (over shaved ice) because the cask-strength whiskey needed the dilution.

2 ounces Old Potrero single malt rye whiskey
1 ounce Pierre Ferrand dry curaçao
2 dashes of Dale DeGroff's Pimento Aromatic Bitters
Flamed orange zest coin (see page 62), for garnish

Shake all the ingredients (except the garnish) with ice and serve over shaved ice in a rocks glass. Garnish with the flamed orange zest coin.

SALTY DOG RETOOLED*

Lime wedge, for frosting the glass
Sea salt, for frosting the glass
1½ ounces Absolut vodka
¾ ounce St-Germain elderflower liqueur
4 ounces fresh grapefruit juice
¼ ounce fresh lime juice
2 dashes of Dale DeGroff's Pimento Aromatic Bitters
Fresh basil sprig, for garnish

Frost half of the rim of a highball glass with the lime and sea salt (see page 63). Build the ingredients (except the garnish) over ice and stir. Garnish with the fresh basil sprig.

SANGRIA

SERVES 6

3 orange wheels, plus more for garnish
3 lemon wheels, plus more for garnish
1 (750 ml) bottle dry Spanish red wine or your favorite, well chilled
3 ounces Marie Brizard orange curaçao
2 ounces fresh lemon juice
2 ounces Simple Syrup (page 225)
3 ounces white grape juice
3 ounces fresh orange juice
3 ounces club soda
7 or 8 green grapes (see Note), for garnish

Place the orange and lemon in the bottom of a large glass pitcher. Using a long wooden spoon or muddler, gently press the fruit to release some juice and some oil from the zest; leave the fruit in the pitcher. Add the remaining ingredients and stir well. Serve over ice in wineglasses. Garnish with additional orange and lemon wheels, cut in half to fit easily in the glassware, and the green grapes.

NOTE You can add other favorite seasonal fruits as garnish.

Lemon or lime wedge, for frosting the glass
Kosher or sea salt, for frosting the glass
1½ ounces Blue Shark vodka
1½ ounces vodka
4 ounces fresh grapefruit juice

Frost the rim of a highball glass with the lemon or lime and salt (see page 63). Fill the glass with ice and build the drink. Stir and serve.

SATAN'S WHISKERS

Adapted from an Embassy Club recipe from Hollywood, circa 1930, this is a sinfully rich version of the Bronx Cocktail (page 97), and like everything else in Hollywood, if it costs more it must be better.

1 ounce Fords gin
½ ounce Martini & Rossi sweet vermouth
½ ounce Niolly Prat Original dry vermouth
½ ounce Grand Marnier
1 ounce fresh orange juice
Dash of Angostura bitters
Dash of Regan's Orange Bitters No. 6
Flamed orange zest coin (see page 62), for garnish

Shake all the ingredients (except the garnish) with ice and strain into a chilled cocktail glass. Garnish with the flamed orange zest coin.

SAZERAC

Popular lore has it that the Sazerac is based on bitters created by Antoine Amédée Peychaud, who opened a pharmacy in New Orleans in 1841. Peychaud held the highest position in his Masonic lodge and entertained fellow Masons after hours at the pharmacy, which offered the opportunity to promote his aromatic bitters, dashing it in cups of Cognac. For many years, the most popular Cognac in New Orleans was Sazerac de Forge et Fils, and some point to this as proof of the birth of the Sazerac, but no actual documentation exists to support that theory.

Historian and author David Wondrich has given in once again to his inescapable addiction to actual facts—like the fact that the drink never appeared in print until 1898, and even then, absinthe was not a part of the recipe. John Schiller may have officially christened the Sazerac Coffee House in 1859, but it had nothing to do with the cocktail. And when Thomas H. Handy took over the bar, he had nothing to do with the Sazerac cocktail. If you are one of those who insist on relying on facts, visit NOLA.com and look for Mr. Wondrich's detailed July 2015 article, which is riddled with facts about what the Sazerac is and is not. I had my own twist on the Sazerac recipe at the Rainbow Room; see my mix below of Cognac *and* bourbon, Peychaud's *and* Angostura, and that's a fact!

1 small sugar cube
2 dashes of Peychaud's bitters
2 dashes of Angostura bitters
1 ounce Pierre Ferrand Ambre Cognac or your favorite VSOP Cognac
1 ounce Wild Turkey 101 rye whiskey
Splash of Jade Esprit Edouard Absinthe Supérieure
Lemon zest coin (see page 62)

Chill a rocks glass with crushed ice and set aside. In another rocks glass, muddle the sugar cube and both bitters to crush the cube and create a flavor paste; a tiny splash of water may help this process along. Add the Cognac, rye whiskey, and 2 or 3 good-size ice cubes and stir to chill. Toss the crushed ice out of the first glass, splash the absinthe into it, and swirl; give it a spinning toss in the air if you have high ceilings and if you're brave—oh, and be sure to catch it on the way down! Strain the chilled drink into the absinthe-seasoned glass and express the oil from the lemon zest over the drink and discard. Serve promptly. Drink slowly.

SCORPINO

This was, and maybe still is, Julia Roberts's favorite drink. She actually said so herself; I'm not making that up.

2 ounces Wyborowa vodka
2 ounces heavy cream
1 ounce Cointreau
1 big scoop of Italian lemon sherbet
Grated lemon zest, for garnish

In a blender, pulse the vodka, cream, Cointreau, and sherbet and pour the mix into a large cocktail glass. Sprinkle the lemon zest over the top and serve.

SCORPION

Here's a variation on the Victor Jules Bergeron (Trader Vic) recipe. Bergeron suggests pulsing this drink in a blender.

1½ ounces Appleton Estate Signature Blend Jamaica rum
¾ ounce Camus Ile de Ré Fine Island Cognac
¾ ounce fresh lemon juice
½ ounce Simple Syrup (page 225)
1 ounce fresh orange juice
½ ounce orgeat
1 cup cracked ice
½ ounce Smith & Cross Jamaica rum
Edible Karma orchid, for garnish (see Notes)

Assemble the first seven ingredients in a blender and pulse to blend. Pour into a double old-fashioned glass. Float the Smith & Cross rum and clip the stem of the orchid over the rim of the glass for a garnish.

NOTES Orchids and other edible flowers are available by mail order from MarxFoods.com.

If you prefer not to blend the drink, the ingredients can be shaken with cracked ice and strained into a double old-fashioned glass over ice cubes; float the Smith & Cross rum on top.

SCREWDRIVER

This was one of the drinks used by John Martin to promote Smirnoff vodka after the World War II. Lore has it that the name comes from the oilmen in Texas, Oklahoma, and California who stirred the vodka and OJ with their screwdrivers. Or Martin, a notorious gorilla marketer, may have made that up.

1½ ounces Blue Shark vodka
5 ounces fresh orange juice
Half orange wheel, for garnish

Build the vodka and orange juice over ice cubes in a highball glass. Garnish with the orange wheel.

SEA BREEZE

The Sea Breeze was created by Ocean Spray company in the 1960s to take advantage of the growing popularity of vodka to promote cranberry juice. They even participated in the release of a new spirit product called Tropico that was a blend of Don Cossack vodka and cranberry juice. Seagram's tried to glom onto the popularity of the Sea Breeze to promote its aged gin, Ancient Bottle golden gin, but it was a losing battle. Gin was out and vodka was in.

1½ ounces Blue Shark vodka
3 ounces fresh grapefruit juice
3 ounces cranberry juice
Lime wedge, for garnish

Pour the vodka into a chilled highball glass. Pour in the grapefruit juice and top with the cranberry juice and stir. Garnish with the lime wedge.

VARIATIONS For the Bay Breeze, substitute pineapple juice for the grapefruit juice. For the Madras, substitute orange juice. For a Shore Breeze, use rum instead of vodka.

SETTING SUN*

This after-dinner selection from the *DeGroff Collection* (1993), a pamphlet produced by Angostura bitters and Bacardi, is like an adult Orange Julius.

2 ounces Bacardí Reserva Ocho rum
1 ounce heavy cream
1 ounce fresh orange juice
½ ounce Cointreau
2 dashes of Angostura bitters
Grated orange zest, for garnish
Pinch of ground cinnamon, for garnish

Shake all the ingredients (except the garnishes) well with ice and strain into a large coupe glass. Garnish with the grated orange zest and dust with cinnamon.

SEVILLA*

I created the Sevilla for a cocktail dinner at Jeroboam restaurant in Dallas for their onion-and-cheddar soup.

3 ounces Stolichnaya Ohranj vodka
¾ ounce Lustau East India Solera sherry
Flamed orange zest coin (see page 62), for garnish

In a mixing glass, stir the vodka and sherry with ice to chill and strain into a chilled cocktail glass. Garnish with the flamed orange zest coin.

SEX ON THE BEACH

1½ ounces Blue Shark vodka
½ ounce DeKuyper Peachtree schnapps
¼ ounce Chambord
2 ounces cranberry juice
1 ounce fresh orange juice
1 ounce fresh grapefruit juice
Bordeaux cherry, for garnish
Lemon wheel, for garnish
Orange wheel, for garnish

Shake all the ingredients (except the garnishes) and strain into a chilled highball glass. Place the cherry in the center of the two fruit wheels, pinch them around the cherry and skewer through all three to hold the cherry in the center. Add to the drink.

SHANDYGAFF OR SHANDY

The modern recipe is a pint glass of lager beer mixed half-and-half with lemonade (lemonade in England refers to sparkling lemon-lime soda). Below is the original recipe from the time of Dickens.

½ pint ale
½ pint ginger beer, homemade (page 222)
or store-bought
1½ ounces Marie Brizard orange curaçao
½ ounce fresh lemon juice
Lemon zest coin (see page 62), for garnish

Build the ingredients (except the garnish) in a mug and garnish with the lemon zest coin.

SIDECAR

The year was 1978. I was working at the bar at the Hotel Bel-Air. I had just finished making a Sidecar one afternoon, when an older gentleman looked at me and said, "You know what a real Sidecar is, son?" I thought I did until I heard him describe the recipe. After four years of tending bar, I finally began to collect proper recipes.

Lemon wedge, for frosting the glass
Sugar, for frosting the glass
1½ ounces Cognac
1 ounce Cointreau
¾ ounce fresh lemon juice
Flamed orange zest coin (see page 62),
for garnish

Frost a cocktail coupe glass with the lemon and sugar (see page 63). Shake the remaining ingredients (except the garnish) with ice and strain into the prepared glass. Garnish with the flamed orange zest coin.

SIMMER DOWN+

Original recipe by award-winning bartender Jason Cousins.

1½ ounces Louis Royer Force 53 VSOP Cognac
1 ounce Russo Antica Distilleria Nocino walnut
liqueur (see Note)
1½ ounces Caffè Borghetti espresso liqueur
(see Note)
2 dashes of Dale DeGroff's Pimento Aromatic
Bitters
Flamed orange zest coin (see page 62),
for garnish

Stir all the ingredients (except the garnish) in a mixing glass with ice and strain into a chilled Nick & Nora glass. Garnish with the flamed orange zest coin.

NOTE The walnut liqueur is available from Wine-Searcher.com. The espresso liqueur is available from TotalWine.com.

SINGAPORE SLING

Created at the Long Bar in Singapore's Raffles Hotel about 1915 by bartender Ngiam Tong Boon, the recipe varies from book to book. Robin Kelley O'Connor, the Bordeaux wine expert, sent me a telegram from Raffles while he was staying there in 1990: "I've never tasted a better version." Apparently in the interim, the recipe at Raffles suffered with different management but now it's back.

1½ ounces Fords gin
½ ounce Herring cherry liqueur
¼ ounce Cointreau
¼ ounce Bénédictine
2 ounces pineapple juice
½ ounce fresh lime juice
Dash of Angostura bitters
2 ounces club soda
Orange slice, for garnish
Bordeaux cherry, for garnish

Shake all the ingredients (except the club soda and garnishes) with ice and strain into a highball glass. Top with the soda. Garnish with the orange slice and cherry.

SLOE GIN FIZZ

1 ounce Plymouth sloe gin
1 ounce Plymouth gin
¾ ounce fresh lemon juice
¾ ounce Simple Syrup (page 225)
3 ounces club soda or seltzer
Orange slice, for garnish
Bordeaux cherry, for garnish

Shake the first four ingredients with ice and strain into an ice-filled highball glass. Top with the soda and stir. Garnish with the orange slice and cherry.

JIM'S SCOTCH AND SODA

I can't imagine a cocktail book without a mention of the scotch and soda. From the day charged water was invented, it has been adopted by the whiskey drinker to replace the water that dilutes and livens up a glass of whiskey. There is even a song named after the drink! But I have a much more important reason to list the scotch and soda: It gives me the chance to tell the story about advertising man and title holder for endurance cocktailing Jim Callaway, "a real larger-than-death character," as his business partner Ron Holland characterized him when Jim was diagnosed with cancer.

In 1987, Jim had major surgery to remove a tumor from his brain. A week after surgery, he was back with us at the bar in Charley O's, bald head covered with a stocking cap, double scotch in an old-fashioned glass and also a Diet Coke in front of him. Jim carefully instructed that if his wife walked through the door, whoever spied her first would pick up his scotch, take a large gulp, and set it down in front of himself.

Conversation carried on as we kept 360 degrees covered, but somehow in the blink of an eye, there was his wife, standing right behind Jim as he was raising his scotch to his lips. We all sat there hopelessly wondering how he'd get out of this one. Seeing the panic in our eyes, Jim slammed down the scotch and choked out, "This is not my Diet Coke!"

SMITH AND KEARNS

The proper name, when this was created in 1952, was Smith and Curran. It was named by bartender Gerbert Doebber at the Blue Blazer Lounge after two customers, Wendell Smith and James Curran. It seems that people heard the name and just spelled it phonetically.

2 ounces Kahlúa
3 ounces whole milk or half-and-half
2 ounces club soda

Build the Kahlúa and milk in a chilled highball glass and top with the soda.

VARIATION For a Colorado Bulldog, substitute Coca-Cola for the club soda.

SMUGGLER'S NOTCH+

"Now the naming part. I scribbled ideas in my Moleskin until I came up with 'Smuggler's Notch.' Most of the ingredients [real spirits] were illegal and had to be smuggled into the United States during Prohibition. I tested my GM, David Rosoff, on the drink in the middle of busy service.

'Great. You made a rum old-fashioned, and I'll bet you got a clever name. . . . I don't really care. Can you please just take care of table five? It's stressing me out they don't have drinks.'" —Eric Alperin, partner in The Varnish, Los Angeles

Splash of Pernod absinthe
1 brown sugar cube, or 1 barspoon of Brown Sugar or Demerara Syrup (page 223)
2 dashes of Bitter Truth orange bitters
Splash of water
2 ounces Bacardi Reserva Ocho rum (or some contraband Havana Club 7-year-old rum)
1 large (2 × 2-inch) ice cube
Orange zest coin (see page 62), for garnish

Rinse an old-fashioned glass with a splash of Pernod and toss the remainder out. Muddle the sugar cube, or stir if using syrup, with the bitters and a splash of water in the glass. Add the rum and the ice cube and stir. Garnish with the orange zest coin.

EGGS IN COCKTAILS

Drinks that call for eggs, egg whites, or egg yolks are tricky. Our eggs today are larger than in the past. Following older recipe instructions that call for a whole egg or the white of an egg while using today's bigger eggs will throw the drink out of whack. The solution is to beat the whole egg(s) or the egg white(s) with a whisk to emulsify them, break them down, so they will pour and can be measured like any other ingredient. I often bottle them in a plastic squeeze bottle for easy use. In recipes that call for a whole egg or egg white, I typically use no more than ¾ ounce of emulsified egg or egg white for a single drink. Always refrigerate any egg products.

SOUTH BEACH*

I created this one for the now shuttered Paddington Corporation in 1992 to showcase Campari cocktails that were less bitter and would appeal to the American palate. That sounds crazy now that Americans seem to have finally awakened to the glories of the bitter aperitif. The recipe below worked back then as an entry level to the complexity of Campari bitters. Today the Negroni (page 175) is sweeping the country.

¾ ounce Campari
¾ ounce Disaronno Originale amaretto
2 ounces fresh orange juice
Flamed orange zest coin (see page 62), for garnish

Shake all the ingredients (except the garnish) with ice and strain into a chilled cocktail glass. Garnish with the flamed orange zest coin.

SOURS

Sours first appeared in *How to Mix Drinks* (1862) by Jerry Thomas. The sour drinks are the benchmark of the professional bartender and are the biggest challenge for the amateur. The difficult factor is balancing the sour ingredient, typically fresh lemon and/or lime juice. Follow the formula below for all your sweet-and-sour drinks—collins, fizz, margarita— and they'll be in "the window of drinkability" for 90 percent of people. In the nineteenth century, the sour category included "Fixes" that had the same ingredients as a sour but in slightly different proportions and were garnished extravagantly with fresh seasonal fruit.

BASIC SOUR FORMULA

1½ to 2 ounces base liquor
¾ ounce sour ingredient (lemon or lime juice or both in equal parts)
¾ ounce sweet ingredient, usually Simple Syrup (page 225)

The sweet can vary; simple syrup made with equal parts (by volume) sugar and water works fine in the formula. But if a liqueur like Cointreau, which is 40% alcohol and much drier than simple syrup, is used, then it should be bumped up to 1 ounce. A sour using any substitute sweet ingredient will require tasting to determine if the formula holds true.

With good ice, at least 1-inch solid cubes, shake all the ingredients very hard for a slow ten count to create a really lively drink with the right dilution. With chipped or cracked ice, shake hard to a five count to chill the drink and avoid over-dilution.

The other issue associated with sours is egg white. The practice of adding egg white to create foam is very popular in the craft bar movement, and it is appreciated by some, but others find a trace flavor of albumen unpleasant. Always ask the guest before using eggs in the recipe. Don't overuse egg white; ¾ ounce or less is more than enough in a cocktail. To properly measure egg white, "emulsify" it by using a whisk to break down the albumen and bottle it in a plastic squeeze bottle for easy use. *Always* keep egg products under refrigeration. (For more information on using eggs in cocktails, see page 204.)

SOUTHSIDE

This was the house drink of the famous 21 Club for years—a kind of Mint Julep for the Gin-and-Tonic crowd.

2 fresh mint sprigs
¾ ounce fresh lime juice
¾ ounce Simple Syrup (page 225)
2 ounces Beefeater 24 gin
1½ ounces club soda

Bruise 1 of the mint sprigs with the lime juice and simple syrup in the bottom of a Boston shaker glass. Add the gin and ice and shake well. Pour into a goblet over cracked ice, add the club soda, and stir until the outside of the glass frosts. Garnish with the remaining mint sprig.

SPICY ABBEY COCKTAIL*

Inspired by the classic Abbey Cocktail (page 72).

1½ ounces Don Julio reposado tequila
½ ounce Lillet Rosé
½ ounce fresh orange juice
¾ ounce fresh lemon juice
¾ ounce agave nectar
1 teaspoon red pepper jelly
Dash of Angostura Bitters
Orange zest coin (see page 62), for garnish

Assemble all the ingredients (except the garnish) in a cocktail shaker and shake well with ice. Fine strain into a double old-fashioned glass over ice. Express the oil of the orange zest coin over the drink and drop it in.

WINE SPRITZER

Fill the wineglass two-thirds with white wine and top with club soda. Most drinkers prefer ice with a spritzer; if serving without ice, keep all the ingredients cold. Garnish with lemon peel. Boston has its own take on the classic wine drink: called the Wine Cooler, Boston style is red table wine mixed with 7UP in a goblet over ice with a lemon zest garnish.

ST. BRUNO†

This is a specialty of Jimmy's bar and restaurant in Aspen, Colorado, where all things agave have a cozy American home.

1 orange slice
1 fresh mint sprig
Dash of Peychaud's bitters
2 ounces El Tesoro Platinum tequila
½ ounce green Chartreuse V.E.P.
Orange zest coin (see page 62), for garnish

Lightly muddle the orange slice and the mint sprig with the bitters in a mixing glass. Add the tequila and the Chartreuse and stir with ice. Fine strain into a Nick & Nora glass. Express the orange zest coin over the drink and drop it in.

STILETTO

1 ounce Disaronno Originale amaretto
½ ounce banana liqueur (I recommend Marie Brizard No 12)
1 ounce fresh orange juice
1 ounce pineapple juice
Flamed orange zest coin (see page 62), for garnish

Shake all the ingredients (except the garnish) well with ice. Strain into a chilled coupe glass. Garnish with the flamed orange zest coin.

STINGER

This classic New York nightcap dates back to 1900. Some decorate it with a mint sprig, but in days gone by, this drink was an adult after-dinner mint, a way to cleanse the palate after a multicourse, extravagantly rich meal; nothing edible came anywhere near the drink, so no garnish. This drink was also popular midcentury with equal parts of brandy and white crème de menthe, but the American palate is much drier today.

2 ounces Martel VSOP Cognac
1 ounce Marie Brizard No 33 white crème
  de menthe

Shake the ingredients hard with ice and strain into an old-fashioned glass filled with crushed ice.

STONE FENCE

Adapted from *Recipes of American and Other Iced Drinks*, by Charlie Paul (1902).

2 ounces Maker's Mark bourbon
5 ounces fresh apple cider
½ ounce fresh lemon juice
3 dashes of Simple Syrup (page 225)
4 dashes of Dale DeGroff's Pimento Aromatic
  Bitters
Granny Smith Apple slice, for garnish

Build the ingredients in a highball glass with ice (except the garnish) and stir. Garnish with the apple slice.

STONE SOUR

I don't know who coined the name first, but I suspect it came from California. As a matter of fact, Stone Sours are also called California Sours. Stone Sour just indicates the addition of a little fresh orange juice.

1½ ounces Bulleit bourbon
¾ ounce fresh lemon juice
¾ ounce Simple Syrup (page 225)
1 ounce fresh orange juice
Orange slice, for garnish
Bordeaux cherry, for garnish

Shake all the ingredients (except the garnishes) with ice and serve in a rocks glass over ice. Garnish with the orange slice and cherry.

STONEHENGE PUNCH

Adapted from an original recipe from The Stonehenge Inn, in Ridgefield, Connecticut.

1 ounce Four Roses bourbon
1 ounce Mount Gay Extra Old rum
½ ounce fresh lemon juice
½ ounce Simple Syrup (page 225)
Dash of Dale DeGroff's Pimento Aromatic Bitters
Bordeaux cherry, for garnish
Pineapple wedge, for garnish
Half-orange wheel, for garnish

Shake the ingredients hard with ice and strain into an old-fashioned glass filled with crushed ice. Garnish with the Bordeaux cherry, pineapple wedge, and half-orange wheel.

STORK CLUB COCKTAIL

I had this beauty on my menu for years at the Rainbow Room, but credit goes to the great Nathaniel Cook. He sounds like a Revolutionary War hero, but he was chief barman at the legendary Stork Club.

1½ ounces Fords gin
½ ounce Joseph Cartron Curaçao Orange
¼ ounce fresh lime juice
1 ounce fresh orange juice
Dash of Angostura bitters
Flamed orange zest coin (see page 62), for garnish

Shake all the ingredients (except the garnish) well with ice and strain into a chilled cocktail glass. Garnish with the flamed orange zest coin.

This unusual combination of hoppy IPA brew, gin, and pineapple was created by bartender Thomas Waugh of Death & Co., an early craft cocktail bar in New York City. It is so much better than it sounds!

2 ounces Tanqueray No. Ten gin
¾ ounce John D. Taylor's Velvet Falernum
1 ounce unsweetened pineapple juice
½ ounce fresh lemon juice
3 ounces hoppy IPA beer (I suggest Green Flash)
Fresh mint sprig, for garnish

Shake the first four ingredients with ice and strain into a pilsner glass without ice. Top slowly with the beer. Garnish with the mint sprig.

STRAWBERRY DAIQUIRI, FROZEN

Fresh-fruit versions of the frozen daiquiri are fun to prepare when seasonal fruit is available. Here is one for fresh strawberries. Note that frozen drinks require a lot more sweetening than shaken drinks because of the additional dilution from the ice.

2 ounces Caña Brava rum
½ ounce Luxardo maraschino liqueur
4 to 6 medium strawberries, hulled and cut up
2 ounces Simple Syrup (page 225)
1 ounce fresh lime juice
1 cup of cracked ice
1 whole fresh strawberry, for garnish

Blend all the ingredients (except the garnish) and pour into a copa grande glass. Garnish with the whole strawberry by making a cut on the bottom of the strawberry and perching it on the rim of the glass.

STRAWBERRY NIRVANA*

1 quarter-size piece of peeled fresh ginger
¼ ounce John D. Taylor's Velvet Falernum
   (see Note)
1½ ounces Plymouth gin
1 ounce mixed strawberry-lychee purée (see Note)
¼ ounce fresh lemon juice
1 whole fresh strawberry, for garnish

Mash the ginger in the bottom of a cocktail shaker with the Falernum. Add the remaining ingredients (except the garnish) and shake well with ice. Fine strain into a chilled coupe glass to remove the ginger bits. Garnish with the strawberry.

NOTE Velvet Falernum is available from Alpenz.com. I recommend flash-frozen products from the Perfect Purée of Napa Valley (www.perfectpuree.com).

SUFFERING BASTARD

This is basically a Mai Tai with orange juice.

1½ ounces Zacapa Centenario rum
¾ ounce Pierre Ferrand dry curaçao
½ ounce orgeat
¾ ounce fresh lime juice
1½ ounces fresh orange juice
½ ounce Smith & Cross Jamaica rum
Lime slice, for garnish
Orange slice, for garnish

Shake the Centenario rum, curaçao, orgeat, and lime and orange juices well with ice. Strain into an ice-filled double old-fashioned glass and float the Smith & Cross rum on top. Garnish with the sliced fruit.

SURE THING*

A cross between the Sundowner and the Tiger Lilly from Ted Saucier's 1951 edition of *Bottoms Up*.

1½ ounces Mount Gay Eclipse rum
½ ounce Martel VSOP Cognac
½ ounce Pierre Ferrand dry curaçao
½ ounce John D. Taylor's Velvet Falernum
½ ounce fresh lime juice
½ ounce fresh blood orange juice
Dash of Angostura bitters
Lime slice, for garnish
Blood orange slice, for garnish

Shake all the ingredients (except the garnishes) well with ice. Strain into an ice-filled double old-fashioned glass and garnish with the fruit.

SWIZZLE

The swizzle drinks are named after the Jamaican swizzle—a very thin stick about twelve inches long with "branches" radiating out of one end, though they are actually the root structure that has been cut short. The swizzle is surprisingly sturdy for what looks like a twig that could easily be snapped in half. To use the thing, it is placed in a tall drink with the root cluster in the drink and rotated rapidly between the palms, agitating the drink as an electric mixer would.

RUM SWIZZLE

1½ ounces Mount Gay Eclipse rum
¼ ounce John D. Taylor's Velvet Falernum (see Note)
½ ounce fresh lime juice
½ ounce Simple Syrup (page 225)
Dash of Dale Degroff's Pimento Aromatic Bitters
Lime wedge, for garnish

Place all the ingredients (except the garnish) in a tall glass with crushed ice. Holding the swizzle between your palms, rapidly rotate it to mix the drink. Remove the swizzle and garnish with the lime wedge.

NOTE Velvet Falernum is available at Alpenz.com.

TAYLOR MADE*

2 ounces Colonel E.H. Taylor small batch bonded bourbon
¼ ounce John D. Taylor's Velvet Falernum (see Note)
¾ ounce fresh grapefruit juice
¼ ounce Honey Syrup (page 224)
Dash of Bitter Truth grapefruit bitters
Half grapefruit wheel, for garnish

Shake all the ingredients (except the garnish) with ice. Strain into an iced double old-fashioned glass. Garnish with the half grapefruit wheel.

TEQUILA SUNRISE

The original Tequila Sunrise of the 1940s is a tequila collins with crème de cassis poured through after adding the seltzer. It originally appeared in *The Roving Bartender* by Bill Kelly (1946.)

1½ ounces Milagro Silver tequila
4 to 5 ounces fresh orange juice
¾ ounce grenadine, homemade (page 224) or
  store-bought, or crème de cassis

Chill a highball glass. Add the tequila, pour in the fresh orange juice, and pour the grenadine or cassis through the orange juice.

THAT'S AMORE

In 1936, Dave Chasen and his silent partner, Harold Ross of *The New Yorker* magazine fame, opened Chasen's in Beverly Hills. It started out as a chili joint, but it soon turned into a celebrity hangout visited by everyone from presidents and monarchs to the Rat Pack. Dean Martin was at the bar once and asked veteran barman Pepe Ruiz to create a drink especially for him. The next time Martin came in, Pepe took a whole navel orange and cut the peel into large strips. He poured a little La Ina fino sherry into a chilled cocktail glass, swirled it around, and threw it out. He expressed the orange oil through a lit match, coating the inside of the glass with the flamed orange oil. Next, he shook vodka with ice, strained it into the cocktail glass, and garnished it with another flamed orange zest. He called it the Flame of Love Martini (see page 124). When Frank Sinatra saw the drink, he got so excited that he told Pepe to "water the infield," a colorful way to say I'm buying everyone a drink, in this case one of the new libations. I suppose Pepe had just a moment of regret as he instructed the staff to bring out a case of oranges.

TOASTED ALMOND

Add vodka to make this a Roasted Almond.

¾ ounce Disaronno Originale amaretto
¾ ounce Kahlúa
2 ounces heavy cream

Shake all the ingredients with ice and strain into a small cocktail glass.

TOM AND JERRY

This was on the bar at every establishment in New York City during the holidays in the Gay Nineties.

FOR THE BATTER
12 fresh large eggs, separated
6 cups sugar
1½ teaspoons ground cinnamon
½ teaspoon ground cloves
½ teaspoon ground allspice
2 ounces añejo rum
1 teaspoon creme of tartar (optional)

FOR EACH INDIVIDUAL DRINK
2 tablespoons batter
1½ ounces brandy
½ ounce añejo rum
3 to 4 ounces boiling water or hot milk
Freshly grated nutmeg, for garnish

To make the batter: In a large bowl, beat the egg yolks until combined. While continuing to beat, gradually add the sugar, spices, and rum and beat until the mixture is thick and pale. Beat the egg whites separately until stiff. Fold the egg whites into the egg yolks and stir until the consistency is of a light batter. Add teaspoon of cream of tartar, if desired, to prevent the sugar from settling to the bottom of the batter.

To prepare each drink: Put the batter in the bottom of a ceramic mug, add the spirits and the boiling water or hot milk and stir. Dust with nutmeg and serve.

TODDIES

In his 1801 book, *The American Herbal, or Materia Medica,* Samuel Stearns offered this recipe for the toddy: water, rum or brandy, sugar, and nutmeg. It was considered to be a salutary (healthy) beverage and was especially popular in the summer.

In his 1862 *How to Mix Drinks,* Jerry Thomas lists toddies and slings together. He indicates that the only difference between them is a little grated nutmeg on top of a sling. Thomas served toddies and slings hot and cold, and used only spirits, sugar, and water (except for the apple toddy, which is made with a baked apple). By the 1890s, lemon juice and lemon peel were introduced to the toddy, and it was on its way to becoming a lemon-and-honey, hot water or tea, teaspoon of whiskey, cure for colds, dispensed by mothers and grandmothers everywhere.

APPLE TODDY

Jerry Thomas's original recipe from *How to Mix Drinks* resembles a colonial-style drink one would find in an eighteenth-century inn.

- **½ baked apple**
- **1 tablespoon fine white sugar**
- **1 wineglass (2 ounces) of cider brandy (Laird's applejack)**
- **4 ounces boiling water**
- **Whole nutmeg, for grating**

Put the baked apple, sugar, and cider brandy in a bar glass or large mug. Fill the glass two-thirds full of boiling water, and grate a little nutmeg on top.

NOTE If there is a question whether the glass is tempered for extremes of hot and cold, place a silver spoon in the glass before adding the boiling water.

HOT TODDY

- **½ ounce brandy, rum, or scotch**
- **1 teaspoon honey**
- **½ ounce fresh lemon juice**
- **4 ounces boiling water or tea**

Combine the first three ingredients in a mug and fill with the boiling water or tea.

TOM COLLINS

This drink is from the Planter's Hotel in St. Louis in the 1850s. Bartenders like Jerry Thomas and Harry Johnson were filled with wanderlust, which is also the case with the craft bar crowd today. The Planter's Hotel it seems was happy to host these celebrity mixologists and did so on a regular basis; both Johnson and Thomas did stints there.

1½ ounces gin
¾ ounce fresh lemon juice
¾ ounce Simple Syrup (page 225)
3 to 4 ounces club soda
Orange slice, for garnish
Bordeaux cherry, for garnish

Shake the first three ingredients with ice and strain into a collins glass. Add the club soda and stir. Garnish with the orange slice and cherry.

TRE AMICI⁺

George Delgado, the head bartender of The Greatest Bar on Earth at Windows on the World restaurant, and I were presenting a hands-on guest seminar on tequila and tequila cocktails on September 10, 2001, in the Skybox lounge overlooking the main bar. We stayed for drinks and dinner after the event and both left around 1:30 in the morning, about seven hours before the first plane hit the south tower. George was off the morning of the tragedy, but many of his friends and mine were there.

1 ounce Amaro Montenegro
1 ounce Punt e Mes
1 ounce Martini Riserva Speciale Rubino
   vermouth
4 dashes of Fee Brothers orange bitters
Orange wedge
Orange zest coin (see page 62), for garnish

Shake the first five ingredients with ice and strain into an old-fashioned glass over ice. Garnish with the orange zest coin.

TRINIDAD SOUR⁺

Created by Giuseppe González. Anyone who has met Giuseppe understands that the words "hey, you can't do that" are the primary reason for doing "that." The recipe below has fully an ounce of Angostura bitters, which is usually administered in dashes. Giuseppe decided the right amount was an ounce. And so it is. A nineteenth-century advertisement for Angostura bitters depicts a comely, well-to-do young woman sipping from a copita of Angostura bitters, proving that Giuseppe is on the right side of history in the choice he made.

½ ounce 100-proof bonded rye whiskey
   (see Note)
1 ounce Angostura bitters
1 ounce orgeat
¾ ounce fresh lemon juice
Lemon peel, for garnish

Shake all the ingredients (except the garnish) well with ice. Strain into a Nick & Nora glass. Garnish with the lemon peel.

NOTE With only ½ ounce total in the drink, the 100-proof rye is an important choice. A lower-proof rye would not make enough impact in the drink.

THE SPICE BOX

Colonial inns kept a spice box with equal parts of ground nutmeg, ground cinnamon, ground ginger, and dried and ground orange zest. One teaspoon of the mix was used per drink for flips and toddies.

TROPICAL ITCH

Harry Yee, legendary Oahu bartender, created this and many other Hawaiian tropical drinks, like the Blue Hawaiian. Harry had a lot of firsts in the tropical drinks world, including using those beautiful purple Vanda orchids.

1 ounce Wild Turkey 101 bourbon
1 ounce Lemon Hart Original 1804 rum
½ ounce Joseph Cartron Curaçao Orange
6 ounces sweetened passion fruit juice
Dash of Angostura bitters
¼ ounce Lemon Hart 151 overproof rum
Chinese back scratcher, for garnish (yes the wooden one—Harry's touch)

In a shaker, combine the bourbon, rum, curaçao, fruit juice, and bitters. Add ice and shake. Strain into a chilled hurricane glass. Float the overproof rum on top. Insert the Chinese back scratcher (no kidding—Harry Yee cornered the back scratcher market with this drink!).

TUXEDO

The Artistry of Mixing Drinks, the privately published book of Frank Meier, the Ritz Paris's legendary bartender, channels the turn-of-the-century American dry martini–style recipes that first appeared in Charles S. Mahoney's *Hoffman House Bartender's Guide* (1905), with even the same brands that were popular in Mahoney's recipes. I was surprised to find out why. Frank Meier apprenticed with the great Charles S. Mahoney of the Hoffman House Hotel bar in New York City. (David Wondrich found this historical nugget in his research.) It seems that the cocktail profession was as nomadic in the nineteenth century as the craft cocktail community is today. I am not sure how long Frank Meier stayed at the Hoffman House, but he must have seen Prohibition on the horizon; he started at the Ritz Paris in 1921.

2 ounces Plymouth gin
1 ounce Noilly Prat Original dry vermouth
2 dashes of Luxardo maraschino liqueur
2 dashes of Marie Brizard anisette

Stir the ingredients with ice and strain into a chilled cocktail glass.

TWENTIETH CENTURY

2 ounces Fords gin
¼ ounce Tempus Fugit crème de cacao
½ ounce Lillet Blanc
¼ ounce fresh lemon juice

Shake all the ingredients with ice and strain into a chilled cocktail glass.

209 EAST COCKTAIL*

If you wish, coat the rim of the glass with a mix of superfine sugar and powdered strawberry. To make powdered strawberry, pulverize freeze-dried strawberries in a spice grinder or with a mortar and pestle.

1½ ounces Herradura reposado tequila
¾ ounce Cointreau
½ ounce Marie Brizard No 22 strawberry liqueur
1 ounce fresh lime juice

Shake all the ingredients with ice and strain into a chilled cocktail glass.

UNDER SIEGE+

This was created by Simon Ford to showcase his London dry Fords gin.

2 ounces Fords gin
½ ounce Aperol
¾ ounce fresh grapefruit juice
½ ounce fresh lemon juice
¾ ounce orgeat
Dash of Peychaud's bitters
Grapefruit zest coin (see page 62), for garnish

Shake all the ingredients (except the bitters and garnish) with ice and strain into a highball glass over ice. Strike with the bitters. Garnish with the grapefruit zest coin.

UPTOWN HAIRY NAVEL

Cousin of the Fuzzy Navel.

1 ounce Blue Shark vodka
1 ounce Marie Brizard No 11 peach liqueur
4 ounces fresh orange juice
Fresh peach slice, for garnish

Build the first three ingredients in a highball glass over ice and stir. Garnish with the peach slice.

VALENCIA 11

This drink was served at the Roosevelt Hotel in Hollywood in the 1930s. I'm sure that the huge citrus groves over the Santa Monica pass in the San Fernando Valley provided inspiration for this orange-drenched beauty. I added the "11" because there is another Valencia, a dry martini recipe with the same name that substituted fino sherry for vermouth.

½ ounce Marie Brizard Apry liqueur
1 ounce fresh orange juice
2 dashes of orange bitters
Champagne
Flamed orange zest coin (see page 62), for garnish

Shake the first three ingredients with ice and strain into a chilled champagne flute. Top with Champagne. Garnish with the flamed orange zest coin.

VENDOME

This was the house drink of the Vendome Club, Hollywood, circa 1930.

1 ounce Dubonnet Rouge
1 ounce Beefeater gin
1 ounce Noilly Prat Original dry vermouth
Lemon peel, for garnish

Stir all the ingredients (except the garnish) with ice and strain into a chilled cocktail glass. Garnish with the lemon peel.

VERMOUTH CASSIS

¾ ounce Maison Trenel Fils Crème de Cassis de Bourgogne
3 ounces Noilly Prat Original dry vermouth
Lemon zest coin (see page 62), for garnish

Fill a white-wine glass three-quarters full of ice. Pour in the cassis and fill with the vermouth. Garnish with the lemon zest coin.

VIRGIN KIR ROYALE* (NONALCOHOLIC)

¼ ounce Monin raspberry syrup
5 ounces Sutter Home Fre alcohol-removed
  sparkling Brut
Lemon peel spiral (see page 62), for garnish
Fresh raspberry, for garnish

Pour the raspberry syrup into a champagne flute and fill slowly with the brut. Garnish with the lemon peel spiral and raspberry.

VIRGIN ROYAL HAWAIIAN* (NONALCOHOLIC)

The original Royal Hawaiian (page 196) was the special drink of the Royal Hawaiian Hotel in Honolulu many years ago and was made with gin.

3 ounces pineapple juice
½ ounce orgeat
¾ ounce fresh lemon juice
½ ounce Simple Syrup (page 225)

Shake all the ingredients with ice and strain into a London dock glass.

VODKA STINGER (AKA THE WHITE SPIDER)

1½ ounces Blue Shark vodka
¾ ounce white crème de menthe
Generous fresh mint sprig, for garnish

Shake the vodka and crème de menthe well with ice and strain into an old-fashioned glass filled with crushed ice. Garnish with the mint sprig.

WALDORF

Albert Stevens Crockett's *Old Waldorf Bar Days* (1931) calls for equal parts of absinthe, sweet vermouth, and whiskey. I have done a complete retooling of those proportions in my version below.

3 dashes of Jade Nouvelle Orléans Absinthe
  Supérieure
2 ounces bonded rye whiskey
¾ ounce Martini Riserva Speciale Rubino
  vermouth
2 dashes of Angostura bitters
Lemon zest coin (see page 62), for garnish

Pour the absinthe into a mixing glass and swirl to coat the glass. Pour out the excess, then add the rye whiskey, the vermouth, the Angostura bitters, and ice cubes. Stir and strain into a chilled Nick & Nora glass. Garnish with the lemon zest coin.

WARD EIGHT

This was created in 1898 at the Locke-Ober restaurant in Boston by Tom Hussion to celebrate the victory of Martin Lomasney, a member of Boston's Hendricks Club political machine, to the state legislature from the Eighth Ward. Lomasney ended up a Prohibitionist and was embarrassed that his ward was becoming famous because of a drink.

2 ounces bourbon whiskey
½ ounce Simple Syrup (page 225)
¾ ounce fresh lemon juice
½ ounce grenadine, homemade (page 224)
  or store-bought
Orange slice, for garnish
Bordeaux cherry, for garnish

Shake all the ingredients (except the garnishes) with ice and strain into an old-fashioned glass or a special sour glass. Garnish with the orange slice and cherry.

WATERMELON PUNCH*

SERVES 12

I made a batch of this every day during the month of August at Blackbird Bar. Use the top third of the hollowed-out watermelon to create a stand for the melon "punch bowl" by placing it stem side up on a cutting board. Cut at a 45-degree angle all the way around the stem to create a ring of watermelon rind 5 to 6 inches wide. Set this piece on a large plate as a stand and place the hollowed-out watermelon punch bowl on top.

1 large watermelon
6 ounces Marie Brizard triple sec
8 ounces Bacardí Limón
4 ounces Luxardo maraschino liqueur
4 ounces fresh lemon juice
Lemon wheels, for garnish
Sliced strawberries, for garnish

Cut the top third off the watermelon and hollow out the inside, saving the top, the melon flesh, and the rind. Be careful not to puncture the rind; it will be used to serve the punch.

Mash the melon flesh through a large chinois or fine-mesh strainer into a large bowl to express the juice. You will need 45 ounces (5¾ cups) of juice. Add the remaining ingredients (except the garnishes) to the watermelon juice and mix well. Chill the rind as well.

Pour the punch into the hollowed-out watermelon. To serve, ladle the punch into goblets over ice. Garnish with lemon wheels and strawberry slices.

WATERPROOF WATCH+

Original cocktail by Sother Teague of Amor y Amargo bar on East Sixth Street in New York City.

1½ ounces Hendrick's gin
¾ ounce Amaro Montenegro
¾ ounce Aperol
2 dashes of Dale DeGroff's Pimento Aromatic Bitters
2 dashes of Angostura bitters
Orange zest coin (see page 62), for garnish

Pour all the ingredients (except the garnish) into a mixing glass filled with ice and stir well. Strain into a rocks glass over ice cubes. Express the orange zest coin over the drink and drop it in the glass.

WET 'N' TAN*

Original cocktail I created for Angostura Aromatic Bitters in 1995.

1½ ounces gin or vodka
½ ounce Noilly Prat Original dry vermouth
2 dashes of Angostura bitters
Lemon zest coin (see page 62), for garnish

Pour all the ingredients (except the garnish) into a old-fashioned glass over ice and stir. Express the lemon zest coin over the drink and drop it in the glass.

WHISKEY AND JOE*

I created this cocktail for the whiskey bars aboard the Holland America Line ships.

1½ ounces **Compass Box Hedonism scotch whisky**
½ ounce **Tia Maria coffee liqueur**
¼ ounce **Tempus Fugit crème de cacao**
1 ounce **cold espresso**
Sweetened cocoa powder, for garnish

Shake the first four ingredients well with ice; the espresso will foam up nicely into a crema. Strain into a chilled old-fashioned glass. Dust the espresso foam with powdered chocolate.

WHISKEY DAISY

This is adapted from the original 1888 edition of *Harry Johnson's New and Improved Illustrated Bartender's Manual.* What interested me was the illustration that went along with the drink, showing fruit at the bottom of the glass as if it had been muddled.

2 ounces **Wild Turkey 101 rye whiskey**
¾ ounce **fresh lemon or lime juice**
¾ ounce **Simple Syrup (page 225)**
½ ounce **yellow Chartreuse**
Bordeaux cherry, for garnish

Pour all the ingredients (except the garnish) into a double old-fashioned glass filled three-quarters full with crushed ice. Stir and garnish with the cherry.

WHISKEY PEACH SMASH*

This is the summer seasonal variation on the original Whiskey Smash I created for Bobby Flay's Bar Amercain.

¾ ounce **Simple Syrup (page 225)**
½ **lemon, cut into quarters**
1 **small peach, cut into quarters**
3 **fresh mint leaves**
2 ounces **Maker's Mark bourbon**
1 **fresh mint sprig, for garnish**
Peach slice, for garnish

Muddle the ingredients (except the bourbon and garnishes) in a Boston shaker glass. Add the bourbon and shake with ice. Fine strain into an ice-filled rocks glass and garnish with the mint sprig and the peach slice.

WHISKEY PLUSH

This is a variation on the White Plush, a whiskey-and-milk drink from *How to Mix Drinks* by Jerry Thomas (1862). It is another adult egg-cream-style drink.

1 ounce **Powers Irish whiskey**
1 ounce **Baileys Irish cream**
½ ounce **Simple Syrup (page 225)**
2 ounces **milk or heavy cream**
1½ ounces **club soda**

Shake all the ingredients (except the club soda) well with ice and strain into a highball glass filled three-quarters full with ice. Stir in the club soda.

WHITE BAT*

This drink is a variation on the Colorado Bulldog (see page 112).

1½ ounces Bacardí rum
½ ounce Kahlúa
1½ ounces milk or half-and-half
3 ounces Coca-Cola

Build all the ingredients in a tall glass over ice. Stir and serve with a straw.

WHITE LADY

From Harry Craddock's *The Savoy Cocktail Book* (1934).

1½ ounces Beefeater gin
¾ ounce fresh lemon juice
1 ounce Cointreau
½ ounce emulsified egg white

Shake all the ingredients well with ice until the egg is fully emulsified and strain into a cocktail glass.

YELLOW BIRD*

This tasty cocktail hasn't gotten much play recently.

2 ounces Mount Gay Eclipse rum
¾ ounce Joseph Cartron Curaçao Orange
½ ounce Galliano
¾ ounce fresh lime juice
Lime peel, for garnish

Shake all the ingredients (except the garnish) with ice and strain into a chilled cocktail glass. Garnish with the lime peel.

YUZU GIMLET*

1½ ounces Bombay dry gin (white label)
½ ounce fresh lime juice
¼ ounce yuzu juice
1 ounce Triple Syrup (page 225)
Thin lime wheel, for garnish
Shiso leaf, for garnish

Shake the ingredients (except the garnishes) with ice and strain into a chilled cocktail glass. Garnish with the lime wheel and shiso leaf.

ZOMBIE

Created by Donn Beach, owner of Don the Beachcomber, who was born Ernest Raymond Beaumont Gantt. (I see why Ernest legally changed his name to Donn Beach.)

1 ounce Cruzan aged rum
1½ ounces Appleton Estate Reserve Blend Jamaica rum
1 ounce Lemon Hart 151-proof Demerara rum
1 ounce Joseph Cartron Curaçao Orange
½ ounce John D. Taylor's Velvet Falernum
¾ ounce fresh lime juice
½ ounce Don's Mix (see Note)
¼ ounce grenadine, homemade (page 224) or store-bought
2 dashes of Angostura bitters
Dash of absinthe
½ cup cracked ice
Sprig of fresh mint, for garnish

Assemble all the ingredients (except the garnish) in a blender and blend for 7 seconds. Pour into a chimney glass and garnish with the mint sprig.

NOTE To make Don's Mix, dissolve 1 part cinnamon sugar into 2 parts white grapefruit juice.

WHISKEY SMASH*

I created this whiskey smash recipe for the opening menu of Bobby Flay's Bar Americain in 2005.

½ lemon, cut into quarters
2 or 3 fresh mint leaves
¾ ounce Simple Syrup (page 225)
2 ounces Maker's Mark bourbon
Sprig of fresh mint
Lemon wheel, for garnish

Muddle the lemon, mint leaves, and simple syrup in the bottom of a Boston shaker glass. Add the bourbon and ice cubes and shake well. Strain into an old-fashioned glass filled with crushed ice. Garnish with the mint sprig and lemon wheel.

BASIC RECIPES

AGAVE SYRUP

Dissolve equal parts by volume of agave nectar and water.

AUDREY'S GINGER BEER

MAKES 1 GALLON

Fresh ginger beer is strongly recommended in Audrey's Gin Gin Mule. Commercial ginger beers are overly sweet and insipid.

- 1 gallon spring water
- 1 pound fresh ginger, peeled and broken into small pieces
- 8 ounces hot water
- ½ cup light brown sugar
- 2 ounces fresh lime juice

Put the spring water in a pot and bring to a boil. Put the ginger into a food processor with the hot water and process to a mulch consistency. Add the ginger mixture to the boiling water and turn off the heat. Stir and cover; let rest for 1 hour.

Strain the mixture through cheesecloth into a large bowl, pressing on it to get the sharpest ginger flavor and a cloudy appearance. Add the brown sugar and lime juice and stir to dissolve the sugar. Let cool, then store in bottles in the refrigerator for up to 2 weeks.

AUDREY'S GINGER BEER, SMALL BATCH

MAKES 1 CUP

- 8 ounces water
- 2 tablespoons finely grated fresh ginger
- ½ teaspoon fresh lime juice
- 1 teaspoon light brown sugar

In a saucepan, boil the water. Remove the pan from the heat and add the ginger and lime juice. Cover and let stand at room temperature for 1 hour. Stir in the brown sugar, then strain it through a fine-mesh strainer, pushing down on the solids to express the ginger extract. Bottle and refrigerate.

BLUEBERRY SHRUB

MAKES 32 OUNCES

- 6 very fresh thick-skinned lemons
- 1½ cups sugar
- 2 pints blueberries
- 12 ounces spring water
- 12 ounces fresh lemon juice

Remove only the yellow zest of the lemons—no pith—and then juice the lemons. Store the juice for later in the fridge.

In an open-mouth quart container with a top, layer 4 tablespoons sugar, lemon zest, and blueberries as follows: sugar, one-quarter of the lemon zest, sugar, a half-pint of blueberries, and another layer of sugar, then repeat the process for the remaining lemons and blueberries. Leave this to rest for 2 hours, then press everything down with a muddler and leave it for at least another hour. When the sugar has turned to a slurry, add the reserved lemon juice and the spring water and stir to dissolve the remaining sugar. Strain off the liquid, then cover and refrigerate until use. If you're not using the shrub immediately, add a couple ounces of pisco to slow the fermentation

BROWN SUGAR OR DEMERARA SYRUP

1 pound Demerara sugar
1 quart spring water

Mix the sugar and water in a saucepan and heat gently over a low simmer, stirring until the sugar dissolves; never boil the mixture. Remove from the heat. Cool and store in the refrigerator; it will be good for up to 2 weeks.

NOTE For a rich version, use 2 parts sugar to 1 part water.

CINNAMON SYRUP

MAKES 1 QUART

10 Ceylon cinnamon sticks, broken
2 cups Demerara sugar
16 ounces water

Combine the ingredients in a saucepan over low heat and simmer, covered, for 1 hour; do not boil. Cool, strain into a bottle, and refrigerate for up to 2 weeks.

CONCORD GRAPE SYRUP

MAKES 20 OUNCES

1½ cups Concord grapes, stems removed
½ cup sugar
4 ounces water

In a blender, pulse the grapes a few times on low speed, then purée them on low for a few seconds, until the grape skins are chopped and the grape flesh is slightly broken down. Combine the rough grape purée with the sugar and water in a small saucepan. Cook over very low heat for 15 minutes, stirring frequently. The mixture should simmer only for about the last 3 minutes of its cooking time. Remove from the heat and strain through a fine-mesh strainer, gently pressing the solids to extract any liquid. Refrigerate until completely cool. Store in the refrigerator in a closed container for up to 2 weeks.

DALE'S LEMON AND ORANGE SHRUB

1 SHRUB FOR EACH LITER BOTTLE OF BASE SPIRIT

4 firm, thick-skinned fresh lemons
1 ounce firm fresh navel orange
1 cup sugar
8 ounces fresh lemon juice
8 ounces water

Remove the zest only (the yellow and orange parts, not the white pith) from all the fruits and combine the zests and the sugar in a liter-size container with a lid. Pound the mixture with a muddler to work the sugar into the zests, then cover and shake everything very well. Set aside for 3 hours. Juice the lemons and orange and set the juices aside. After 3 hours, check to see if the sugar is all gooey and liquefied, and pour the lemon juice over the flavored, gooey sugar. Stir and/or shake until the remaining sugar is dissolved. Strain the liquid from the zests and refrigerate in a closed container until use; this is your shrub. Retain the zests for a second wash with water. Add the water to the remaining zests, cap the container, and shake. The water will remove the remaining citrus sugar; add the water to your shrub and put it back into the fridge until use. Now the zests can be discarded or they can be dehydrated (which can be done on a cookie sheet in a warm 250°F oven overnight or with a dehydrator, if you have one). Grind the peels in a spice grinder or coffee grinder and mix them with some granulated sugar; they make a pleasant frosting for the rims of glasses.

GINGER SYRUP

MAKES 30 OUNCES

1 pound fresh ginger, peeled and julienned (cutting only with the grain)
Juice of 4 limes
4 cups Demerara sugar
1 quart water

Combine the ginger, lime juice, and sugar with the water in a saucepan. Simmer, but do not boil, until the sugar is dissolved. Strain, cool, and bottle for use.

HOMEMADE GRENADINE

MAKES 28 TO 30 OUNCES

24 ounces pomegranate juice
1 cup sugar

Mix the ingredients in a saucepan and cook over low heat to dissolve the sugar; do not boil.

HONEY SYRUP

Honey is wonderful in drinks, but at full strength it is difficult to use. A practical way of preparing honey for use in drinks is to turn it into a thinner syrup, similar to simple syrup (page 225). To do so, combine 1 part honey with 1 part warm water and stir until all the honey is dissolved. Store in the fridge for 2 weeks.

IBÉRICO FAT-WASHED BOURBON

MAKES 1 LITER

100 grams (3¾ ounces) rendered Ibérico ham fat
1 liter bourbon

Mix the fat with the bourbon in a large open container. Cover and place in the freezer for 48 hours. The fat will rise to the top, clarifying the liquid. Remove the fat from the top of the liquid and strain to get any leftover bits of fat, then rebottle the whiskey for use.

LIME ACID

MAKES 105 ML (3.5 OUNCES)

The resulting liquid here has the exact same acidity as lime juice and will allow you to produce a clear sour-style drink.

4 grams citric acid (see Note)
2 grams malic acid (see Note)
94 grams filtered or spring water

Dissolve the citric acid and malic acid in the filtered water. Store for up to 3 weeks.

NOTE Both citric and malic acids can be purchased online at Modernist Pantry (www.modernistpantry.com/).

LEMON MANGO SHRUB

MAKES 20 OUNCES

4 firm thick-skinned fresh lemons
2 ripe mangos
1 cup sugar
8 ounces fresh lemon juice
8 ounces spring water

Remove the zest from all the lemons, avoiding the white pith. Peel the mangos, remove the pits, and cut the flesh into long, flat pieces. In an open-mouth quart-size container fitted with a watertight lid, layer the sugar, zest, and mango, as follows: one-quarter of the sugar, half of the lemon zest, sugar, half of the mango pieces, and another layer of sugar, then repeat the process for the remaining lemon zest and mango pieces. Set aside for 2 hours, then press the ingredients with a muddler and set aside for at least another hour. When the sugar has turned to a slurry, add the lemon juice and stir to dissolve any remaining sugar. Screw down the lid and shake well to dissolve. Strain the liquid off the peels, pressing the fruit down to get all the juice, then add the spring water to the spent peels and shake again. Strain the water, add it to the juice already collected, and discard the peels; refrigerate and cover until ready to use. If the shrub is not for immediate use, add a couple ounces of pisco to retard fermentation.

PINEAPPLE SYRUP

Mix equal parts simple syrup (page 225) and unsweetened pineapple juice.

SIMPLE SYRUP

Dissolve equal parts by volume of granulated sugar and water. This can be done by the cold method of simply shaking the mixture until the sugar is dissolved or by warming the sugar and water in a saucepan without boiling. Boiling will concentrate the syrup and that will change the ratio of sweet to sour.

Rich Simple Syrup is 2 parts granulated sugar dissolved in 1 part water. In this new edition, you will notice that I have become more exacting in my simple syrup production and, like the rest of the world, my sours are 2 parts strong to 1 *measured* part each of the sweet and sour. The industry standard is 2:1:1, strong to sweet to sour. At the Rainbow Room, I used decorative Spanish bottles as vehicles for the syrup on the bar; they gave an attractive appearance to the bar top as well. I always kept a couple ready to go.

SPICED SIMPLE SYRUP

MAKES 32 OUNCES

2 quarts water
1 cup dried orange zests
12 whole cloves
6 Ceylon cinnamon sticks (the smaller curls)
8 cups sugar

Combine all the ingredients in a saucepan over low heat. Simmer slowly until just under a boil, then remove immediately from the heat. Strain and cool before bottling.

TRIPLE SYRUP

Prepare simple syrup (page 225), agave syrup (page 222), and honey syrup (page 224). Mix the three together in the following proportions: 1 part simple syrup, ½ part agave syrup, and ¼ part honey syrup.

UNSWEETENED HAND-WHIPPED IRISH-COFFEE CREAM

To speed up the whipping, chill a stainless steel pitcher or bowl beforehand (or if it is possible, rest the pitcher in a container of ice while whipping).

1 pint heavy whipping cream

Whisk the cream until all the air bubbles disappear, but stop short of stiff. The cream should still pour slowly.

Gently pull the cream with the whisk, layering it on top of the coffee drink and taking care not to allow the cream to mix in with the coffee. If the cream mixes in it, this indicates either that the cream was underwhipped or the pour was too rapid. The end product should show a perfect definition between the black coffee and the white cream when viewed through the side of an Irish-coffee glass.

For sweetened whipped cream: Add sugar to taste, 1 tablespoon at a time, while whipping, plus a couple drops of vanilla extract. Never use sweetened whipped cream in coffee drinks—sweeten the coffee, not the cream.

PART THREE

RESOURCES

TOOLS & BOOKS

COCKTAIL KINGDOM
cocktailkingdom.com
Elegant and state-of-the-art bar tools, including signature collections and authentic reproductions of historical cocktail books. A unique look into the history of all things cocktail through their products and their books.

THE CRAFTY BARTENDER
thecraftybartender.com
An online cocktail supply shop with modern and classic barware, including a huge selection of bitters and the Blue Blazer mug recommended for serving Jerry Thomas's famous drink (see page 86).

EUVS VINTAGE COCKTAIL BOOKS
euvs-vintage-cocktail-books.cld.bz
The Exposition Universelle des Vins Spiritueux (EUVS) is a spirits and cocktail museum on the French island of Bendor. The site offers searchable copies of rare and out-of-print cocktail books. It's an invaluable resource for any cocktail geek.

THE MODERN MIXOLOGIST
themodernmixologist.com
A selection of Tony Abou-Ganim (TAG) bar tools, Boston shakers, lime squeezers, Mojito kits, and muddlers.

OXO GOOD GRIPS
oxo.com
A line of ergonomically designed bar tools, including Hawthorne strainers, channel knives, wine openers, paring knives, and bottle openers.

PINEAPPLE BAR TOOLS
A full line of bar tools and storage cases available at Amazon.com and Williams-Sonoma.com.

CLASSES & SEMINARS

BARSMARTS
barsmarts.com
Pernod Ricard USA offers BarSmarts to select establishments that require their staff to complete the program. There are no registration fees for accounts taking part in this offer. It's comprehensive, engaging, and results-driven online instruction in bartending. Also, BarSmarts Advanced is a daylong session providing education and hands-on mixology instruction, plus testing and certification.

BEVERAGE ALCOHOL RESOURCE (BAR)
beveragealcoholresource.com
This is a comprehensive, innovative course on distilled spirits and mixology offered by six of the world's leading spirits and cocktails authorities. The BAR 5-Day Certification Program is revolutionizing the way in which spirits and cocktails are viewed, understood, and appreciated.

DIAGEO BAR ACADEMY
diageobaracademy.com
An immersive training program for bar professionals across the globe, Diageo Bar Academy is made up of physical trainings and online learnings, covering many aspects of the industry, from service skills and product knowledge to high-level techniques and the business operations of your venue.

INSTITUTE OF CULINARY EDUCATION
ice.edu/newyork/explore-ice/mixology-center
#take-a-mixology-class
The Mixology Center provides hands-on training in beverage service using state-of-the-art bars and equipment. Students also learn beverage management, how to cost drinks based on the needs of their establishment, and other key elements of a successful bar program.

MUSEUM OF THE AMERICAN COCKTAIL
southernfood.org/cocktail-museum
Featuring permanent collections in Los Angeles and New Orleans, this museum provides educational resources to professionals and enthusiasts in the fine art of crafting the cocktail through a series of seminars and other programs conducted by the world's foremost experts in locations across the country and globe, among them Los Angeles, New Orleans, New York, and Washington, D.C.

NATIONAL FOOD & BEVERAGE FOUNDATION (NATFAB)

Southern Food & Beverage Museum
southernfood.org

Dedicated to the discovery, understanding, and celebration of food, drink, and its related culture and folklife in America and the world, the National Food & Beverage Foundation is home to several entities: the Southern Food & Beverage Museum, the Museum of the American Cocktail, the John & Bonnie Boyd Hospitality & Culinary Library, and Pacific Food and Beverage Museum. NatFAB continues to grow into the nation's most comprehensive cultural institution studying food and drink. Programs and events are offered at both the New Orleans and Los Angeles area facilities.

SPIRIT, WINE & COCKTAIL COMPETITIONS

INTERNATIONAL WINE & SPIRIT COMPETITION

iwsc.net

This annual wine and spirit competition founded in 1969 by the German/British oenologist Anton Massel. Each year the competition receives entries from more than ninety countries worldwide. The awards given by the competition are considered high honors in the industry.

SAN FRANCISCO WORLD SPIRITS COMPETITION

sfspiritscomp.com

Founded in 2000, the SFWSC is one of the oldest competitions of its kind and has one of the world's most respected spirits competitions due in large part to its esteemed judges.

ULTIMATE SPIRITS CHALLENGE

ultimate-beverage.com

This competition provides the most expert and authoritative evaluation of spirits for producers, marketers, importers, distributors, and retailers available. You'll find careful, meticulous evaluation of each product as well as powerful marketing support and collateral that helps build brands and further promotion of products.

NEWSLETTERS & BLOGS

BEVERAGE MEDIA GROUP

beveragemedia.com

Together with Beverage Media Group, BevAccess publishes the United States' premier beverage and alcohol trade magazines, and it also serves as the national office for the Beverage Network, delivering timely information to more than 140,000 beverage alcohol licensees in forty-eight markets each month.

CAMPER ENGLISH

alcademics.com

Alcademics is the website from Camper English, a cocktails and spirits writer, speaker, consultant, and sometimes event bartender who has contributed to publications including *Popular Science*, *Saveur*, *Details*, *Whisky Advocate*, and *Drinks International*.

COCKTAILDB

cocktaildb.com

Martin Doudoroff and Ted Haigh (aka Dr. Cocktail) have developed this extensive database, which also includes a bibliography, extensive recipe library cross-referenced by ingredients, and an active and regularly updated message board.

DIFFORD'S GUIDE

diffordsguide.com

Difford's Guide is the world's first and most definitive directory of cocktails, bartenders, bars, beer, wine, and spirits information.

HERITAGE RADIO NETWORK, THE SPEAKEASY (PODCAST)

heritageradionetwork.org/author/sotherteague/

Heritage Radio is a food-and-beverage station hosting many food and beverage professionals, including Sother Teague from the cocktail world, who discusses cocktails, spirits, wine, beer, and all things liquid, with guests ranging from bartenders and brewers, alchemists and ambassadors, roasters and regulars, and every expert and enthusiast in between.

HOME BAR BASICS
homebarbasics.com
Dave Stolte's site is a great stop for cocktail lovers with lots of not-so-basic information.

IMBIBE MAGAZINE
imbibemagazine.com
This is hands-down the best all-round beverage industry magazine on the rack. You will find it online as well as in hard copy.

JAMIE BOUDREAU
spiritsandcocktails.com
From simple garnishes to the most complex molecular mixology, tips and techniques that are paramount to today's bartender are offered here.

JEFFREY MORGENTHALER
jeffreymorgenthaler.com
Offering bartending and cocktail advice since 2004, Morgenthaler, bar manager at Clyde Common and Pepe Le Moko in Portland, Oregon, shares recipes and opinions. Comments and participation are encouraged.

LIQUOR.COM
All-round good resource for everything cocktail and spirits related.

MINISTRY OF RUM
ministryofrum.com
From Ed Hamilton, dedicated to all things rum, with a special emphasis on rhum agricole.

PROOF66
proof66.com
Literally thousands and thousands of spirits are listed, with reviews, ABV information, production information (when available), and consumer comments.

PUNCH
punchdrink.com
This James Beard award–winning online magazine, in collaboration with Ten Speed Press, focuses on narrative journalism—both written and visual—about wine, spirits, beer, and cocktails.

SPIRIT JOURNAL
spiritjournal.com
F. Paul Pacult's *Spirit Journal* is a quarterly newsletter covering spirits, wine, and beer.

THE WEBTENDER
webtender.com
Here's a great place for regularly updated drink forums, plus mixing terms, bar measurements, stocking your bar, and more.

SPIRITS, FRUITS, MIXERS, JUICES & GARNISHES

CONNOISSEUR MARKET
connoisseurmarketplace.com
Purveyor of southern staples, diet specialties, and cocktail essentials.

DALE DEGROFF'S PIMENTO AROMATIC BITTERS
kingcocktail.com/bitters.htm
Dale DeGroff's Pimento Aromatic Bitters is a blend of Jamaican allspice, with a hint of green anise and other herbs.

DIRTY SUE OLIVE JUICE
dirtysue.com/store
Premium olive juice and hard-stuffed garnishes.

FILTHY FOOD PREMIUM DRINK GARNISHES
filthyfood.com
Filthy Food's premium cocktail garnishes add new and creative twists to drinks.

FRESH ORIGINS
freshorigins.com
Microgreens, edible flowers, and other culinary specialties.

FRESH VICTOR
freshvictor.com
A line of premium, fresh, juice-based cocktail mixers for mixing consistently delicious and efficient cocktails. Five different blends—all available in food service size—make it easy to find the right flavors that seamlessly integrate into your cocktail menu.

HAUS ALPENZ

alpenz.com

Long-tail market portfolio of amari and liqueurs, wines and sparkling wines, vermouth and fortified wines and spirits.

MARX FOODS

marxfoods.com

Orchids and other edible flowers.

NATURAL BLONDE BLOODY MARY MIX

naturalblondebloodymary.com

This is made from all-natural ingredients, including yellow tomatoes. Delicious, fresh, and healthy, with low sodium and under twenty calories per serving, this makes a perfect Bloody Mary.

ROYAL HARVEST

amazon.com/Royal-Harvest-Bordeaux-Maraschino-Cherries/dp/B00J9ZNJVO

Natural Bordeaux maraschino cherries with stems.

TRADER VIC'S

tradervics.com

From the originator of the Mai Tai cocktail, this is a wonderful source for tiki glasses, Ko-Ko Kreme coconut syrup, orgeat syrup, grenadine syrup, rock candy syrup, passion fruit syrup, and hot-buttered-rum batter.

MEASURES

Pony/cordial glass = 1 ounce
Cocktail glass = 2 ounces
Wineglass = 2 ounces
Gill = 4 ounces

STANDARD U.S. BAR MEASUREMENTS

Pony = 1 ounce = 30 ml
1 ounce = 3 centiliters = 30 ml
Jigger, shot = 1½ ounces = 45 ml
Mixing glass = 16 ounces
Splash = ½ ounce = 15 ml
6 drops = 1 dash = ⅙ teaspoon

OTHER MEASURES

1 drop = 0.14 ml
6 drops = 1 dash
1 dash = 0.8 ml
36 dashes = 1 ounce = 30 ml
3 dashes = ½ teaspoon
1 standard barspoon = 1 teaspoon = 4 ml
6 teaspoons = 1 ounce = 30 ml
3 teaspoons = 1 tablespoon
1 tablespoon = ½ ounce = 15 ml
2 tablespoons = 1 ounce = 30 ml
¼ cup = 2 ounces
½ cup = 4 ounces
1 cup = ½ pint = 8 ounces
2 cups = 1 pint = 16 ounces
4 cups = 2 pints = 1 quart = 32 ounces

BOTTLE SIZE

Split = 187 ml = 6.3 ounces
Half bottle = 375 ml = 12.7 ounces
Fifth = 750 ml = 25.4 ounces
Liter = 33.8 ounces
Magnum =1.5 liters = 2 wine bottles
Jeroboam = 3 liters = 4 wine bottles
Rehoboam = 6 wine bottles
Methuselah = 8 wine bottles
Salmanazar = 12 wine bottles
Balthazar = 16 wine bottles
Nebuchadnezzar = 20 wine bottles
Sovereign = 34 wine bottles

MIXING TERMS & TECHNIQUES

BRUISE Bruising is a gentle pressure for mint leaves and delicate herbs. It is done with a muddler. Herbs like mint, verbena, and borage, and spices like ginger are used more and more to flavor drinks. These should be bruised first to release more flavor; they should not be torn apart.

BUILD refers to preparing a drink in the glass in which it will be served, usually by pouring the ingredients in the order listed and then stirring.

CREAM drinks should always be made with heavy cream—people expect the rich flavor. Substitute half-and-half or milk for dieters.

DIRTY DUMPING means pouring the entire contents of the cocktail shaker into the serving glass after shaking. The Caipirinha (page 102) is made with this technique.

DISCARD the ice used to shake a drink and strain the drink over fresh ice, unless the recipe indicates otherwise, as in the Caipirinha (page 102).

DOUBLE STRAIN Straining a cocktail by using both the julep strainer and the Hawthorne strainer. Place the Hawthorne strainer on top of the cocktail shaker and hold the julep strainer over the top of the glass. Pour through the julep strainer to keep the finer bits of herbs or muddled fruit from entering the drink.

DRY SHAKE see Shaking a drink.

FAT WASHING infuses a spirit with liquid fat, like butter, bacon fat, duck fat, or peanut butter, and chilling the spirit allows the fat to solidify on top. The fat is then removed, but the spirit retains its flavor. The ratio of fat to spirit is 4 to 8 ounces of fat to one 750 ml bottle of spirit. Use lighter fats at the higher proportion (8 ounces) and heavy ones, like bacon fat, at the lower concentration (4 ounces). See the recipe for Ibérico Fat-Washed Bourbon on page 224.

FINE STRAIN means using a fine-mesh tea-style strainer to remove seeds, ice shards, and other bits from cocktails.

FLAG refers to the standard garnish of an orange slice and cherry. It is used in sours, old-fashioneds, and many tropical drinks. A slice of fresh pineapple is sometimes added to the flag garnish.

FRAPPÉ AND MIST DRINKS are served over crushed or shaved ice.

IN AND OUT refers to a style of martini preparation. A small amount of dry vermouth is dashed into the mixing glass over ice, swirled around, and then tossed out. Then the gin or vodka is poured over the seasoned ice, stirred to chill, and strained into the serving glass.

LAYERING Floating drink ingredients one on top of another, beginning with the heaviest and adding according to weight. Brix or sugar content determines the weight of the liquid. The Pousse-Café (page 187) is an example, and often starts with a layer of grenadine as the base, since it is a nonalcoholic sugar syrup and the heaviest. A float of overproof rum is sometimes layered on top of a rum punch, because the high alcohol content makes the overproof spirits the lightest and easiest to float as the final ingredient.

MUDDLING More vigorous than bruising. I bruise mint leaves to avoid tearing them into little pieces while still releasing some essence. I muddle limes in a Caipirinha (page 102) more aggressively to extract the juice and the oil from the skin. This easy step can add so much to a cocktail.

NEAT Spirits served at room temperature without stirring or adding ice.

ON THE ROCKS Indicates a drink served in an old-fashioned or rocks glass over ice.

ROLLING OR TOSSING Pouring the assembled ingredients for a drink back and forth between two large bar glasses to mix without agitating too much. This technique is used for drinks with tomato juice to avoid destroying the texture of the juice on the tongue. Rolling or tossing Martinis and Manhattans is popular in Europe, especially in Spain and Italy.

SEASON OR WASH Dash a small amount of the spirit you wish to season with into the glass, then rotate the glass and toss out the excess.

SHAKING A DRINK The ingredients and the ice are assembled in a cocktail shaker and shaken well, then strained into a serving glass. Dry shake is a technique developed by Chad Solomon, co-owner of the Midnight Rambler in Dallas, Texas, when he worked at Pegu Club in New York City to lessen the impact of shaking egg drinks on his ailing back. The egg white and other ingredients are shaken without ice first, to emulsify and integrate the egg white, and then the ice is added and the drink is shaken again for a short time just to chill. The practice was adopted by many in the craft community to create a silkier texture and more and finer foam on sours with egg white, and to raise a statuesque foam "hat" on a Ramos or New Orleans Fizz (page 127). I'm not sold on the technique's benefits versus the time it adds to drink production. It also tends to lead to overuse of egg white in drinks. I find that too much foam on top of a Ramos or New Orleans Fizz is stealing from the liquid below, the part I am most interested in!

SHAKING FRESH FRUIT in a cocktail will always improve the flavor. For example, when shaking a Whiskey Sour, throw in an orange slice and a cherry, bruise the fruit with a muddler, and shake. Strain the drink, and always use a fresh garnish unless the recipe indicates otherwise.

SHOOTERS These small tastes served in shot glasses are fun crowd-pleasers, but they also present a dilemma to the host: they're invariably ordered when guests already have drinks in front of them, so how do you as a host provide a fun, recreational environment and at the same time serve in a responsible way? Here is how: All shooters should be ¾ ounce to 1 ounce, no larger. Buy special shot glasses just for shooters if they are popular with your crowd. Choosing the right recipes will allow some control over the alcohol content. My trick was to take a really tasty cocktail like the French

Flamingo (page 130) and re-create it as a shot. The drink doesn't have a high alcohol content, and the recipe calls for a total liquid content of 3¾ ounces. By shaking well with ice, you add an additional 1½ ounces of liquid and have a very tasty new shot that will serve six people, taste great, and spread 2½ ounces of alcohol over 6 shots. Straight shots of spirits as shooters can also be served in a ¾-ounce to 1½-ounce shot glass and priced accordingly. The check will look better at the end of the night and so will the guests.

STIRRED Assemble ingredients in the glass portion of a cocktail shaker with ice and stir with a long cocktail spoon before straining into a serving glass.

STRAIGHT-UP A style of drinks stirred over ice and strained into a chilled glass.

STRAIGHT UP drinks are stirred or shaken with ice and strained into a chilled cocktail glass without ice.

SWIZZLE A punch-style drink mixed by rotating a wooden Caribbean swizzle stick between the palms of the hands. That modern swizzle stick, often placed in or to the side of a highball drink, allowing the guest to stir their drink, is a spinoff of the original Caribbean swizzle stick. Authentic swizzle sticks can be sourced at kegworks.com.

GLOSSARY

ABBOTT'S BITTERS
American-made bitters that were discontinued after Prohibition.

ABRICOTINE
A liqueur or eau-de-vie made from ripe apricots rather than the natural or synthetic flavor of apricot. Morand makes both versions, and Marie Brizard Apry is the liqueur version.

ABSINTHE
A distillate originally based on grape eau-de-vie but today it's based on high-proof beet-sugar spirit and steeped with several herbal and botanical ingredients, including wormwood, hyssop, lemon balm, anise, Chinese aniseed, fennel, coriander, and other roots and herbs. Wormwood (*Artemisia absinthium*) was responsible for the nearly worldwide ban on absinthe at the end of the nineteenth century. Today, there is scientific agreement that absinthe's high 130 proof was more problematic than the tiny amount of psychoactive ingredients liked thujone. Absinthe is currently legal for purchase in the United States and European Union countries, where higher levels of thujone are permitted.

ADVOCAAT
A Dutch liqueur made with egg yolk and brandy and flavored with vanilla, among other flavorings.

AGAVE, MAGUEY
A large plant indigenous to Mexico that looks like a cross between a giant pineapple and a cactus. The plant is actually a member of the lily family. There are hundreds of varieties of agave, both cultivated and wild. The Weber's Blue agave is the variety used to make tequila (see Blue Agave Tequila, page 237). *Maguey* is the traditional Taíno word for agave.

AGED
The process of storing wine and spirits in oak or other wood barrels for a period of time to soften harsh flavor notes and to add specific characteristics found in the wood. The age, previous use, and size of the barrels determine the wood's effects. The barrels are often toasted or charred inside to introduce additional flavors from the caramelized sugars in the wood.

AGUARDENTE BAGACEIRA
Portuguese brandy distilled from grape pomace; similar to Italian grappa. The French version is marc.

AGUARDIENTE
Literally translated as "burning water," this is the word used in Spanish-speaking countries for brandy.

AGUARDIENTE DE CAÑA
Spirit derived from sugarcane, such as cachaça or rum.

AGUARDIENTE DE COLOMBIA
An anise-flavored liqueur from Colombia.

AGUARDIENTE DE PALMA
A Philippine spirit derived from palm sugar.

ALCOHOL, ETHYL
Beverage alcohol widely believed to be derived from the Arabic word *al-kohl. Kohl*, however, was a fine powdered cosmetic used by Arabic women for eye shadow. I am still looking for the connection.

ALE
A beer made with yeast that floats to the top during fermentation. Ale is the oldest style of beer, usually made with less hops and served fresh without aging.

ALEMBIC STILL
The original single-batch pot still, thought to have originated in China and been brought to the West by the Moors, who introduced it to Continental Europe on the Iberian Peninsula, where the first distilling of any kind in Europe probably took place. The root of the word is *al-inbiq*, the Arabic word for "still."

AMARETTO DI SARONNO
Almond-flavored liqueur from Saronno, Italy. Legend has it that Bernardino Luini, a student of the da Vinci school, was painting frescoes for Sanctuario della Beata Vergine dei Miracoli and used as a model a young woman who worked at the inn where he stayed. She showed her gratitude by making him this sweet liqueur with almonds and apricots. It's a nice story.

AMARO
The Italian word for "bitter" and also a category of bittersweet liqueurs traditionally made from grape eau-de-vie and bitter herbs, usually served after a meal as a *digestivo*.

AMER PICON

A French bitter liqueur flavored with quinine, orange zest, gentian, and other bitter herbs; it is 39% alcohol. The French distiller-turned-soldier Gaetan Picon first made it for the French troops fighting in Algeria in 1837. It's no longer available in the United States.

AÑEJO RUM

Rum aged in oak barrels; the aging requirements vary.

ANGOSTURA BITTERS

J. G. B. Siegert, a young German army doctor who volunteered to fight for Simón Bolívar and Venezuelan independence, first created Angostura bitters in 1824 as a stomach tonic for Bolívar's jungle-weary troops. His first production plant was in the town of Angostura; when the government became unstable, he moved offshore to the island of Trinidad, where the factory remains to this day in Port of Spain. The formula for Angostura is secret, but the top flavor notes are cinnamon, allspice, and clove. Angostura is officially categorized as a food additive, even though it is 40% alcohol.

ANISETTE

A liqueur made in many countries (but originally France) that is flavored with aniseed.

APERITIF

A drink before the main meal to stimulate the palate, from the Latin word *aperire,* "to open." Aperitifs can encompass anything from wine to flavored, aromatized, and fortified wines to cocktails to Champagne.

APPLEJACK

Whiskey made from a mash of at least 51 percent apples that is fermented, then distilled. The Laird & Company started in New Jersey and has been making applejack since colonial times, thus the drink is sometimes referred to as Jersey Lightning. Applejack is usually bottled at 40% alcohol.

APRICOT BRANDY, FRUIT BRANDIES

Misnomer for a flavored neutral spirit, in many cases apricots or any other fruit, that is then sweetened and bottled at 35 percent alcohol. *See* Brandy; Eau-de-Vie for information on spirits made from a mash of the fruit itself that is fermented and then distilled.

APRY

A proprietary apricot liqueur by Marie Brizard.

AQUA VITAE

Literally means "water of life"; Latin for "spirits."

AQUAVIT

Grain-based vodka-like spirit made in Scandinavian countries, flavored with different herbs, the most common of which are caraway and fennel seeds.

ARAK, ARRACK, RAKI

A distillation originally made from date palm, now also from rice and sugarcane. Arak was the base for the first punch drinks in the seventeenth century, a tradition taken from India to England by British traders. Today it is made in the Middle East, India, and Southeast Asia. See the two-part article by David Wondrich in the *Daily Beast* about the most famous of all, batavia arrack: "Rediscovering the World's First Luxury Spirit" (part one) and "The Rebirth of an Essential Cocktail Ingredient" (part two).

ARMAGNAC

French brandy from the department of Gers in southern France. Single distilled in a special still, Armagnac is considered a stronger style than Cognac. There are three regions in Armagnac as defined by the AOC: Bas-Armagnac (the best), Armagnac-Ténarèze, and Haut-Armagnac.

AROMATIZED WINES

Wines that are flavored with herbs, spices, and fruits; examples include vermouth and other aperitif wines.

ARROPE

Grape juice boiled down and added to a concentrated wine to make Pedro Ximénez, a sweetener for amoroso-style sherry. Arrope is also added to whiskey for color.

AVERNA AMARO

A bittersweet Italian liqueur served as a *digestivo*, bottled at 34% alcohol. Like most of the bitter liqueurs of France and Italy, it is flavored with herbs and quinine from the bark of the cinchona tree.

BACARDI LIMITED

Bacardi Limited is the largest privately owned spirits company worldwide, with headquarters in Hamilton, Bermuda. Holdings include the largest rum production in the world, with distilleries in several countries. Other holdings include blended and malt scotch whiskies, tequila, Martini & Rossi and Noilly Prat vermouths and aperitifs, American whiskey, vodkas including Grey Goose vodka, and Bombay gin. The Bacardí family originated in Cuba, but Fidel Castro nationalized the company facilities in 1960, and the family began producing in Puerto Rico and elsewhere.

BACK

Water or soft drink served with or behind a drink of spirits. Classic nineteenth-century bar service called for a water back to be served with every alcoholic beverage.

BAGASSE
The fiber left after the juice has been removed from sugarcane; traditionally used in rum distilleries to fuel the fire in the still. Today it is used for biofuel, pulp, and even insulation.

BAILEYS IRISH CREAM
A proprietary Irish liqueur made from fresh dairy cream, Irish whiskey, and sugar. Baileys was the first cream liqueur to solve the problem of separating and curdling.

BARBANCOURT
Haitian rum made from sugarcane juice instead of molasses, whose reputation rests on French distilling techniques borrowed from Cognac. Today Barbancourt rum is distilled twice, first in a column and then in a pot still. All Barbancourt rum is aged in oak; 3 star is aged four years, 5 star is aged eight years, and the Réserve du Domaine is aged fifteen years.

BARSPOON
A long-handled spoon for stirring cocktails. Some are made in one piece with a twisted stainless handle to aid in twirling the spoon; others are made in two pieces, with a shaft that revolves inside a sleeve.

BARTENDER, BARMAN, DOCTOR, CHEMIST
The individual who prepares and serves alcoholic beverages across the bar in an on-premises establishment. Many nicknames have grown popular over the years, like chemist, which dates to the nineteenth century, when bartenders were responsible for manufacturing many of the products they used. Doctor was another nickname that referred to the practice many neighborhood bartenders adopted of commenting on and even warning regular patrons of individual health problems. In early nineteenth-century hotels in the United States, the desk clerk often doubled as the bartender.

BATHTUB GIN
Illegal gin made literally in the bathtub during Prohibition by adding juniper oil to grain alcohol.

BEEFEATER GIN
James Burrough established this iconic distillery in London in 1863 and began producing gin, including a dry style called London dry gin and an Old Time–style gin. But his big success was a gin called Beefeater that included a selection of nine botanicals. The London dry brand eventually became the generic name for the category of dry gin made in that style.

BEHIND THE STICK
Slang for working behind the bar; the "stick" is the beer tap.

BENDER
Slang for a bout of heavy drinking; there are dozens of descriptions for a heavy-drinking event: on a tear, off the wagon, and binge drinking, to name a few.

BÉNÉDICTINE D.O.M.
A French liqueur, originally made by Bénédictine monks, that dates back to the sixteenth century. The base is grape eau-de-vie from Cognac, which is flavored with herbs, citrus peel, and aromatics. "D.O.M." on the label stands for the Latin *Deo Optimo Maximo*, a Bénédictine indulgence for "God most good, most great." At 40% alcohol, it is one of the higher-proof liqueurs. Today Bénédictine is owned by Bacardi Limited.

BIBBER
British slang term for heavy drinker.

BLACKBERRY BRANDY
Misnomer for a flavored neutral spirit, in this case blackberry flavored, that is sweetened and bottled at no more than 35% alcohol. *See* Brandy for the real deal.

BLENDED AMERICAN WHISKEY
A minimum of 20 percent straight whiskeys at 100 proof, blended with neutral-grain whiskey or light whiskey.

BLENDED MALT WHISKY
Scotch single malts blended together were called vatted malts until the Scotch Whisky Association renamed them blended malts.

BLENDED SCOTCH
The malt and grain whiskies that are blended together must be aged in used oak barrels a minimum of three years. They are blended from single-malt whiskies and mixed-grain whisky made in Scotland and distilled at less than 166.4 proof.

BLENDED SCOTCH WHISKY
A blend of single-malt scotch whiskies and mixed grain whisky. Made in Scotland, usually from mixed grains. The grain whisky is distilled at 94% and usually made from a mash of malted barley, maize, and wheat. The whiskies are aged separately but for the same amount of time, then blended and married for several months in casks before being reduced to bottling strength. Blends used to be the choice for mixing in cocktails, but with the dawn of the craft cocktail, big flavor is the order of the day, and malt scotches have found their way into many cocktails, like the modern classic Penicillin (page 181).

BLENDED STRAIGHT WHISKEY

A blend of 100 percent straight whiskeys of the same type, e.g., rye, bourbon, or corn, from different distillers or from different seasons within one distillery.

BLIND TIGER, BLIND PIG

An attempt to circumvent the law and licensing procedures by giving away a "free" glass of booze to anyone who would pay to see the "blind tiger" or "blind pig."

BLUE AGAVE TEQUILA, TEQUILA PURO

One hundred percent blue agave tequila is distilled from the fermented sugars of only the Weber's Blue agave plant and must be made and bottled in Mexico. Like all tequila, 100 percent blue agave tequila can be aged or unaged. German botanist Frédéric Albert Constantin Weber classified this variety (*Agave tequilana* 'Weber's Blue') in 1905.

BLUECOAT AMERICAN DRY GIN

Bluecoat American dry gin is rectified in Philadelphia from mixed grain spirit with four organic botanicals—dried citrus peels, juniper, coriander seeds, and angelica root; made in the London dry style.

BOLS COMPANY

Erven Lucas Bols founded the Bols Company of Holland in 1575. It began as a gin distillery but expanded to develop many fruit liqueurs, including the famous orange liqueur curaçao, made with the bitter curaçao oranges brought back from the New World. Many of the early *liqueuristes* from Europe learned their craft by studying at the Bols distillery. Bols also purchased grape eaux-de-vies from the big distilling regions—Armagnac, Cognac, and Jerez—to use in liqueur production.

BONDED WHISKEY

Whiskey bottled "in bond" is stored in a government warehouse, aged four years minimum, and bottled at 100 proof under government supervision. It is not taxed until after it is bottled. The practice became law in 1897 with the Bottled in Bond Act.

BOOTH'S GIN

Possibly the first of the London dry gin distillers, established in 1740. Today, Booth's is made by license in the United States.

BOSTON SHAKER

A two-piece cocktail shaker comprised of a sixteen-ounce mixing-glass half and a slightly larger metal half that fits over the glass half, forming a seal. The craft cocktail bartenders have switched almost without exception to the metal-over-metal version of the Boston shaker.

BOURBON

American whiskey made from a mash of between 51 and 79 percent corn; a small amount of barley; then either rye or wheat fills out the rest of the mash bill. Aged a minimum of two years in new charred oak barrels. Distilled at not more than 160 proof.

BRANCH

Water from a small spring-fed stream used for mixing with bourbon whiskey, as in bourbon and branch.

BRANDY

Distilled spirit derived from fermented fruit.

CACAO

See Crème de Cacao.

CACHAÇA

A sugarcane spirit made in Brazil, usually distilled from fresh-cut cane and bottled without oak aging, with some spectacular exceptions.

CALVADOS

Calvados is an aged brandy made from a mash of up to forty-eight different apples and even a few pear varieties in the Calvados Département in the Normandy region of France. Cider for Calvados ferments for a minimum of six weeks, then is double distilled in a pot still and aged for a minimum of two years.

CANADIAN WHISKY

Aged in used oak barrels a minimum of three years, this whisky style is distilled from mixed grains: rye, corn, wheat, and barley malt. Canada has less regulation than other countries, and flavor additives are allowed that cannot be used elsewhere.

CAMPARI

An Italian spicy, bitter *aperitivo* based on quinine that was originally colored with cochineal, developed in the 1860s by Gaspare Campari in Milan. Campari, bottled at 24% alcohol, is used in many well-known cocktails, including the Americano Highball (page 77) and the "it" cocktail of today, the Negroni (page 175).

CARPANO, PUNT E MES

The Carpano family in Turin, Italy, was the first to make the proprietary spiced wines in the vermouth category, developed in the late eighteenth century. The name Punt e Mes translates to "point and a half," referring to the popular ratio of wine to mixer among the traders who frequented the Carpano café: one point of the wine and a half point of the mixer. There is another product from the Carpano label that is a relative newcomer to the American market, Carpano Antica Formula, with a decided vanilla-flavor profile. Punt e Mes is good in cocktails like the Negroni (page 175) and the Classic Manhattan (page 157) in place of regular vermouth.

CASSIS OR CRÈME DE CASSIS

A liqueur made from black currant that originated in the town of Dijon, in Burgundy, but is now made throughout France. It is wonderful in a drink called a Kir (page 151), a small amount of cassis in a glass of white table wine. The Kir Royale (page 151) is the same drink made with Champagne.

CENTILITER (CL), MILLILITER (ML)

Measures used in European cocktail recipes equal to one-hundredth of a liter. One ounce equals about 3 cl or 30 ml.

CHAMBORD

A proprietary raspberry liqueur made in France, Chambord was adopted by the disco generation as a cocktail ingredient in drinks like Sex on the Beach (page 202), the Brain Tumor, and the Purple Hooter.

CHAMPAGNE

A sparkling wine made in the Champagne region of northeast France, primarily from the Pinot Noir and Chardonnay grapes. After the first fermentation, the special character of the wine is created during a second fermentation in the bottle, with the addition of sugar and yeast to create the famous bubbles. This process is called the *méthode champenoise,* or "Champagne method," and it is the benchmark of style for sparkling wines—though the word *Champagne* is protected by an appellation d'origine contrôlée

(AOC) established in 1927. The United States is one of the few countries that permits the use of the word *champagne* on domestic wine labels. The major styles of Champagne are determined by sugar content, from the driest style (*brut*) or *natural* to *extra dry* to *demi-sec,* and then the sweetest, *doux.*

CHARGED WATER

Water saturated with carbon dioxide gas. This was the nineteenth-century name for club soda.

CHARTREUSE

A French herbal liqueur made in two styles: yellow, bottled at 80 proof, and green, bottled at 110 proof. Originally made by Carthusian monks in Voirons, France, then, beginning in 1901, in Tarragona, Spain, when a French law was passed against production by the religious order. Production has since returned to France. An aged version designated V.E.P. (for *vieillissement exceptionnellement prolongé*) is also available.

CHERRY BRANDY

See Apricot Brandy.

COBBLER

The cobblers were wine- or spirit-based drinks made with sugar and water over lots of shaved ice and decorated with a generous garnish of fresh fruit. Some cobblers were shaken with fruit, like the Whiskey Cobbler (page 115).

COCO LÓPEZ

Coconut-flavored paste used for Piña Coladas (page 183); widely available in grocery stores.

COFFEE LIQUEUR

Made around the world, usually bottled between 25% and 30% alcohol. Two well-known brands

are Kahlúa (see page 242), made in Mexico and Denmark, and Tia Maria, from Jamaica.

COINTREAU

A premium proprietary version of triple sec orange liqueur made in France. Its many cocktail applications include the Sidecar (page 202), Margarita (page 160), and White Lady (page 220).

CONGENERS

Impurities carried along with the molecules of alcohol vapor during distillation. They may derive from the base fruit or grain used in the original mash or from other organic chemicals encountered during the different stages of beverage alcohol production. The congeners are the elements that give a spirit its distinctive taste and aroma. The chemical bonds between the congeners and the alcohol vapor can be broken by fractional distillation in column stills.

CONTINUOUS OR PATENT STILL

The two-column still that was invented in Ireland by Aeneas Coffey in 1831.

CORDIAL GLASS

The original pony glass was only one ounce, and it was shaped like a small version of a port or dessert wineglass. Today, most bars serve a large portion, and the pony is seldom used as a measure.

CORDIALS/LIQUEURS

The word *cordial* in the United States refers to sweet liqueurs flavored with fruits, herbs, botanicals, and spices. The U.S. Alcohol and Tobacco Tax and Trade Bureau (TTB) requires liqueurs to have a minimum of 2 percent sugar content. The words *cordial* and *liqueur* are interchangeable in the United States, but in Europe *cordial* refers to nonalcoholic flavored syrups.

CORN WHISKEY

Aged in new or used oak barrels and sometimes not aged but "rested." Made from a mash of at least 80 percent corn.

COURVOISIER VS

A proprietary Cognac rated Very Superior, which indicates a minimum of two years in oak for the youngest brandy in the blend.

CRÈME DE BANANA

Banana-flavored liqueur used in cocktails like the Banshee (page 82), Rum Runner (page 196), and Yellow Bird (page 220).

CRÈME DE CACAO

Liqueur made from cocoa beans, bottled in two styles, dark or clear, at 25% alcohol.

CRÈME DE FRAISES

Strawberry-flavored liqueur. Used in the 209 East Cocktail (page 215).

CRÈME DE FRAMBOISE

Raspberry-flavored liqueur.

CRÈME DE MENTHE

Mint-flavored liqueur made in two colors: green and clear (white). The green is traditionally served frappé-style over crushed ice in the Grasshopper (page 138), and the white or clear is an ingredient in classics like the Stinger (page 207).

CRÈME DE NOYAUX

A low-proof almond-flavored liqueur that is used in the Pink Squirrel cocktail (page 184).

CRÈME DE PRUNELLE

A French liqueur made with wild plums, called sloe berries.

CRIADERA

The numbered layers of barrels in a solera aging room used in the production of sherry in Spain.

CRUSTA

A nineteenth-century drink created by Joseph Santina, a New Orleans saloon keeper, that featured a sugar-rimmed (crusted) stem glass garnished with a long spiral of lemon peel. The drink could be made with any spirits, the most common of which were gin, brandy, whiskey, and rum, then mixed with lemon juice, simple syrup, bitters, and a sweet liqueur (such as maraschino), shaken, and served over crushed ice. (See page 96 for my recipe.)

CUPS

Wine-based drinks flavored with liqueurs, spirits, fruits, and herbs, iced, and topped with seltzer.

CURAÇAO

A liqueur first made by the Bols Distillery in Holland from small, bitter curaçao oranges. Now made in many countries, it comes in white, orange, and blue—the color being the only difference. Curaçao was a superior cocktail ingredient used in the early days of the cocktail, much the way vermouth was used later. Curaçao is a great match with rums, lime, and juices.

CYNAR

An artichoke-flavored Italian *aperitivo*.

DALE DEGROFF'S PIMENTO AROMATIC BITTERS

Allspice bitters created in 2009, by Dale DeGroff and master distiller Ted Breaux. Originally produced at the Combier Distillery in Saumur, France. Moved production to the Sazerac Company in Louisville, Kentucky.

DAMSON GIN

Damson plums macerated in gin and sugar syrup.

DIASTASE

The enzyme that is formed in the barley kernel when it is germinated or malted. Diastase helps transform the starch chains in the grain into simple sugars.

DISTILLATION

The process of separating parts of a liquid mixture through evaporation and condensation. Distillation is used to produce concentrated beverage alcohol, called ethanol.

DRACHM

Scottish for *dram*, or small quantity, it has an apothecary's weight of ⅛ ounce.

DRAMBUIE

A scotch-based sweet liqueur made with heather honey.

DUBONNET ROUGE

French aperitif wine fortified with grape eau-de-vie, originally made in the nineteenth century from the red wines of Roussillon, flavored with quinine, and used to protect soldiers from malaria in tropical colonial outposts. Also made in Bardstown, Kentucky, by Heaven Hill. They recently changed the formula to be more in line with the European flavor profile. See header note at the Dubonnet Cocktail (page 121)

DUNDER

Unique to rum production in Jamaica, dunder pits grow yeast and bacteria on the mash from previous fermentation that are carried forward to the next batch of mash; funky stuff that gives the rum "hogo," a sort of gamey funk.

EAU-DE-VIE

French for "water of life," but more specifically, a type of brandy made from a fermented mash of fruit, usually unaged. Eau-de-vie has evolved to define a group of unaged digestif brandies made from stone fruits and other fruits like raspberries and strawberries. It can also be generic for any ardent spirits.

EIGHTY-SIX

Slang for "out-of-stock" products behind the bar or for customers who are barred from entering the premises. It's thought to have originated during Prohibition at Chumley's, a bar at 86 Bedford Street in New York City, which did brisk business as a speakeasy.

ESTERS

Acid compounds resulting from distillation that give aroma to spirits.

ETHYL ALCOHOL

Beverage alcohol produced by the fermentation of a sugar solution.

FALERNUM

A sugar syrup from the island of Barbados flavored with almonds, lime, and spices; it comes in alcoholic and nonalcoholic versions. The alcoholic version is 11% ABV and available in the United States under the John D. Taylor brand.

FEE BROTHERS

The Fee Brothers of Rochester, New York, have a line of eighteen flavored bitters products that includes peach, mint, aromatic, and orange. They also produce flavored syrups, botanical waters, mixers, and brines for cocktail preparation.

FERMENTATION

A process that describes the consumption of sugar by yeast organisms, the by-products of which are carbon dioxide gas and ethyl alcohol. Yeast organisms reproduce rapidly in a solution containing sugar and continue to work until the alcohol content in the host solution reaches a concentration that is lethal to the yeast organisms.

FINO SHERRY

The driest style of sherry, a popular predinner aperitif wine in Spain.

FIX

A nineteenth-century drink made like a sour, but garnished extravagantly with fruits.

FIZZ

A sour with club soda or some other sparkling finish. The fizz coincided with the appearance of "charged water" in the mid-nineteenth-century bars.

FLIP

Flips were originally colonial drinks made either with beer, sherry, rum, or a combination of alcohol bases with egg and sugar. The mixture was sometimes heated with a hot loggerhead, or a fire iron with a ball on the end that was placed in the fire and used to heat drinks. Flips became much more sophisticated in the cocktail age, when they were made with sugar, a whole egg, and sherry or some spirit, shaken very well and served in a cocktail glass.

FOR THE MONEY

A post Prohibition–era expression indicating a larger serving. A waiter would order "two Cokes; one back and one for the money," indicating to the bartender that one Coke was a back (free with the spirit) and one was a larger serving for the money.

FORBIDDEN FRUIT

An American liqueur produced by the Jacquin Company with grapefruit and other citrus fruits, sweetened with honey. Not produced since 1970.

FORTIFIED WINES

Wines with alcohol added, like port, Sauternes, Madeira, and sherry. Not to be confused with aromatized wines like vermouth, which are also fortified with alcohol.

FRANGELICO

A proprietary liqueur from Italy flavored with hazelnuts.

FRAPPÉ

Drink served over snow or crushed ice. It is also referred to as a "mist," e.g., a scotch mist.

FRUIT PURÉE

Fruit broken down to liquid by a food processor. Restaurants often use flash-frozen fruit purées as the base for sorbet. My favorites are available from Perfect Purée of Napa.

GALLIANO

An Italian herb liqueur made with unaged grape brandy. The Harvey Wallbanger (page 141) cocktail put Galliano on every American bar forty-five to fifty years ago.

GIFFARD CRÈME DE VIOLETTE

A violet-blossom liqueur available from Rothman & Winter. Used primarily in the Aviation Cocktail (page 81).

GILL

Wineglass measuring a 4-ounce pour in the nineteenth-century cocktail recipe books.

GIN

Grain spirit flavored with botanicals, specifically juniper, and others, including coriander, lemon zest, fennel, cassia, anise, almond, gingerroot, orange zest, angelica, and many more.

GINGER BEER

A spicy soft drink, usually carbonated, made from gingerroot; originated in Jamaica.

GLASS RAIL

The inside channel on a bar top used for dirty glasses and cocktail tools. The channel should be about four inches wide to accommodate a liquor bottle or mixing glass.

GODIVA LIQUEURS

American proprietary chocolate and caramel liqueurs. The name and the logo are licensed from the Belgian chocolate company of the same name.

GOLDSCHLÄGER

A Swiss proprietary cinnamon liqueur, bottled at 87 proof, with 24-carat-gold flakes in the bottle.

GRAIN NEUTRAL SPIRITS

Spirits distilled from mixed grain at above 190 proof and unaged.

GRAIN SPIRITS

Spirits distilled from mixed grain at above 190 proof, then stored in oak containers instead of stainless steel, and bottled at not less than 80 proof.

GRAND MARNIER

A French proprietary orange and brandy liqueur that is made with curaçao oranges. Two levels are widely available: Cordon Rouge (the standard); Cuvée du Centenaire (100th anniversary).

GRAPPA

Poor man's brandy, or so it was originally. Grappa is made from pomace, the skins, seeds, and stems left over after grapes are pressed for wine. Grappa is usually unaged. Today grappa has become fashionable in fine-dining restaurants and is being made from single varietal grapes and bottled in expensive designer bottles.

GRENADINE

Sweet red syrup used in alcoholic and nonalcoholic drinks. The original flavor base was pomegranate, but many brands now use artificial flavor. A homemade version can be made with sugar and pomegranate juice; see page 224.

GUINNESS STOUT

Top-fermenting Irish beer that is almost black in color as a result of the heavily toasted malt used to make it. Dublin-made Guinness Stout is dry with a slightly bitter aftertaste.

HEADS

Volatile spirits from the beginning of a distillation run that are usually redistilled or removed from the spirit.

HIMBEERGEIST

Eau-de-vie distilled from raspberry and not aged or sweetened. These fruit brandies were traditionally made in Alsace, Germany, and Switzerland, but now they are made in the United States. They are served after a meal as a digestif and range from 80 to 90 proof.

INFUSION

A process similar to making tea—but on a bigger scale. In beer and whiskey making, the grains and malted grains are soaked in hot water several times, often with increasingly higher temperatures, resulting in a sweet liquid called wort. Infusion is also used in the production of fruit liqueurs, where fruit and other flavors are steeped in brandy for any extended time. After infusion, the mixture is strained, lowered to bottle proof with water, sweetened with sugar syrup, and then bottled.

IRISH CREAM

A liqueur made from Irish whiskey, sugar, and fresh cream. *See* Baileys Irish Cream.

IRISH MIST

Irish whiskey liqueur made from a blend of four whiskeys, two pot distilled and two grain, sweetened with three kinds of honey, including heather and clover.

IRISH WHISKEY

A triple-distilled whiskey from Ireland, thought to be the first whiskey. Irish whiskey is aged in oak barrels a minimum of three years. Modern Irish whiskey is made with pot-distilled malted and unmalted barley whiskey that is blended with column-stilled grain whiskey. Irish whiskey has a completely different character than its neighbor Scotland's whisky, mostly because the malt is not kilned or toasted with peat, so there is no smoky quality in the flavor. Today distillers are looking back to traditional methods and ingredients. Several 100 percent pot-distilled Irish whiskeys are being made, many at the Midleton distillery in Dublin; Green Spot, and Redbreast are among them.

JADE LIQUEURS

An absinthe and liqueur distilling company in the Combier Distillery in Saumur, France. Master distiller Ted Breaux produces Esprit Edouard Absinthe Supérieure, 1901 Absinthe Supérieure, Nouvelle Orléans Absinthe Supérieure, and C. F. Berger Absinthe Supérieure.

JÄGERMEISTER

A German liqueur made from fifty-six herbs that has a bittersweet flavor.

Jägermeister has been produced since 1934, but when Sidney Frank Importing began to import and promote the product in 1972, it went from 500 cases a year to 2 million cases a year in 2005. Mast-Jägermeister UK bought Sidney Frank Importing in 2015. They have been repositioning the brand, and the releasing of a super-premium bottling called Manifest was the first big step in that direction.

JOHN D. TAYLOR VELVET FALERNUM

Velvet Falernum was originally a sugar syrup flavored with almond, lime, and clove. The liqueur version was dosed with a small amount of alcohol to make it accessible to wider sales by liquor distributors in the United States.

JULEP

A popular American drink that originated in the late eighteenth century and is still popular today. It was originally made with Cognac and peach brandy, but it evolved into a bourbon drink mixed with fresh mint and sugar, served in a frosted silver cup over shaved ice. The Mint Julep (page 149) was one of the first American iced drinks to be celebrated abroad. England's Oxford University has a Mint Julep Quarterperson, whose job is providing Mint Juleps to all the membership of the Junior Common Room on June 1 in honor of the 1845 visit to Oxford by William Heyward Trapier of South Carolina, who was shocked that the butler had never heard of the Mint Julep and shared his family recipe.

KAHLÚA

A proprietary coffee liqueur from Mexico, arguably the best known of the coffee liqueurs. All Kahlúa sold in the United States is made in Mexico, but Kahlúa sold in Europe is made under a license by the Cherry Heering Company in Denmark. In 2017, De Kuyper Royal Distillers acquired Cherry Heering.

KOLD-DRAFT ICE

An American ice machine company that pioneered the moving water reservoir technique of ice making. They produced a large 1¼-inch-square ice cube and dominated the ice machine market into the late 1970s, when faster, more efficient Japanese technology prevailed in the industry.

LAST CALL

The traditional phrase in bars announcing the last round of drinks before closing.

LAYERED

Maintaining separate, visible layers in a drink by slowly pouring over the back of a spoon held inside the glass. The most famous layered drink is the Pousse-Café (page 187) after-dinner drink.

LICOR 43

A proprietary Spanish liqueur with forty-three herbal ingredients and grape eau-de-vie—though the resulting flavor is distinctly vanilla; it is bottled at 34% alcohol.

LILLET

Lillet or Lille is a French wine-based aperitif that is produced in three styles: Lillet Blanc, Lillet Rosé, and Lillet Rouge. The Blanc is produced from Sauvignon Blanc and Semillon grapes mixed with a concentrate prepared by macerating several fruits in brandy. The Rouge is made from Cabernet and Merlot grapes mixed with a similar concentrate. Lillet has a sweet, fruity taste and finds a home in several well-known cocktails, such as the Vesper, created for James Bond in *Casino Royale*. Often referred to in older recipe books as Kina Lillet, an older recipe with a bit more bitter quinine.

LIQUEURS

See Cordials.

MACERATION

The process of steeping a flavoring agent in water or alcohol, then either redistilling the resulting product or adding it to a larger batch for flavoring. The same flavoring agent will extract differently in water than in alcohol; alcohol tends to extract more bitter notes.

MADEIRA

Fortified sweet red wine from the Portuguese island of Madeira that is aged in soleras, like the brandies of Spain. Madeira is reputed to be among the longest-lived wines in the world, lasting well over one hundred years in some cases. The island of Madeira was often the last stop for ships sailing to the New World, and the barrels of wine were loaded for ballast as well as freight. The wine seemed to thrive in the steaming holds of the ships and had improved in flavor at the end of long voyages. Today, Madeira makers re-create this "cooking" of the wine in a process called *estufagem,* whereby the temperature in the aging warehouses is raised to over 100°F to simulate the heat in the hold of a sailing vessel.

MAHOGANY, ACROSS THE MAHOGANY

A slang word for a bar top.

MALT SCOTCH

Aged in used oak barrels not less than three years, but in practice almost never less than five years, and usually between eight and eighteen years. Pot distilled from a mash of 100 percent malted barley, dried partially in peat-fired kilns for flavor. Made in Scotland.

MALTING
Germinating grain, usually barley or rye. *See* Diastase.

MARASCHINO LIQUEUR
A sweet, clear liqueur made from Marasca cherries and cherry pits. Maraschino was a popular ingredient in early punches and cocktails; it is almost never drunk straight. The talented bartenders of Cuba in the 1920s made maraschino popular by adding it to their Daiquiris.

MARC
The skins and seeds left over from the pressing in winemaking in France. Marc is fermented and distilled into an unaged brandy of the same name, similar to grappa.

MARSALA
A fortified wine from Marsala, Sicily, it is more processed than the other great fortified wines from Portugal, Spain, and Madeira. After the base wine is made, concentrates of boiled-down wine and concentrated grape juice mixed with spirits are blended into the wine. The wine then begins its journey through the solera system for aging.

MEZCAL
The general category of which tequila is a subcategory. To be clearer, all tequila is mezcal, but mezcal is not tequila. Mezcal is made primarily in Oaxaca, Mexico, from the *espadín* and several other types of agave. The worm has been retired, and premium mezcals are now available from several makers, including Del Maguey. Traditional mezcal has a smoky quality from the slow baking of the agave piña in rock-lined pits.

MIDORI
A proprietary melon liqueur from the Suntory distillery in Japan, it is popular in cocktails for the green color it brings to drinks, such as the Midori Margarita.

MIST
Any spirit served over crushed ice.

MISTELLE
A blend of raw grape juice and spirits sometimes used as a base for aperitif fortified wines, such as vermouth, and sometimes bottled as a stand-alone product, as in Pineau des Charentes.

MIXTO TEQUILA
Mixto is a tequila that is at least 51 percent derived from the blue agave, but it also contains sugars from cane or other sources. One hundred percent agave tequilas are referred to as *puro*.

MOUNT GAY RUM
Touted as the oldest brand of rum (1703), made by Abel and William Gay at the St. Lucy Estate on the island of Barbados. Mount Gay is made from molasses and a very closely guarded yeast recipe. The rum is a blend of pot-still and continuous-still rums. The aging takes place in small barrels that are used a maximum of three times to avoid depletion, and the aging lasts between two and ten years. The blender then takes over, exercising his art to marry the older and younger rums. Mount Gay produces four products: Eclipse Barbados rum (standard) and the Premium White, both aged two years; Mount Gay Extra Old rum, blended with a larger percentage of the ten-year-old rum; and the very rare Sugar Cane Brandy, which is not widely available.

MUDDLER OR TODDY STICK
A wooden tool shaped like the grinding tool of a mortar and pestle (between six and nine inches long) used to mash fruit and herbs with sugar or liqueur in the bottom of a bar mixing glass. This technique is essential for making Old-Fashioneds (page 176) and the Caipirinha (page 102).

MULLED WINE
Wine cooked with spices and sugar.

OJEN
Spanish anise-flavored liqueur.

OLD-FASHIONED GLASS
Holds eight to ten ounces in a short, stout shape. Often referred to as the "on the rocks" or simply "rocks" glass. Double old-fashioned glasses, also called buckets, were popularized by drinks like the Mai Tai (page 156).

OLD POTRERO 18TH CENTURY STYLE WHISKEY
An unusual American malted rye whiskey made by the Anchor Distillery. It is made from malted rye and aged for two to five years in new and used toasted barrels, and for that reason, the word *rye* is not in the title of the whiskey. Old Potrero is bottled at 51.2% alcohol.

OLD TOM GIN
A sweetened London dry style gin very popular in the nineteenth century, and recently having a comeback. There are no rules here, and some of the modern versions are not sweetened. A broader explanation of this unofficial category can be found in the *Daily Beast* article (March 17, 2017) by David Wondrich titled simply "Solving the Riddle of Old Tom Gin."

ON PREMISE

A trade term for a licensed liquor business that serves spirits, wine, and beer by the glass, i.e., bars and restaurants. Off-premise licensed, businesses sell retail packaged alcoholic beverages.

ORANGE BITTERS

Alcohol-based bitters flavored with orange zest and other botanicals, made in the United States by the Fee Brothers in Rochester, New York, and in Kentucky at the Sazerac Distillery under the name Regan's orange bitters. Also made in Germany by the Bitter Truth company but widely distributed in the United States. Orange bitters was an ingredient in early dry Martini recipes, but it was dropped in later recipes. It has multiple applications in cocktails traditional and new.

ORANGE-FLOWER WATER

Water flavored with orange blossoms and used in baking and cooking. It is the critical ingredient in the famous New Orleans cocktail, the Ramos or New Orleans Fizz (page 127).

ORGEAT

A milky, sweet almond syrup used extensively in baking; also called orzata. Orgeat is an ingredient in Victor Bergeron's classic Mai Tai cocktail (page 156).

OUZO

Greek anise-flavored liqueur.

PASSION FRUIT PURÉE

A sweet, thick juice made from sugar water and passion fruit. Fresh passion fruit is a wonderful addition to tropical cocktails, but it needs a lot of sweetening.

PEACH BITTERS

See Fee Brothers.

PEACHTREE SCHNAPPS

This was the spirit that began the whole fruit schnapps craze; it is produced by De Kuyper USA in Louisville, Kentucky, and is 30 proof. De Kuyper Holland was the first company to contract distill in the United States, in Kentucky after Prohibition.

PEPPER VODKA

Vodka made by steeping hot peppers or pepper oil in vodka.

PERFECT

A modifying term in the Manhattan cocktail recipe indicating a mix of half sweet and half dry vermouth, as in a Perfect Manhattan.

PERNOD

Created as an absinthe substitute. *See* Absinthe.

PERRY

Cider made from pears or a combination of pears and apple.

PETER HEERING CHERRY LIQUEUR

A superior cherry liqueur made in Denmark from native Stevns sour cherries with an intense bittersweet flavor. Made by Heering, it is a famous ingredient in the true Singapore Sling (page 203).

PEYCHAUD'S BITTERS

Antoine Peychaud, owner of an apothecary shop in New Orleans, created an all-purpose flavoring and health tonic in the 1830s from herbs and Caribbean spices. Lore has it he combined the bitters with a French Cognac imported to New Orleans and produced by Sazerac de Forge et Fils, and that was the inspiration for the Sazerac cocktail. David Wondrich, our historical oracle in the cocktail community, is skeptical of the connection between the two.

PHYLLOXERA VASTATRIX

An American insect from the aphid family that was exported to Europe on root splicings and decimated wine-producing grapes in many countries. The aphids attack the roots, and American vines were resistant. Whiskey makers in northern Europe and in the United States, as well as absinthe producers, were the accidental benefactors of the disaster after the brandy makers in southern Europe were ruined.

PIMENTO DRAM LIQUEUR

Liqueur made in Jamaica from allspice berries. Available only sporadically in the United States.

PIMM'S CUPS

Pimm's Cups were cocktail creations of James Pimm, a barman in London in the 1840s. In the 1870s former colleagues and customers used the formulas to create bottled cocktails under the name Pimm's. No. 1 (gin based), No. 2 (whiskey based), No. 3 (brandy based), No. 4 (rum based), No. 5 (rye based), and No. 6 (vodka based). In the United States only No. 1 is available, but in England No. 1 and No. 6 are still available.

PINEAU DES CHARENTES

A blend of raw grape juice and Cognac that is aged and bottled. Often served as an aperitif or mixed in cocktails; see Rainbow Sour (page 189).

PISCO

Pisco is a grape brandy made in Peru and Chile (don't tell the Peruvians; they claim sole ownership) from the ancient Muscat and other sweet grape varieties brought from the Old World to the Spanish colony called the Viceroyalty of Peru in the 1500s.

POMEGRANATE MOLASSES

Thick syrup made from cooked and concentrated pomegranate juice, found in Middle Eastern grocery stores. Pom Wonderful fresh pomegranate juice has eclipsed some of its use by bartenders.

PONY GLASS

A small, stemmed glass measuring one ounce.

PORT

Fortified wine from the Douro Valley of Portugal; it comes in several styles, including vintage, vintage character, ruby, tawny, and white. The grape varieties are numerous, including Touriga Nacional and Francisca, Bastardo, Tinta Roriz, Tinta Cão, and Souzão.

PUNCH

From the Persian word *panj* or the Hindi *panch,* meaning "five" (ingredients): spirit, sugar, lime juice, spice, and water. Similarly, an ancient Greek drink called *pentaploa* ("fivefold") was also made with five ingredients: wine, honey, cheese, flour, and oil. The drink was presented to the winner of a race from the Temple of Dionysus in Athens to the seacoast at Phaleron. Punch originated in India and became the fuel of high society social gathering in seventeenth- and eighteenth-century Europe. Shrub-based punches—a blend of spice, sweet, sour, strong and weak—were the blueprint for the American iced drink called the cocktail.

PUNT E MES.

See Carpano.

RAMAZZOTTI

Sometimes called "Amaro Felsina Ramazzotti," it is made from thirty-three herbs and spices and has a bittersweet flavor. Produced by the same company in Milan since 1815.

REAL MCCOY

During Prohibition, Captain William J. McCoy turned his luxury yacht *Arethusa* into a rumrunner sailing from multiple locations to the U.S. East Coast, unloading illegal spirits from overseas onto smaller boats while moored beyond the three-mile limit. His spirits were always high quality, hence the phrase "the real McCoy." Bill McCoy was arrested in 1925 and spent several months in a New Jersey jail before retiring to Florida, where he built sailing vessels. Real McCoy rum is distilled in Barbados.

RECTIFYING

This is an often-misunderstood word because it can describe many different operations. Basically, it means to change a spirit in some way after it has been distilled. Those changes can include redistilling, adding flavor or color, and adding water to lower the bottle proof strength.

RICARD, PERNOD

See Absinthe.

ROSE WATER

A food- and beverage-flavoring agent made by steeping rose petals in alcohol. Used extensively in the Middle East. Good in lemonade drinks.

RUBY PORT

See Port.

RUM

Made from molasses, sugarcane juice, or sugarcane syrup, it is considered the first spirit of the New World. First produced in Barbados and Jamaica, traditionally double distilled. *Rhum agricole* is made from sugarcane juice, not molasses.

RUM SWIZZLE

Created at the Georgetown Club in British Guiana by putting rum, bitters, lime, and ice in a tumbler, then mixing it with a long swizzle stick until the outside of the glass frosted over.

RYE WHISKEY

Whiskey aged two years in new charred oak barrels. Made with 51 to 100 percent rye in the mash.

ST RAPHAËL

An aromatized wine flavored with quinine, herbs, and spices. Used by the French government to protect their troops in Algeria from malaria.

SAKE

Japanese wine made from fermented rice. A special yeast called koji that is grown on grain cakes gives sake its special flavor.

SAMBUCA

Anise-based, licorice-flavored Italian after-dinner liqueur often taken with coffee. Black sambuca was recently introduced to the American market under the names Opal Nera and Della Notte.

SANGAREE

An early colonial beverage made from wine, usually Madeira, water, and spices and served as a tall refresher in the summer. Mulled wine is a winter version of the sangaree, served hot.

SANGRIA

A beverage originating in Spain made with red or white wine, sugar, and fruits, and garnished with fresh fruits and berries.

SANGRITA

A spicy mix with lime juice, Maggi Seasoning, Tabasco, Worcestershire sauce, and other flavorings, used as a companion shot with a tequila shot.

SAZERAC
See Peychaud's Bitters.

SCHNAPPS
A Scandinavian and German term for strong, colorless spirits. Also known as snaps, they may be flavored or unflavored. It is also used as slang for any strong spirit. Today schnapps is a popular category of low-end fruit and spice spirits made by companies like DeKuyper, Mohawk, and Leroux.

SCOTCH
Whisky distilled in Scotland from malted barley.

SHERRY
Spanish fortified wine from the province of Cádiz. Sherry has a long second fermentation during which the wine is in contact with the air, and a yeast cap, known as flor, grows on top of the wine. The wines with the thickest layer of flor will be marked for fino, and continue a biological aging period. Resulting fino sherry is drier with less alcohol. If the flor breaks prematurely, the resulting barrel will be marked for amontillado or for oloroso sherry, fuller bodied with more alcohol added. All sherry is fermented dry, and some oloroso sherry is sweetened with Pedro Ximénez, a sweetened concentrated wine made by boiling down wine and adding arrope (boiled grape juice). Sherry is a blended wine that is aged by the solera system. The wine is preserved by the addition of alcohol distilled from local grapes. There are two broad categories of sherry: dry (fino) and fuller body, sometimes sweeter (oloroso)

SHOOTERS
One-ounce shots of cocktails or straight spirits like Jägermeister that are downed in one gulp.

SHRUB
Punch base made with lemon peel, sugar, and lemon juice. See pages 222, 223, and 224.

SINGLE-MALT SCOTCH
A Scottish barley-based spirit produced by a single distillery in one season. Bottled straight or used as a blending agent in blended scotch.

SKIN
A category of drinks from the nineteenth century made with lemon juice, spirits, and hot water.

SLING
In the early nineteenth century, a sling was described as a toddy (spirits, sugar, and water with nutmeg grated on top), a poor man's punch. The first definition of the cocktail in print in 1806, described the cocktail as a "bittered sling."

SLOE GIN
A gin flavored with wild plums called sloe berries.

SOLERA AGING
Spanish brandy and sherry are both aged in this system of barrels; the bottom layer of barrels is the solera and the other layers are the criaderas. During the solera aging process, the wine or spirit is moved through the criaderas by blending younger wines or brandies in with older barrels. In this way the wine or brandy takes on an age character beyond its years, or as the Spanish say, the old brandy teaches the young brandy.

SORGHUM
A type of grass grown in the Plains states of the United States that

is boiled down to make a type of molasses. Sorghum is the base for some baijiu and especially the official spirit of China, Moutai baijiu, made by Kweichow.

SOURS
Cocktails made with a strong, sweet, and a sour ingredient. Those ingredients can vary widely from one sour to the next, but the proportions should remain the same. The proportions I have determined to appeal to the widest audience are three-quarters part sour to one part sweet to two parts strong. *See* Fix.

SPANISH BRANDY
See Solera Aging.

SPRITZER
A mix of white wine and club soda over ice.

STOLICHNAYA OHRANJ
Orange-flavored vodka from Russia. Russian vodka and Scandinavian aquavit were the first flavored vodkas.

STREGA
Italian liqueur that is a blend of seventy different herbs and barks. Great over ice cream.

SUNTORY, BEAM SUNTORY
The best-selling brand of Japanese whiskey, Suntory is also one of Japan's largest alcohol beverage companies, with two main distilleries, Hakushu and Yamazaki. Suntory Holdings purchased Beam Inc., in 2014.

SWIZZLE
See Rum Swizzle.

TAILS
Spirits from the end of a distilling run are usually high in acrid fusel oils and removed by the distiller for redistillation.

TAWNY PORT

Wood-aged port blended from several vintages and aged from five to forty years in oak. Tawny starts out dark red like ruby or vintage ports, but the oldest ones take on the light copper color from which the name is derived.

TENNESSEE WHISKEY

Made similar to bourbon, with the exception of a charcoal-filtration process called the Lincoln County Process that is required for all Tennessee sour mash whiskeys. Aged in charred oak barrels a minimum of two years but usually bottled not less than four to six years. The filtration process prohibits use of the word *bourbon* on the label.

TEQUILA

Produced in Mexico, derived from the *Agave tequiliana* 'Weber's Blue', one of the 400 varieties of the agave plant, a member of the lily family. Tequila comes in two main categories: *mixto* and *puro*, 100 percent blue agave. Mixto is at least 51 percent agave with other sugars (usually from cane) added to the agave during fermentation.

TIA MARIA

Coffee-flavored liqueur from Jamaica.

TODDY

A sap derived from palm, wild date, and palmyra trees. In India it was the base for a nonalcoholic sweet drink and a lightly alcoholic fermented drink. *Toddy* came to be known as a hot or cold beverage made of spirits, sugar or honey, and water. My Nana, on the Italian side of the family, was not averse to a splash of some sort of spirit with the honey, lemon, and hot water she gave us even as kids.

TONIC WATER

A carbonated water that contains quinine and sugar. There is a rich historical background to research, from the impact of this beverage on the health of the British military serving in the colonies in the tropics all the way to a cultlike following of the Gin and Tonic in modern-day Spain.

TRIPLE SEC

A liqueur made from the curaçao oranges, first in Holland but now produced in many countries. Triple sec, with the exception of Cointreau, is mostly a mixer and is almost never taken straight.

TUACA

An Italian sweet liqueur, flavored with citrus and with a top note of vanilla.

UISGE BEATHA (CELTIC) OR USQUEBAUGH (GAELIC)

Both translate literally to "water of life." These are the old words for "whisky" in the British Isles. Some believe the Celtic pronunciation led to the English word *whisky*.

UNDERBERG BITTERS

Stomach bitters sold everywhere. They were once labeled Underberg Boonekamp Bitters.

UNICUM BITTERS

Beverage bitters made in Hungary by the Zwack family. It is a maceration of forty herbs in alcohol that is aged in oak casks.

VERMOUTH

Fortified and aromatized wines made in sweet or dry styles, used in cocktails and as an aperitif. The word originated from the German word for the wormwood plant, *Wermut*.

VODKA

From *voda*, the Russian word for "water," vodka is distilled from grain, potatoes, grapes, and even sugarcane in the Caribbean. It is distilled to above 190 proof and bottled at a minimum of 40% alcohol. No additives or flavoring are permitted, with the exception of water and minute parts per million of citric acid and glycerin.

VS, VSOP, XO COGNAC

These are designations used in Cognac to indicate minimum aging for their brandies: Very Special (VS), two year minimum in French oak; Very Superior Old Pale (VSOP), four year minimum in French oak; and Extra Old (XO), ten years minimum in French oak.

WHISKEY/ Y

From the Gaelic *usquebaugh,* or "water of life," whiskey is made from grain that is ground into grist, then cooked with water to release starches. Malt is added to convert the starch into sugar, and then yeast to begin fermentation. The low-proof liquid after fermentation is called beer, which after distillation becomes whiskey.

WHITE CRÈME DE MENTHE

See Crème de Menthe.

WORMWOOD

The all-important herbal ingredient in absinthe. The Latin name for wormwood is *Artemisia absinthium.*

YELLOW CHARTREUSE

See Chartreuse.

YUKON JACK

Canadian whisky slightly sweetened with honey.

ŻUBRÓWKA

Polish vodka flavored with sweet-scented buffalo grass.

BIBLIOGRAPHY

Arnold, Dave. *Liquid Intelligence.* New York: W. W. Norton & Company, Inc. Publishing, 2014.

Barr, Andrew. *Drink: A Social History of America.* New York: Carroll & Graf Publishing, 1999.

Barty-King, Anton, and Hugh Massel. *Rum: Yesterday and Today.* London: Heidelberg Publishing, 1983.

Bergeron, Victor J. *Trader Vic's Rum Cookery & Drinkery.* New York: Doubleday, 1974.

Boothby, William T. *Cocktail Boothby's American Bartender.* San Francisco: H. S. Crocker Company, 1891.

Buzza, George. *Hollywood's Favorite Cocktail Book.* Hollywood, CA: Buzza-Cardoza of Hollywood, 1933.

Byron, H. O. *Modern Bartenders' Guide, or Fancy Drinks and How to Mix Them.* New York: Excelsior Publishing House, 1884.

Carson, Gerald. *The Social History of Bourbon.* New York: Dodd, Mead & Company, 1963.

Christian, Paul, and Donald G. Kyle. *A Companion to Sport and Spectacle in Greek and Roman Antiquity.* Malden, MA: Wiley Blackwell, 2014.

Craddock, Harry. *The Savoy Cocktail Book.* London: Constable and Company, 1930.

Crockett, Albert Stevens. *Old Waldorf Bar Days.* New York: Aventine Press, 1931.

Cunningham, Stephen Kittredge. *The Bartender's Black Book.* Self-published, 1994.

David, Elizabeth. *Harvest of the Cold Months: The Social History of Ice and Ices.* New York: Viking Press, 1994.

de Fleury, R. *1800 and All That: Drinks Ancient and Modern.* London: St. Catherine Press, 1937.

Edmunds, Lowell. *Martini, Straight Up: The Classic American Cocktail.* Baltimore: Johns Hopkins University Press, 1998.

Embury, David A. *The Fine Art of Mixing Drinks.* New York: Doubleday, 1948.

Foley, Raymond, and Jaclyn Foley. *The Williams-Sonoma Bar Guide.* New York: Williams-Sonoma/Time Life, 1999.

Funderburg, J. Anne. *Rumrunners: Liquor Smugglers on America's Coasts, 1920–1933.* Jefferson, NC: McFarland & Company, 2016.

Gale, Hyman, and Gerald F. Marco. *The How and When.* Chicago: Marco Importing Company, 1940.

Goodwin, Betty. *Hollywood du Jour.* Santa Monica, CA: Angel City Press, 1993.

Grimes, William. *Straight Up or On the Rocks.* New York: Simon & Schuster, 1993.

Haas, Irvin. *Inns and Taverns.* New York: Arco Publishing, 1972.

Haimo, Oscar. *Cocktail and Wine Digest.* New York: Cocktail, Wine, Beer and Spirit Digest, Inc., 1945.

Hamilton, Edward. *The Complete Guide to Rum.* Chicago: Triumph Books, 1997.

Haney, Jesse. *Haney's Steward & Barkeeper's Manual.* New York: Jesse Haney & Co., Publishers, 1869.

Hills, Phillip. *Appreciating Whisky: The Connoisseur's Guide to Nosing, Tasting and Enjoying Scotch.* New York: HarperCollins, 2000.

Jeffs, Julian. *Little Dictionary of Drink.* London: Pelham Books, 1973.

Johnson, Harry. *New and Improved Bartender's Manual.* New York: Harry Johnson, Publisher, 1882.

Jones, Andrew. *The Aperitif Companion.* New York: Knickerbocker Press, 1998.

Kaplan, David, Fauchald, Nick, Day, Alex. *Death & Co: Modern Classic Cocktails.* Berkeley California: Ten Speed Press, 2014

Kappeler, George J. *Modern American Drinks.* New York: The Merriam Company, 1895.

Mahoney, Charles S. *Hoffman House Bartender's Guide.* New York: Richard K. Fox Publisher, 1905.

Mason, Dexter. *The Art of Drinking.* New York: Farrar & Rinehart, Inc., 1930.

Meier, Frank. *The Artistry of Mixing Drinks.* Paris: Fryam Press, 1936.

Mendelsohn, Oscar A. *The Dictionary of Drink and Drinking.* New York: Hawthorn Books, Inc., 1965.

Muckensturm, H. M. Louis. *Louis' Mixed Drinks.* Boston: Caldwell Co., 1906.

Nowak, Barbara. *Cook It Right: The Comprehensive Source for Substitutions, Equivalents, and Cooking Tips.* South Dennis, MA: Sandcastle Publishing, 1995.

Pacult, F. Paul. *Kindred Spirits.* New York: Hyperion, 1997.

Page, David, and Barbara Shinn. *Recipes from Home.* New York: Artisan, 2001.

Paul, Charlie. *Recipes of American and Other Iced Drinks.* London: Farrow & Jackson Ltd., 1902.

Poister, John. *The New American Bartender's Guide.* New York: Signet, 1999.

Pokhlebkin, William. *A History of Vodka.* London: Versoo, 1991.

The Practical Housewife: A Complete Encyclopedia of Domestic Economy and Family Medical Guide. Philadelphia: J. B. Lippincott and Company, 1860.

Price, Pamela Vandyke. *Dictionary of Wine and Spirits.* London: Northwood Books, 1980.

Ricket, Edward. *The Gentleman's Table Guide.* Published by the author, 1873.

Schmidt, William. *The Flowing Bowl.* New York: Charles L. Webster Co., 1891.

Schumann, Charles. *The Tropical Bar Book.* New York: Stewart, Tabori & Chang, 1989.

Spalding, Jill. *Blithe Spirits: A Toast to the Cocktail.* Washington, DC: Alvin Rosenbaum Projects, Inc., 1988.

Spencer, Edward. *The Flowing Bowl.* London: Grant Richards, 1903.

Stearns, Samuel. *The American Herbal, or Materia Medica.* Walpole, MA: Thomas & Thomas, 1801.

Tartling, W. J. *Café Royal Cocktail Book.* London: Pall Mall Ltd., 1937.

Taussig, Charles. *Rum, Romance and Rebellion.* London: William Jarrolds Publishers, 1928.

Thomas, Jerry. *Bar-Tender's Guide: How to Mix Drinks or the Bon Vivant's Companion.* New York: Dick & Fitzgerald Publishing, 1862.

Vermeire, Robert. *Cocktails: How to Mix Them.* London: Herbert Jenkins, 1930.

Visakay, Stephen. *Vintage Bar Ware.* Paducah, KY: Schroeder Publishing Co., 1997.

Werner, M. R., *Tammany Hall.* New York: Doubleday, Doran & Company, 1928.

SPECIAL THANKS

To my wife, Jill, whose art has surrounded us with beauty, thank you for your patience, your thoughts, and your suggestions as they eased me through a long and difficult process.

A huge thank you to Audrey Saunders for providing the classic Pegu Club lounge as the venue for the photography. We made good use of every table and the stunning bar as the backdrop for some great photography. To Cocktail Kingdom for supplying the glassware and the Café Brûlot apparatus. To photographer Daniel Krieger, it was an honor to work with you. I marveled at your relaxed approach each day; we never rushed but somehow we managed twelve to fifteen setups a day and ended up with stunning pictures. To Robert Oppenheimer, my old friend and general manager of the Pegu Club, for your support during the days of the photo shoot. And to Pegu Club bartender Raul Flores for your careful drink preparations and the creative garnish suggestions. It was a pleasure to work with such an accomplished professional. To Kenta Goto for your generous hospitality in offering Bar Goto as a venue for our final few photos.

Thank you to the team at Random House and Clarkson Potter, especially to Angelin Borsics for guiding me through the publishing world, which, even after my third immersion, still feels like a foreign country that I am visiting for the first time. To Ian Dingman, thank you for the dancing font that gives the pages a fun, lively look. The cocktail has become more culinary, but it still remains a diversion for the weary and work-worn masses. To Joyce Wong for her editorial expertise, and to Jessica Heim for proofing the images and producing a beautiful book. To Anthony Giglio for his invaluable help in condensing the first edition into one book!

To Ron Holland for introducing me to the New York City bar and grill. To Gerry Holland for his memory. To Abbie Schiller for the title. To Cynthia Fagan for giving me the King cocktail moniker that has become my trademark. To Brian Rea for opening his library to me and for all his support over the years. To Harry, Zane, and Arnold for their wonderful stories from my Hotel Bel-Air bar days. I've been dining out for years on those stories! To my family for their love and their meatballs! And to the bar staff from my Rainbow Room days. And to all my customers over the years for their thirst and their good cheer.

And a special thanks to Joe Baum for taking me to a place where troubles melt like lemon drops …

INDEX

Published in the United States by Clarkson Potter/
Publishers, an imprint of Random House, a division
of Penguin Random House LLC, New York.
clarksonpotter.com

CLARKSON POTTER is a trademark and POTTER
with colophon is a registered trademark of Penguin
Random House LLC.

Originally published in hardcover in the United
States in a slightly different form, by Clarkson Potter,
an imprint of Penguin Random House LLC, in 2002,
and subsequently in eBook format by Clarkson
Potter, an imprint of Penguin Random House LLC,
New York, in 2010.

Library of Congress Control Number: 2020936112.

ISBN 978-1-9848-2357-1
Ebook ISBN 978-1-9848-2358-8

Printed in China

Book design by Ian Dingman
Illustrations by Steven Noble

10 9 8 7 6 5 4 3

First Revised Edition